KURT COBAIN
THE NIRVANA YEARS

CARRIE BORZILLO

CARLTON
BOOKS

*For my husband Chris Vrenna and my parents
Ron and Paula Borzillo*

THIS IS A CARLTON BOOK

Text copyright © 2000 Carrie Borzillo
Design copyright © 2003 Carlton Books Limited

This edition published by Carlton Books Limited in 2013
20 Mortimer Street
London W1T 3JW

A CIP catalogue for this book is available from the British Library.

ISBN: 978-1-78097-400-2

CONTENTS

INTRODUCTION

With their unique blend of punk aggression, pop sensibilities, and a pained voice that tore into the hearts and souls of anyone listening, Nirvana became the most important band of the '90s. And, Kurt Cobain not only emerged as the unwitting voice of a generation and our greatest musical loss since John Lennon, but also one of the most misunderstood geniuses ever. This book will hopefully separate fact from fiction and clear up some of the myths and untruths that have grown up around the band and their singer's troubled life by bringing you a straightforward, day-by-day account of their career and lives.

When I was first approached to write this book, my initial reaction was "Well, I love Nirvana, but you want me to *what*?" I mean, trying to compile a timeline of anyone's life or career is a next-to-impossible task, let alone the career of a band that would go for months at a time lying dormant.

I for one can't recall what I did last Tuesday, and the same seems to go for any human being, including those involved with Nirvana. For instance, Chad Channing, drummer from 1988–1990, can't for the life of him recall the date he joined the band. Kurt Cobain himself had innocently told different journalists that his parents divorced when he was seven, eight, or nine. And even Geffen Records erred when they listed January 5, 1994 as the date of a show on the band's *From the Muddy Banks of the Wishkah* album, when in fact the show was January 7. But, I took the assignment once I accepted the fact that, yes – it is impossible to know what the band did on every single day. And I hope the reader accepts that fact as well.

A bit needs to be said about how this was put together. To nail down the dates of key events – and squeeze out some interesting anecdotes about them – my first stop was interviewing as many people as possible who worked with the band, played in the band, who knew the band, or who were simply "there" to witness rock history.

As you will see, the majority of the quotes in this book are from fresh interviews I did with 55 people, whom I am forever in debt to for generously providing first-hand accounts, memories, explanations, and/or anecdotes of important moments in Nirvana's career. Those people are: Grant Alden, Gina Arnold, Greg Babior, Scott Becker, Bill Bennett, Nils Bernstein, Danny Bland, Meat Puppets' Derrick Bostrum, Jamie Brown, Chad Channing, Marci Cohen, Flaming Lips' Wayne Coyne, Melora Creager, Charles R. Cross, Donna DeChristopher, Drunk Ted, Jack Endino, Falling James, Robert Fisher, Gillian G. Gaar, Gary Graf, Lisa Gladfelter Bell, Pansy Division's Jon Ginoli, Danny Goldberg, Michael Greene, Helmet's Page Hamilton, Steve Hochman, Daniel House, Megan Jasper, Jack Off Jill's Jessicka, Cheryl Kavolchick, Greg Kot, Dave Lott, Make-A-Wish Foundation, Jim Merlis, Josh Mills, Craig Montgomery, Slim Moon, Posies' Mike Musburger, Dave Navarro, Carlos "Cake" Nunez, Tom Phalen, Jonathan Poneman, Kevan Roberts, Tom Sheehy, Lynda Stenge, Kurt St. Thomas, Susie Tennant, Dave Thompson, Jenny Toomey, John Troutman, Ted Volk, John Wallace, Greg Watermann, and "Weird Al" Yankovic.

Even though media law allows journalists to use a certain amount of material from another source without giving credit, every single quote in this book that isn't from one of my interviews is attributed to its rightful source. I strongly encourage future authors to credit their research material as well. This habit of rewriting other people's work has got to stop – if only out of professional courtesy to those in our field. The authors of the works credited within this book deserve a lot of credit for being among the first journalists to cover Nirvana with the passion that they did.

After the interviews, the next step was to get my hands on as many official documents as possible. This includes official copies of tour itineraries; album/single release schedules; album liner notes; press releases from Geffen, Gold Mountain, or other authorities; letters; and some not-so-pleasant stuff such as police reports, lawsuits, and later the autopsy report and death certificate. I'd like to thank the following for providing useful information, helping to fact-check, sending me articles or documents, providing contact numbers, and/or hooking me up with interviewees: Michelle Andersen, Leah Barker, Tammi Blevins, Jeff Boerio, Michele Botwin, Elizabeth Chanley, Brian Eldridge, Yvonne Garrett, Roy Hamm, Heath, Jennifer Hollman, Bill Kennedy, Michael Lavine, Tristan Laughter, Lookout! Records, Barbara Mitchell, Killing Joke's Paul Raven, Sorrelle Saidman, and Roy Trakin.

I am also grateful to the following Web sites for their help with research: allmusic.com, allstarnews.com, cdnow.com, nirvanaclub.com, duke.edu/~jlb2/nirvgd.htm, flash.net/~mabeyta/nirvana/nirvana.html, subpop.com, geffen.com, riaa.com, billboard.com, http://seds.lpl.arizona.edu/~smiley/nirvana/index.html, geocities.com/SunsetStrip/Towers/6792/rec_sess/main.html, http://ksproul.threadnet.com, walrus.com/~dreamlog/nirvana/, endino.com, latimes.com, arocknid.com/gnr/, ew.com, foofighters.com, calendarhome.com/tyc/, http://members.xoom.com/holeboot/, geocities.com/SunsetStrip/Arena/3342/tour-gnr.html, silverbox.com/nirvana/, southern.com/southern/label/DIS/, and ludd.luth.se/misc/nirvana/faq/ConcertChronology.html.

Special thanks to *Billboard* – past and present – Ken Schlager, Craig Rosen, Melinda Newman, Timothy White, Geoff Mayfield, and Thom Duffy; SCSU; Arthur Levy; Mike Greenblatt; and Anne Leighton, all of whom believed in me early on; to Lucian Randall for giving me this assignment; *Cobain* by the Editors of *Rolling Stone*; to my family for their love and support, especially Chris, the Borzillos, Maguires, Horvaths, and McGills; to Kevin Raub, Donna De Christopher, and Jim Keller and all at allstarnews.com and cdnow.

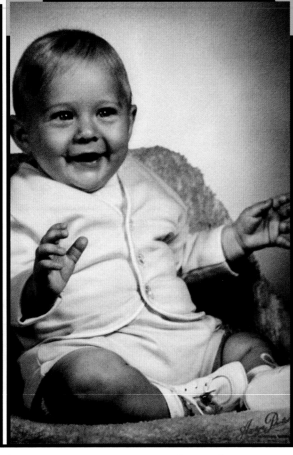

"HEY MAN, LET'S START A BAND!"

MAY 16, 1965:
Krist Anthony Novoselic is born in Compton, California to Krist and Maria Novoselic, who emigrated to the USA from Yugoslavia in 1963. They first lived in Gardena, California where his father was a driver for the Sparkletts bottled water company. Up until around April 1993, Krist used the more common spelling of his name, Chris.

JULY 9, 1965:
Courtney Love Michele Harrison is born in San Francisco to Linda Rissi, a psychiatrist and hippie, and Hank Harrison, a one-time road manager for the Grateful Dead and author of *The Dead* and *Kurt Cobain, Beyond Nirvana: The Legacy of Kurt Cobain*. Throughout the years, Courtney is known by the following names: Courtney Menely, Lorrie Glass, Michele Rodriguez, Courtney Love, Courtney Love Cobain, and Courtney Cobain.

JANUARY 31, 1967:
Chad Douglas Channing is born in Santa Rosa, California to Wayne and Burnyce Channing. His father is a successful radio DJ and television newscaster. Chad, Nirvana's first long-term drummer, moved around a lot due to his father's profession. He has lived all over California, and in Idaho, West Virginia, Alaska, Minnesota, Hawaii, and Washington.

FEBRUARY 20, 1967:
Kurt Donald Cobain is born in Grays Harbor Community Hospital in Aberdeen, Washington to Wendy, a housewife, and Donald Cobain, a gas station mechanic at Chevron in nearby Hoquiam where they lived at 2830 Aberdeen Ave. More of Kurt's childhood will be told in this chapter than the other members of Nirvana, as it served as the foundation for what would later become some of the most engaging songs ever recorded.

AUGUST 1967:

Wendy and Don Cobain and six-month-old Kurt move to 1210 East 1st St. in Aberdeen, Washington. In an early Nirvana bio, Kurt calls Aberdeen "a redneck, loser town," and the city has been described many times as "Twin Peaks without the excitement."

1969

At age two, Kurt develops an interest in music. "He was singing from the time he was two," says Kurt's Aunt Mari (Fradenburg) Earl in Gillian G. Gaar's extensive article "Verse Chorus Verse: The Recording History of Nirvana," published in the record collector magazine *Goldmine.* "He would sing Beatles songs like 'Hey Jude.' He would do anything. You could just say, 'Hey Kurt, sing this!' and he would sing it. He had a lot of charisma from a very young age." Mari, who was a country musician herself and the sister of Kurt's mother Wendy, was the first person to hand Kurt a guitar.

There is an audio clip of Kurt around age two in the controversial documentary by Nick Broomfield, *Kurt & Courtney,* in which Kurt's screaming into the microphone such nonsense as, "Hey monkey." Then you hear him say to his aunt, "I'll do it by myself." "He was a pretty wild little guy," says Mari in the film.

JANUARY 14, 1969:

David Eric Grohl is born in Warren, Ohio to James, a Scripps-Howard newspaperman, and Virginia Grohl, a high school English teacher. He lives in Columbus, Ohio for the first three years of his life.

1970

At age three, Kurt becomes hateful toward policemen, so he concocts this little ditty to sing when they passed by, "Corn on the cops! Corn on the cops! The cops are coming! They're going to kill you!," according to Michael Azerrad's 1993 biography on the band, *Come As You Are: The Story of Nirvana.*

APRIL 24, 1970:

Used to being the center of attention, especially his mother's attention, Kurt now has to share some of the spotlight with his sister Kimberly, born on this day.

1972

At age three, Dave Grohl moves with his family to Springfield, Virginia.

1974

Kurt goes on Ritalin as a treatment for his hyperactivity. The drug fails and makes him more hyper, so the family tries sedatives, which make him too sleepy. They soon decide to just cut out sugar and it seems to work. At age seven, as Kurt would later reveal in his suicide note, he became "hateful toward all humans in general only because it seems so easy for people to get along and have empathy." Also at this age, Aunt Mari gives him a bass drum, which the youth would march around his neighborhood banging loudly.

OCTOBER 1974:

In second grade, Kurt's artwork appears on the cover of his school newspaper, but feeling that his art is unworthy of the cover, he gets angry that it's received such an honor. "My mother encouraged me a lot to be artistic," Kurt tells Roy Trakin of the US music trade publication *Hits* in 1991. "It was written in a contract at an early age that I would be an artist." Kurt was described as an extremely sensitive, bright, and perceptive child.

DECEMBER 25, 1974:

Kurt gets a lump of coal for Christmas. He wanted a five dollar "Starsky and Hutch" gun.

1975

At age eight, Don and Wendy Cobain divorce, leaving a devastating mark on Kurt. Kurt's mother was given legal custody, but he didn't live with her for very long. In the coming years, he moved between his father's house in Montesano, Washington and several sets of aunts and uncles, and grandparents, and later friends and classmates. To express the anger and pain he felt from his parents' breakup, Kurt writes on his bedroom wall: "I hate mom. I hate dad. Dad hates mom. Mom hates dad. It simply makes you want to be sad."

"I remember feeling ashamed, for some reason. I was ashamed of my parents," Kurt explains to Jon Savage in a 1993 *Guitar World* interview. "I couldn't face some of my friends at school anymore, because I desperately wanted to have the classic, you know, typical family. Mother, father. I wanted that security, so I resented my parents for quite a few years because of that." Kurt later told *Spin* magazine that after the divorce he became "extremely depressed and withdrawn."

Also this year, Kurt starts taking drum lessons. And, back on the East Coast, Dave Grohl's parents, Virginia and James, divorce when he is six years old. Dave is raised by his mother.

● **An angelic Kurt Donald Cobain** ●

1976

At age nine, Kurt has said he became manic-depressive and started looking at things differently: "Up until I was nine, I felt I could become a rock star or astronaut or the President. I had total freedom and a lot of support and love from my family or at least my mom's side," Kurt tells the *Los Angeles Times*' Robert Hilburn in 1993.

Before he wanted to be a rock star, Kurt wanted to be just like his hero, Evel Knievel. "I wanted to be a stuntman the first seven years of my life," he tells journalist Roy Trakin. "[I'd] put pillows on the ground and jump off my roof. I was a little baby Iggy Pop."

1977/1978

At age seven or eight, Dave Grohl picks up his first instrument: the trombone.

1978

In sixth grade, Kurt's views on life turn downward yet again. "When I was a kid, I thought everything was so great," Kurt tells journalist Bob Gulla in 1990 for an interview that isn't published until 1999 when it's published on the online music site www.cdnow.com. "I was so excited to grow up. But in sixth grade, I realized 'Wow my whole life really sucks. Everyone I know is an asshole'."

FEBRUARY 1978:

Kurt's father Don remarries and becomes a stepfather to two children. Kurt's not happy with it. "I tried to do everything to make him feel wanted," Don Cobain says in *Come As You Are*. "But, he just didn't want to be there and wanted to be with his mom and she didn't want him." Wendy badmouthed Don in this biography also, claiming that Don threw Kurt across a room when he was six years old. Don denied it.

1979

At age 12, after having seen photos of punk bands like the Sex Pistols in *Creem* magazine, Kurt becomes attracted to punk rock. "I sensed that [I wanted to be in a punk band] before I had an opportunity to even hear any punk rock," Kurt says to *Hits*. "I had a subscription to *Creem* magazine, and I thought, at age 12, that that's exactly what I wanted to do and it took years after that to finally have an opportunity to hear that stuff 'cause I lived in a really small town."

Also this year, while in seventh grade, Kurt starts getting drunk and he goes to his first rock concert: Sammy Hagar. "My friend and I were taken by his sister to the show in Seattle," Kurt tells Gina Arnold in her 1993 book, *Route 666: On the Road to Nirvana*. "And on the way there, we drank a case of beer and we were stuck in traffic and I had to go so bad I peed my pants. And when we got into the concert, people were passing pipes around, marijuana, and I'd never smoked pot before, and I got really high."

Meanwhile, at age 10, Dave Grohl has an important musical experience. "When I was in the fifth grade," Dave later tells Australian journalist Murray Engleheart, "I guess I was 10 years old, my best friend and I went to see that AC/DC movie, *Let There Be Rock*. I had never been to a rock concert or seen a rock movie and that fucking movie changed my life man." He soon forms his first band, the H.G. Hancock Band.

This is also the year that a 14-year-old Chris Novoselic moves to

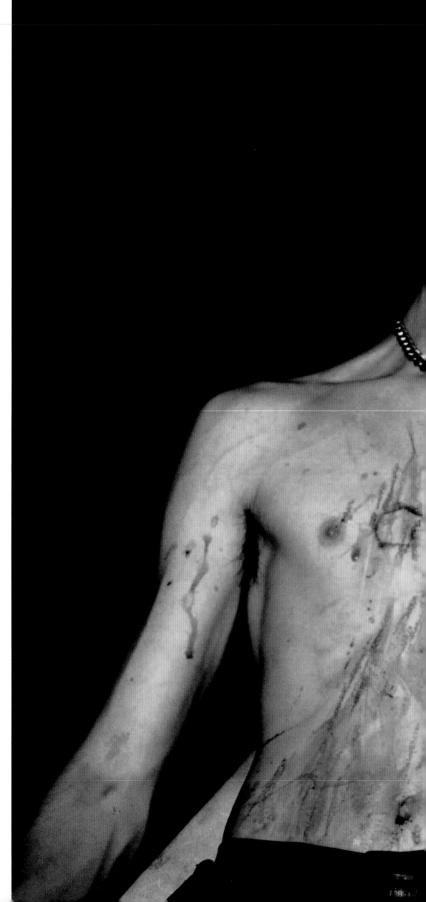

Aberdeen, Washington. (Maria Novoselic tells the *Seattle Times* in 1992 that the reason they moved to Aberdeen was because "there are lots of Croatian people here.") And Chad Channing's family moves him to Washington State as well – first to Port Angeles and then to Bainbridge Island, which is a 20-minute ferry ride from Seattle. Meanwhile, Bruce Pavitt starts a fanzine titled *Subterranean Pop*. He later becomes a co-founder of Sub Pop Records.

JUNE 14, 1979:

Don Cobain tries to get custody of Kurt from the Grays Harbor Superior Court.

JULY 1979:

Suicide ran in Kurt's family. Kurt's Great Uncle Burle Cobain commits suicide with a gunshot to his abdomen on this day, according to *Rolling Stone*. Another uncle, Burle's brother Kenneth, killed himself in 1984 in the same way that Kurt later does: with a gunshot to the head. And Kurt's mother Wendy tells *Entertainment Weekly* that her grandfather also tried to kill himself and ultimately died from his injuries.

In the *EW* piece, Wendy admits that Kurt was probably a "mis- or undiagnosed depressive," which also ran in the family, and that there were tell-tale signs that Kurt had a serious problem with depression: "I now know in hindsight that the sleeping he was doing in his teenage years was the very beginning of it. He was sleeping so much, but that was also masked by just being a teenager. But now I look back and go, 'Aha, that was the very beginning of it.'"

1980

After bouncing between his two parents' houses, Kurt moves again and changes schools to the Miller Junior High School in Aberdeen. Kurt's father makes him join the Babe Ruth baseball team. Not an avid sports fan, Kurt would also be pressured into accompanying his father on a hunting trip and joining the junior high wrestling team. In an act of rebellion and to embarrass his father who is in the audience, Kurt throws a championship match by lying down on the mat instead of fighting back.

While in the eighth grade, Kurt is diagnosed with a minor case of scoliosis, a curvature of the spine. Health problems plagued him all his life. Along with scoliosis and, before that, hyperactivity, he also suffered from chronic bronchitis and severe stomach pains. Kurt would later self-medicate his ailments with heroin and even experiment with a virtual reality machine to help control his physical pain.

JUNE 1980:

Chris also suffered from depression as a child. Worried about it, the Novoselics send Chris to live with his relatives in Croatia for a year.

1981

February 20, 1981: For Kurt's 14th birthday, his Uncle Chuck Fradenburg, Aunt Mari's husband and also a musician, asks him if he'd like a bike or a guitar for his birthday. Kurt chooses a guitar and gets a $125 Lindell. Kurt soon takes lessons from a man named Warren Mason, who was in Chuck's band at the time. Within his first year playing the instrument, Kurt learns to play Led Zeppelin's "Stairway to Heaven," the Cars' "My

Best Friend's Girl," the Kingsmen's "Louie Louie," AC/DC's "Back In Black," and Queen's "Another One Bites the Dust."

MAY 1981:

After only three months, Wendy makes Kurt stop taking guitar lessons. Kurt continues to play.

SUMMER 1981:

The summer before entering into the ninth grade, Kurt meets the Melvins for the first time at their rehearsal space, where the band was playing songs from Cream and Jimi Hendrix. Of his first impression of Kurt, the Melvins' Buzz Osborne (a.k.a. King Buzzo) says to Dave Thompson in *Never Fade Away: The Kurt Cobain Story*: "He looked like a teenage runaway."

The Melvins – the biggest band in Aberdeen at the time – are acknowledged as the godfathers of grunge, and Buzz soon plays a key role in Nirvana's career. He's the one who introduces Kurt to such bands as the Butthole Surfers, Flipper, and MDC; and he also introduces him to his first girlfriend, Tracy Marander, and later on drummer Dave Grohl. Kurt actually auditioned for the Melvins once, but didn't make it. He soon becomes a roadie for them instead, and Chris spent some time roadie-ing for the band as well.

"Until I met the Melvins, my life was really boring," Kurt says to *Spin* in 1992. "All of a sudden, I found a totally different world. I started getting into music and finally seeing shows and doing things I always wanted to do while I was in high school."

DECEMBER 25, 1981:

At age 12, Dave Grohl gets an electric guitar for Christmas.

1981/1982

In the ninth grade, Kurt becomes a heavy pot smoker, and he meets up with Buzz again at Montesano High in Montesano, Washington. Kurt's also teased by classmates this year who think he's gay because he has a homosexual friend. "I didn't even know he was gay, but everyone else did, so there were all these gay bashing rumors going on, like they were going to beat me up," Kurt says in *Route 666*. "There were really bad vibes going on in my P.E. class and then my mom forbid me to hang out with him anymore because he was gay... I was always attracted to him 'cause he was really different."

In his 1993 interview with the prominent gay magazine the *Advocate*, Kurt says, in reaction to these rumors, that he'd start to pretend he was gay "just to fuck with people."

1982

At age 17, Chris attends his first rock concert. "The first concert I ever went to was the Scorpions," Chris says in *Route 666*. "I went with these gay guys 'cause I was the only one with a car. One guy was my age and the other was older. And we were driving up to Seattle, and I looked in the back seat and they were making out and I'm like, 'Jeepers creepers.' I was 17. They didn't bug me or anything. I kind of laughed. I thought it was funny 'cause I never saw gay people before. So we went to the show, it was the Scorpions, and it was totally boring. I stood up front and threw my shirt on the stage."

● The Melvins – an early influence on Nirvana ●

● **The Butthole Surfers** ●

"Most of what I remember about the songs was a lot of distortion on guitar, really heavy bass, and the clucky sound of the wooden spoons," Mari tells *Goldmine*. "And his voice, sounding like he was mumbling under a big fluffy comforter, with some passionate screams once in awhile."

1983

Chris graduates from high school. He's the only member of Nirvana to do so. Shortly after graduation, Chris's parents also divorce. Meanwhile, Kurt transfers schools once again, this time to Aberdeen High School. Now in the 11th grade, Kurt starts skipping classes regularly. Meanwhile, in Virginia, Dave Grohl is voted Vice President of his freshman class at Thomas Jefferson High School in Alexandria where he'd play Circle Jerks and Bad Brains during the morning announcements, according to *Come As You Are*. He was a heavy pot smoker in school too.

1983/ 1984

During his senior year in high school, Chris meets his future wife, Shelli.

1984 MAY 1984:

Wendy remarries to a longshoreman named Pat O'Connor. Kurt soon moves back in with his mother, but only temporarily. According to *Come As You Are*, Kurt had to beg to move back in with his mother. Once he did, he found that all wasn't perfect in the household. He once witnessed a fight between his mother and Pat, which ended with Wendy pulling out a gun and threatening to shoot him. She then took all of his guns and threw them in the Wishkah River. Kurt paid a few friends to fish them out for him, and he sold the guns to buy his first amplifier for his guitar.

SUMMER 1984:

At age 15, Dave joins the band, Freak Baby, where he first plays guitar and then switches to the drums. The group broke up the following summer. Other early bands for Dave were Dain Bramage, Mission Impossible, Fast, and Harlingtox A.D. (Harlingtox A.D. actually never played a show; it was just a 1990 studio project conceived by Dave and Tos Nieuwenhuizen of the Holland band God.)

SEPTEMBER 25, 1984:

Kurt falls in love with Black Flag's "Damaged II" from a mix tape Buzz made him. Kurt sells his record collection to see Black Flag live at the Mountaineer (with Saccharine Trust and Tom Troccoli on the bill) in Seattle with Buzz and Matt Lukin, the Melvins' bass player, who Kurt first met in Montesano High. Matt later joins Mudhoney.

"Buzz was the punk rock guru of Aberdeen. He's the guy who spread the good news around town, but only to the most deserving, 'cause a lot of people in Aberdeen would discount it," Chris Novoselic, who was also the recipient of a mix tape of punk songs from Buzz, says in *Option* magazine. Chris also played guitar in a band with Buzz on bass and the Melvins' original drummer Mike Dillard. Later, under the name Phil Atio, Chris plays in a Mentors cover band.

DECEMBER 1982:

Kurt records a demo tape called "Organized Confusion" at his Aunt Mari's house over his Christmas break from school. The tape features Kurt singing, playing guitar, and playing percussion (he actually bangs on a suitcase to get a drum sound). "I told him, 'Kurt, you're totally welcome to use my computer drummer.' He goes, 'Oh yeah, I don't want to use a computer; I want to keep my music pure,'" Mari says in *Kurt & Courtney*.

1985

MARCH 1985:

Chris and Shelli start dating seriously. The two marry in 1989.

MAY 1985:

The latter part of Kurt's senior year at Aberdeen High was a tough one. "When I was 17, I got kicked out of my mom's house," Kurt tells the *New York Times*' Jon Pareles in 1993. "I was living on the streets and I called my dad, and he said I could come back to stay for a few days, on a trial basis. When I did he had me take the test for the Navy and he had me pawn my guitar. He had the recruiter come to the house two nights in a row."

Kurt also tells *Hits* in 1991 that he was "borderline autistic. I had trouble in school, constantly being kicked out. I quit the last month. I was supposed to go to art school; I had won a couple of scholarships but it was just too much for me to handle, I knew I didn't want to do art. I wanted to do music, so I ran away from home. And became a punk rocker for a few months, living on the streets."

WINTER 1985/1986:

With no place to go and a dead-end job as a janitor at his former high school, Kurt spends some nights sleeping under the bridge over Aberdeen's Wishkah River. The experience is the subject of "Something in the Way" from *Nevermind*.

"I always wanted to experience the street life because my teenage life in Aberdeen was so boring," Kurt tells *Spin*. "But I was never really independent enough to do it. I applied for food stamps, lived under the bridge, and built a fort at the cedar mill. I eventually moved to Olympia."

For eight months starting in early winter of 1985, Kurt stays with Steve and Eric Shillinger and their family. While he lived there, Kurt also had a job teaching swimming to kids aged three to seven at the YMCA. Also this winter, Kurt, who initially sings in a British accent to be more punk, hooks up with bassist Dale Crover (who later becomes the Melvins' drummer, and also plays drums with Nirvana for a brief period) and drummer Greg Hokanson. The three guys record a demo tape on a TEAC four-track at Aunt Mari's house under the name Fecal Matter.

"They set up in my music room and they'd just crank it up. It was loud," Mari tells *Goldmine* of the session. "...I don't recall any of the songs being early versions of anything they did with Nirvana. It just resembled the Nirvana sound." The tape includes "Downer," which is later recorded for Nirvana's debut 1989 album *Bleach*.

"GOD IS GAY AND HOMO SEX RULES".

The band plays a few shows, one of which was as the opening act for the Melvins at the Spot Tavern in Moclips, Washington this December. Kurt also lives with Greg for about six months in 1986. "I don't think he ever slept at home past the age of 15," says Greg in the *Seattle Times*. The story also quotes Greg's mother saying that living with Kurt was like "living with the devil."

Meanwhile, it's the 11th grade for Dave Grohl and he decides to drop out of school.

DECEMBER 1985:

Kurt and Dale Crover (Greg Hokanson is no longer in the group) record another four-track demo at Aunt Mari's house. Some bootlegs of the tape list the songs as "Bambi Slaughter," "Buffy's Pregnant," "Downer," "Laminated Effect," "Spank Thru," "Sound of Dentage," and "Suicide Samurai." However, Mari mentions a song called "Seaside Suicide" in an interview she did in *Kurt & Courtney*.

"I do feel that Kurt was an unstable person before he ever got into the music business," says Mari in the film. "When he was here recording in this room, when he was 17 years old, he and his friend, the drummer he brought along, took off for lunch or something and I kind of sneaked in here and took a look at his lyrics. And there was a song that was in amongst his lyrics that he never did record on that particular tape, but it was called 'Seaside Suicide' and it left me with an impression that he had possibly tried suicide before."

It's the Kurt/Dale tape that attracts Chris to Kurt's music. Chris explains how he and Kurt got together in the interview CD *Nevermind: It's an Interview*: "A little social group came together, and we just kinda hung out, you know, talked about things. And then one thing led to another. Kurt did a tape with Dale Crover from the Melvins and one of the songs on it was 'Spank Thru' and he turned me on to it, and I kinda liked it. It got me excited, so I go, 'Hey man, let's start a band.' We scrounged up a drummer, and we started practicing... took it very seriously too."

One of the first groups Kurt and Chris play together in is the Sellouts, a Creedence Clearwater Revival cover band. The Sellouts include Kurt on drums, Chris singing, and Steve Newman on bass. Kurt and Chris also had a band briefly with a drummer named Bob McFadden. And the two also played together in the Stiff Woodies. Kurt was on drums, Chris sang lead vocals, and other members, such as Buzz Osborne, Dale Crover, Matt Lukin, and Gary Cole came and went. They rehearse in a room (an empty apartment) above Chris' mother's beauty shop, Maria's Hair Design in Aberdeen.

1986

MARCH 1986:

Chris and Shelli move to Phoenix, Arizona to look for better jobs. After six months, they move back to Washington.

JULY 1986:

Jonathan Poneman and Bruce Pavitt launch Sub Pop Records with the release of the compilation, *Sub Pop 100*, featuring U-Men, Steve Fisk, Naked Raygun, Sonic Youth, Big Black's Steve Albini, and Skinny Puppy. This same month, Reciprocal Recording opens its doors in Seattle, where the likes of Nirvana, Green River, and Tad would soon record.

Kurt Cobain later tells the *Chicago Tribune*'s Greg Kot in 1991 of this period: "Around 1985, '86, the hard-core scene seemed exhausted to us. It was boring, so we just started accepting the fact that we liked the music that we grew up on: Alice Cooper, MC5, Kiss. It was almost taboo to admit something like that in '85, but we grew our hair long and said, 'Fuck what everybody else thinks.'"

SUMMER 1986:

Kurt is arrested on a vandalism charge in Aberdeen for spray-painting God is Gay and Homo Sex Rules on cars. He's fined $180 and given a 30-day suspended sentence. His guitar would later boast the sticker: "Vandalism: Beautiful as a Rock in a Cop's Face." This summer, Kurt tries heroin for the first time at age 18. He's previously only smoked pot, drank, and dabbled in pills, such as the tranquilizer Percodan.

DECEMBER 1986:

Kurt and Matt Lukin move into 10001/2 East Second Street in Aberdeen after Kurt's mom put down the $100 deposit for them. This is the apartment where Kurt kept turtles in the living room. Soon after moving in, he gets a job at the Polynesian Hotel in Ocean Shores, Washington. Matt moves out five months later.

WINTER 1986:

Kurt plays his first show with Buzz and Dale under the name Brown Cow at GESSCO Hall in Olympia, a town with an artist community and the hip college radio station, Evergreen State College's KAOS. At the show, Kurt meets Dylan Carlson and the two remain friends until Kurt's death. Kurt also meets Dylan's roommate Slim Moon at a party at Slim's house in Olympia, which was dubbed the Alamo.

Slim is the head of the Olympia, Washington-based indie label Kill Rock Stars and a founding member of the band Lush (not to be confused with the British group who had a 1996 hit with "Ladykillers"), and he was also briefly in Dylan's band Earth.

Of the Brown Cow show, Slim says, "There was some weird thing where Buzz told [promoter] Stan Dunster over the phone what the band was called, and he put the wrong thing on the flyer. It was Brown Towel, but they put Brown Cow. But Buzz and Kurt just seemed to think it was funny that there was confusion, so they wouldn't clear it up. It was a one-time show anyway." As for the show itself, Slim remembers it as being "kind of goofy in a Touch and Go way, if you know Killdozer and Scratch Acid. They were goofy and dire."

The show changed Slim's opinion that Kurt was just another Melvins' hanger-on: "The Melvins were from Aberdeen, which is a pretty backwards place, and this is before Buzz got clean and Matt Lukin – Buzz and Dale, they were kind of party animals back then. So the Melvins, when they came to Olympia or even when they came to Seattle, the Melvins always had this entourage of four or five really backwards kind of guys. Very much *Deliverance*-like. They would just sort of follow them around. And I figured out that Chris, who had a much tighter connection with them than Kurt did at first, was sort of a cut above the rest of the guys that followed around the Melvins. But the first few times I saw Kurt, I just thought of him as another one of those sort of inbred Aberdeen retards that hung out with the Melvins or

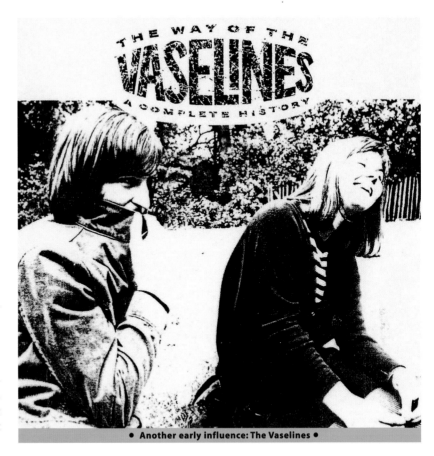

● Another early influence: The Vaselines ●

whatever, and so seeing that show just made me think maybe that guy's got something more going on."

1987

JANUARY/ FEBRUARY 1987:

Kurt and Chris find a new drummer, Aaron Burckhard, who lived down the street from Kurt at the time. The trio soon goes through a series of band names – Skid Row (not the hair band led by Sebastian Bach), Pen Cap Chew, Ted Ed Fred, Throat Oyster, Windowpane, and later Bliss. The name Nirvana didn't come up until early 1988.

EARLY 1987:

Kurt, Chris, and Aaron perform at a house party in Raymond, Washington, which they've often cited as one of their favorite early shows.

"We were really drunk so we started making spectacles of ourselves," Kurt says about the show in *Option*. "Playing off the bad vibes we were giving to the rednecks, you know – jumping off tables and pretending we were rock stars. And Chris jumped through a window. Then we started playing [Flipper's] 'Sex Bomb' for about an hour and our girlfriends were hanging on us and grabbing our legs and doing a mock lesbian scene, and that really started freaking out the rednecks." Their next gig is at the closing night of GESSCO Hall.

● Dylan Carlson: Stayed friends with Kurt until the Nirvana front man's death ●

Slim Moon has fond memories of some of these early parties, though he's not clear of the dates. "Chris would sometimes get drunk and he'd take his clothes off and jump on someone's table at a party until it broke and they would hate him forever. Or at another party he like shot off the fire extinguisher in the middle of the party. He always just meant to be funny, but sometimes it would get out of control and he'd end up making enemies," says Slim. "Kurt was never the life of the party, but when he did talk at parties he'd say things that were really bitingly funny. But usually he'd just hold up the wall."

At another party during this period, at a party house called the Dude Ranch, Slim recalls getting the impression that Kurt was conscious of the perception that some in the scene had of him as being just another part of the Melvins entourage: "I was engaged in some conversation about Big Black and he was coming out to his car or something and heard me talking. And, he goes, loudly, 'I like Big Black.' And then he goes, 'No, really, I do.' The tone of it was like he was saying 'I actually know who they are. I like what they're doing. I'm not some guy from Aberdeen who's heard of the Melvins, but doesn't know music.'"

MARCH 1987:

Kurt, Chris, and Aaron perform at the Community World Theater in Tacoma. "I'm certain their first show after the one at the party was Community World Theater under one of these three names, Skid Row, Ted Ed Fred, or Pen Cap Chew. But I think they were called Skid Row first and then they played Community World and then a show at GESSCO's last night when it suddenly lost its funding," says Slim.

APRIL 17, 1987:

Calling themselves Skid Row, Kurt, Chris, and Aaron perform on Calvin Johnson's radio show, "Boy Meets Girl," on Evergreen's KAOS. Calvin is also the head of the indie label K Records and a member of the band Beat Happening. The songs performed live on the show are "Love Buzz," "Floyd the Barber," "Downer," "Mexican Seafood," "Hairspray Queen," "Pen Cap Chew," "Spank Thru," "Anorexorcist," and "White Lace and Strange" by Thunder and Roses. The tape from this show serves as the band's first demo tape.

SPRING 1987:

Meanwhile, Dave Grohl joins the Washington, DC-based hardcore band Scream as their drummer. The band breaks up in 1990 while on tour in Los Angeles. Scream's releases with Dave in the band include *No More Censorship, Live at Van Hall in Amsterdam*, a self-titled live album, and *Fumble*.

JUNE 1987:

Sub Pop releases Green River's *Dry As a Bone* EP and a new "genre" of music is labeled. "This is actually where the term 'grunge' originated," believes Megan Jasper, who started as the receptionist at Sub Pop and is currently the label's General Manager. "Sub Pop put this in the catalogue where Everett True [writer for the UK music magazine *Melody Maker*] pulled out the descriptions from the album and it says 'ultra loose grunge.' So, Everett took that and called it grunge."

Also in June of 1987, a 14-year-old girl's rape in Tacoma affects Kurt to the extent that he writes a song about the horrible incident. The song

is "Polly." Kurt later explains the song to *Hits* as an "anti-rape song... It's a story about a rapist who captures a sadomasochist and this woman, 'Polly,' is having sex as a way to develop a relationship. He rapes her at first and they have a relationship and they fall in love, then eventually she kills him and runs away. It's not a pleasant thought. I just thought that a standard song about rape would be boring and trite." The true story entails the young girl being kidnapped, raped, and tortured.

SEPTEMBER 1987:

Kurt meets his first steady girlfriend, Tracy Marander, through Buzz.

OCTOBER 1987:

Kurt and Chris place an ad in Seattle's main music paper, the *Rocket*, looking for a new drummer to replace Aaron Burckhard, who parts ways with the group over their heavy practice schedule. The ad reads: "SERIOUS DRUMMER WANTED. Underground attitude, Black Flag, Melvins, Zeppelin, Scratch Acid, Ethel Merman. Versatile as heck. Kurdt 352-0992." (This was Kurt's home phone number in Olympia.) Meanwhile, Dave Grohl heads out on a US tour with Scream.

FALL 1987:

Kurt soon moves into Tracy's apartment at 114 North Pear Street in Olympia (where rent is a mere $137 a month) and they go out for the next three years. "He lived in the apartment in the back," says Slim, his next-door neighbor, who'd sometimes loan him records including his Leadbelly LPs. "When he wasn't on tour later on, he was a total homebody. And Tracy worked all night and slept all day and he was just bored all the time. Kurt and Tracy lived in the studio in the front and it was really crammed in there, and then they eventually moved in the back into a one-bedroom. Me and Dylan lived in the three-bedroom with this guy named Jim Hartley."

While Tracy worked the overnight shift in the cafeteria at Boeing with Chris's girlfriend Shelli, Kurt stayed home and worked on his music. When Tracy complained that he didn't do his fair share of the housework, he threatened to move into his car. "About a Girl" is about their relationship.

DECEMBER 1987:

Kurt and Chris start practicing with Dale Crover on drums to prepare for recording their first real demo tape. According to *Come As You Are*, they practice for three weekends before heading into Reciprocal Recording in January 1988.

Somewhere between October 1987 and February 1988, Chad Channing, Nirvana's drummer from May 1988 through May 1990, first meets Chris and Kurt. He was in Tic-Dolly-Row at the time. "I just met them socially through a friend of mine. They saw Tic-Dolly-Row play at the Community World Theater. I didn't meet them then, but later Damen [Ramero], a friend of mine, was pretty good friends with them and a little while after that – after my band broke up – Damen got a hold of me and said that if I wanted to meet Chris, he was in this band and they were looking for a drummer. And it was at that Community World Theater where I met Chris. It would have been probably '87 or '88. It was really cold out, so between October and February."

Chad says his first impression of Kurt and Chris was that they "seemed like straight-up pretty normal guys."

GUNKA, GUNKA, CLANK

JANUARY 23, 1988:

Kurt, Chris, and Dale Crover record a 10-song demo tape with Jack Endino at Reciprocal Recording in Seattle. Jack, a member of Skin Yard, was *the* person to record with, having recorded several Seattle bands, including Soundgarden, Mudhoney, and Green River. The six-hour session included "AeroZeppelin," "Beeswax," "Downer," "Floyd the Barber," "Hairspray Queen," "Mexican Seafood," "Paper Cuts," "If You Must," "Pen Cap Chew," and "Spank Thru." They booked the session under Kurt's name and when Jack asked what their band name was, they listed a whole series of names that they had used. The show that night at Community World Theater in Tacoma, Washington was under the name Ted Ed Fred.

The tape, which cost them $152.44, is known as the "Dale Demo" and it's this tape that piques the interest of Jonathan Poneman, co-founder of Sub Pop Records. "I would talk to Jack every now and then because there were a lot of bands going into Reciprocal and I'd just ask him, 'Hey did you hear anything that blew you away?' I never did it quite entirely seriously, just feeling my way around, like, 'Hey [mockingly] what's the Next Big Thing?," recalls Jonathan. "He told me, 'There's this

kid who came in who looks like a car mechanic. He came in with Dale Crover. He lives in Olympia and his name is Kurt.' And he says, 'To be honest I don't even really know what to make of this tape. It's awesome, but they just bashed it out and it's really unlike anything I've really heard. The guy's got an amazing voice.'

"I think he was more awestruck than anything that this guy he never heard of came in from the hinterlands and just whipped out this pretty amazing tape," continues Jonathan. "I remember the very first song on the tape was 'If You Must' and listening to the first part of it, it starts off with a little guitar strum, a mellow guitar part, for lack of a better word, it's a little dissonant. Kurt's doing this slurring, quiet vocal over this dark, dissonant guitar and then suddenly, he goes into his classic roar into this chorus. The first time I heard that I just went, 'Ohhhhh my God'. I heard a pain and an angst, but I also think there was a playfulness like with songs like 'Floyd the Barber' [an ode of sorts to the character on 'The Andy Griffith Show']."

Of the session, Jack Endino says that it went smoothly – not many bands and engineers can record and mix 10 songs in one afternoon – and that it "went by so fast that I hardly remember even talking with them. It was one of the fastest sessions I had done. They had a show to get to in Tacoma (30 miles away) and didn't have much money to spend, so they were in a hurry. I obliged."

JANUARY 24, 1988:

The day after the recording, the "Dale Demo," which was just roughly mixed at the time, began making the rounds. Kurt sent copies to various indie labels, as well as to friends. Slim Moon was among the first to hear the demo.

"Kurt gave me a tape the next day after he recorded it," says Slim. "He said basically that it was a rough tape and they still needed to go mix it, but they never did go mix it. I played it a lot and I thought it was great. I hadn't really realized how good they were, and I also thought that they'd really suffer if Dale left. I knew he was a temporary drummer, and that Kurt was a lot better songwriter than I had realized. I didn't really think he had that much ambition then, but I got to know him better and I sort of realized that he really did. He's just really coy about it."

FEBRUARY 20, 1988:

Kurt Cobain turns 21 years old. Strangely, none of the 50-plus people interviewed for this book could remember any birthday, Thanksgiving, or Christmas celebrations. "I think they were a lot like me as far as birthdays go," says Chad Channing. "I just let mine come and go."

February/March 1988: Excited about the tape, Jonathan Poneman meets with Kurt Cobain at a coffee shop called Café Roma on Broadway in Seattle.

"My earliest recollection of Kurt was that he seemed awestruck at life," says Jonathan. "And he was playful. And I think only later he turned into the Kurt Cobain that has become the media sensation. I remember part of the reason why he was talking to me at all was Sub Pop had put out the Soundgarden album [1987's *Screaming Life* EP] and he later went on to say some dismissive things about Soundgarden, but I swear to you at the time he thought they were the cat's meow, as did I for that matter. I thought he was a young guy who was very shy and had a lot of wonderment, a lot of intelligence, sensitivity, a little freaked out like, 'Wow you wanna make a record? Cool.' That sort of thing."

In true indie rock fashion, the relationship between Nirvana and Sub Pop was a casual one at first. After the group met with the label, they decided to release a single together and that single led to an album. It wasn't until around early 1989 – after the band had already recorded for the label – that the band decided they wanted a formal recording contract from Sub Pop.

MARCH 1988:

After the departure of drummer Dale Crover, who moved to San Francisco with the Melvins, the band is in search of yet another drummer and places an ad in the *Rocket* that says: "DRUMMER WANTED: Play hard, sometimes light, underground, versatile, fast, medium, slow, versatile, serious, heavy, versatile, dorky, nirvana, hungry. Kurdt 352.0992."

Around this time, Kurt is constantly writing new songs in his Olympia apartment, including "About a Girl." If you talk to Slim Moon or Nils Bernstein, who helped out with Nirvana's fan mail in the early years

(he was never the fan club president as some have reported) and later worked at Sub Pop, it's easy to see how a simple pop song like this one found its way on to an album of otherwise heavy material as on the band's 1989 debut *Bleach*.

"When you first hear 'About a Girl,' it was kind of like, 'Huh? That's kind of weird for Kurt.' Because that's not the perception people had of Kurt 'cause he was really into Touch and Go bands and he was really into noisy stuff and to write a pop song seemed a little strange," explains Slim. "But he had been living in Olympia for a while. And, because pop, like really simple pop, was kind of a big thing [in Olympia] back then, the kinds of bands that people were listening to were the Vaselines, the Pastels, and Beat Happening. So my perception, and I think other people's perception, was that a song like 'About a Girl' sort of showed that he was influenced by the new music he was listening to at the time. But not that he was making a conscious effort to write a pop song; it was that he had come to understand the sort of legitimacy and coolness of a simple song."

At the same time, something heavier was happening in Seattle. Nils Bernstein, now Matador Records' publicist, notes, "Seattle was a *huge* metal town. *Huge*. And so I always reduced grunge to being, you know, the rockers and the punks were always against each other, and all of a sudden grunge happened, and they were the same. It was weird; it's a combination of metal and punk, and it didn't happen anywhere else."

MARCH 19, 1988:

Billed as "Nirvana: Also known as Skid Row, Ted Ed Fred, Pen Cap Chew, and Bliss," Kurt, Chris, and Dave Foster, who replaced Dale Crover on drums, perform at Community World Theater in Tacoma with Lush on the bill. The flyer for the show says, "Hey kids! Don't buy a gram this weekend. Come see a revelation in progress. It will be a gosh darn... Healing Explosion."

"I saw them play here at least four times," says Slim Moon. "It was pretty much the songs off the demo each time. In one of the songs, instead of playing a solo in the middle, Kurt would just twist his digital

● The Vaselines' Frances McKee and Eugene Kelly ●

• Early performance... •

• ... and publicity •

distortion knob for like a minute and get kind of crazy with it. I remember he dressed really crazy at the time. He'd wear weird layers and he dressed in all these kooky thrift store clothes and platform heels, but it wasn't like, 'Look at me. I'm a rock star.' It was more like a goofy, sarcastic, kitschy kind of vibe."

Chad believes it's this show where he sees the band perform for the first time. "The sound was really bad; it was really, really noisy," remembers Chad. "I liked the way they looked more than the way they sounded, but it was pretty cool 'cause Kurt was wearing these high heels and had these really intense bell bottoms on. But I couldn't really make too much heads or tails on what exactly they were playing. It was a combination of just the sound and the room and everything else; when I heard them the second time, I got a little more of an understanding of what was going on... I got into it when they gave me the tape they did with Dale, I thought, well, this makes a little more sense. I knew things were going to happen for them."

April 24, 1988:
Nirvana play their first show in Seattle at the Vogue. They had attempted a show in town shortly before this date at the Central Tavern, but the only people who showed up were Sub Pop's Jonathan and Bruce, so the band turned around and went home.

Depending on whom you ask, there were only 10, 20, or 50 people in the Vogue crowd this night. "Kurt Cobain was so nervous that he was shaking in his flannels," wrote Dawn Anderson in her review of the show in the *Rocket*. "It just didn't seem like a real show," Kurdt (as he alternately spells his name throughout the years) says of the show in the first feature ever written on the band – for Dawn Anderson's now-defunct *Backlash*. "We felt we were being judged; it was like everyone should've had scorecards. Plus, I was sick. I puked that day. That's a good excuse."

Seattle scenester and photographer Charles Peterson – known for his classic blurred photos of Nirvana – has described the show as "atrocious" and told *Goldmine* that he didn't even take photos at the concert because he didn't think much of the band at the time. Grant Alden, the *Rocket*'s former Managing Editor, wasn't initially impressed either: "They were awful. I think I ended up walking out – just dreadful. Don't think I could tell one song from another."

May 1988:
Chad attends a show by Nirvana outside on the campus of Evergreen State College just weeks before he plays his first show with the group.

Chad replaces Aaron Burckhard, who had been practicing with them again for a short time after Dave Foster was booted out. Of Dave, Slim Moon notes, "No one actually liked him because he had an anger problem and he'd go off on you."

"I met Chris and Kurt again after the show," says Chad of this show. "And they were like, 'Do you wanna play with us or something?' And, I'm like, 'OK sure.' I think it was the following week we got together and jammed. Everyone seemed very cool."

Chad recalls about four or five rehearsals in the basement of Chris's home in Tacoma between seeing them at the Evergreen show and playing his first show with them this month at the Vogue. Of the first rehearsal, he remembers, "It was just kind of, it just seemed like a jam. I'm used to playing with lots of people all the time, so it was like another jam session. It's always kind of weird at first when you play with someone you've never worked with before. Those two guys had been playing together for a long time, so I felt a little bit on the outside of what they were doing. But overall, I enjoyed myself."

Late Spring/ Early Summer 1988:
Photographer Charles Peterson takes the ferry to Bainbridge Island, Washington, where Chad lived, for his first formal photo shoot with Nirvana.

"There's this place on the south end of the island, there's a World War II base that was up there and some facilities and they had this giant reservoir," says Chad. "It's [the shoot] with the photos of us that look like we're up against this giant cement thing, it's really huge, there's also a tower that we used to climb a lot back then. There's some photographs of us at the base of the tower. It was fun, it was cool."

May 16, 1988:
Chris Novoselic turns 23 years old.

June 5, 1988:
Nirvana plays the Central Tavern in Seattle. It's their third show in Seattle and was booked by Nikolas J. Hartshorne, who would later be the King County Medical Examiner at the time of Kurt's death. The band opened for the Leaving Trains, whose lead singer Falling James is

Courtney Love's first husband.

"Nirvana, at the time, was still so new and unknown that they opened the show with the Leaving Trains," says Falling James. "I identified with them for many reasons, including the spontaneous excitement of witnessing for the first time a bunch of simpatico longer-haired slacker types who just didn't give a fuck about image or the then-current faux-metal revival, or *making it*. They reminded me of me. But I felt oddly liberated to see how Nirvana took punk energy and inspiration *and* ideals, and transmuted them into something different, something chaotic and beautiful. I was jealous and proud of them, and felt like I was a part of it somehow."

Out of these early shows, Chad says it's this Central Tavern show that he remembers best. "The biggest thing that stands out was that there were hardly any people there, maybe 12 at the most," says Chad. "We probably played 'Love Buzz,' 'Floyd' for sure. 'Hairspray Queen,' 'Spank Thru,' 'Downer,' a lot of stuff off that first tape that Dale did. It was all kind of cut and dry.

June 11, 1988:

Kurt, Chris, and Chad head to Reciprocal Recording to record their first single, a cover of "Love Buzz" from the Dutch band called the Shocking Blue, which had a 1969 hit with "Venus." They also record the single's B-

side "Big Cheese," "Blandest," and they re-record "Spank Thru," which had been recorded in their January session with Dale Crover on drums. Jack Endino thinks that they might have recorded a version of "Mr. Moustache" as well, and maybe even "Sifting," though the only completed songs were the four above.

"Blandest" was actually their first choice for a B-side, but Jack thought "Big Cheese" was a far better choice for their first original recording. "['Big Cheese'] is a much stronger song and they readily agreed," says Jack. "It wasn't called 'Blandest' for nothing. It was also not a very good take of 'Blandest.' So we went over it later by mutual agreement, expecting to do a much better take, which somehow they never got around to doing. That's why only bootlegs of it exist, taken from cassette rough mixes from that session."

Chad Channing describes the atmosphere during these recordings as "pretty relaxed." "I remember we spent a lot of time tooling with my drums because being that they were North drums and very unusual, we had a funky time trying to get it right," he says. "We just motored through the songs and stuff and I learned that Jack Endino was into chocolate, so we'd get him his candy bars every night. Recording with him was awesome. He just honed in on what we wanted and was able to pull out a lot of what we were looking for. He kept [the songs] the way we'd play them. Most of the stuff we did in one take. The only things different, of course, is double tracking some of the guitars and doing the solos."

June 16, 1988:

Nirvana opens for Bundle of Hiss at the Vogue on this date. But it must be noted that there are likely some tour dates missing from these early years (up until their first European tour in late 1989), mostly because no one saved Nirvana tour itineraries. A few of the band's earliest booking agents, Danny Bland and Michelle Vlasimksy, didn't keep records of the band's tour dates. "I booked them at a time when I had to beg club owners to have the band for $50 on a three-band bill," says Danny. "I wouldn't have thought to keep itineraries." Sub Pop also didn't keep records, and some of the clubs the band played have either closed down or don't have records of shows this old either.

That said, most of the dates and venues for these early shows were culled from interviews I did, from concert reviews in local newspapers, advance show listings and ads in papers, and where noted, from other

books or articles, as well as from show flyers and tour posters. But, ever interviewing people who were there, a common response was, "I wa really drunk around that time" or "All those shows run together in my mind." Bootlegs are often unreliable, and there are a lot of valid Nirvana Web sites with concert information, but unless the date could be verified by at least two sources, it wasn't used.

JUNE 17, 1988:

The band performs at the Hal Holmes Center in Ellensburgh Washington. Slim Moon's band, Lush, was on this bill as well. "The PA was really shitty and you have these great big amps so no one can hear the vocals. Only about 50 kids or so were there," says Slim. "In the very beginning, Kurt really tried to get attention. He'd do those screech vocals, he dressed funny, he moved around more, and later he was more introverted onstage and he'd just get out the weirdness at the enc when he'd smash up his guitar."

JUNE 29, 1988:

Sub Pop stages their first Lame Fest at the Moore Theater in Seattle which was a beautiful old movie theater later used as a concert venue with Nirvana, Tad, and Mudhoney on the bill.

"They weren't that good," recalls former *Rocket* Managing Edito Grant Alden. "Again, honestly, I remember Tad threatening to stage dive on the audience, and [Mudhoney's] Mark Arm talking shit about [*Seattle Times* music scribe] Pat MacDonald, but do I remember Nirvana tha night? No, I really don't." The *Seattle Times* review of the show by Pau DeBarros said, "If this is the future of rock and roll... I hope I die before get much older."

JUNE 30, 1988:

The band does more recording on "Love Buzz," "Big Cheese," and "Spank Thru" at Reciprocal with Jack Endino. ("Blandest" was nixed by this time. Jack believes they must have recorded the songs in the first two sessions (this one, and the aforementioned June 11 session), and then mixed them in the next two sessions.

"Jonathan didn't like the first vocal take [of 'Love Buzz'] for some reason and asked me to ask Kurt to re-sing it," says Jack. "It came ou exactly the same. There are bootlegs of the earlier vocal take... probably one of the earlier sessions though."

Chad describes these early recording sessions and shows as a carefree, optimistic time for everyone in the group. "It's interesting because around when Kurt died, me and Chris had a chance to talk fo a while and he was saying how some of our early days were some of the funnest days. They were hard on us because of the way we had to dea with the touring and all that stuff. But at the same time, we had a lot o freedom as a band, which toward the end, I think they were losing a lo of that."

JULY 3, 1988:

Nirvana plays a Sub Pop Sunday at the Vogue.

JULY 16, 1988:

First day of mixing for "Love Buzz," "Big Cheese," and "Spank Thru." "Love Buzz," which Jack Endino recalls was Jonathan Poneman's suggestion struck some as an odd choice for a first single: a) it's a cover song and b) it's more pop than rock. "I thought it was kind of dopey," says Nils Bernstein. "'Big Cheese' was kind of trashy and 'Love Buzz' was too poppy, but it was kind of neat that it was poppy."

The song originally had a 30-second montage of sounds that Kurt recorded, but it was edited down to just 10 seconds as the intro to the single only. Charles R. Cross, Editor of the *Rocket* since 1986, says, "'Love Buzz' was notable mostly for the guitar playing and that's what people forget about early Nirvana – the main reason people were interested in the band was because of the guitar playing. In the club settings, the vocals were virtually impossible to hear."

JULY 23, 1988:
Nirvana plays the Central Tavern in Seattle.

JULY 30, 1988:
The band plays the Squid Row in Seattle.

AUGUST 1 88:
"It May Be The Devil And It May Be The Lord... But It Sure As Hell Ain't Human," the first article ever written on Nirvana, is published in this August '88 issue of *Backlash*. The article is famous for Dawn Anderson's then-bold declaration, "I honestly believe that with enough practice, Nirvana could become... better than the Melvins!" In the interview, Kurdt admits, "Our biggest fear at the beginning was that people might think we were a Melvins rip-off."

AUGUST 28, 1988:
The blossoming Northwest music scene is the subject of a *Tacoma News Tribune* feature titled "Fresh from the Northwest: Hometown Bands Are Making Big Soundwaves Elsewhere." The article focuses on acts that are breaking nationally such as Soundgarden (who graduated from Sub Pop to A&M this year), the Young Fresh Fellows, and the Dan Reed Network.

"I don't remember the buzz on Nirvana as much as the buzz on Sub Pop," says Gillian G. Gaar, who has written about Nirvana for *Goldmine*,

● Chad rocks the beret look ●

the *Rocket*, and other publications, of this time. "The band that I thought was really gonna break through was Mudhoney, and soon after that Soundgarden signed to A&M and that was a big deal, so it wasn't that much of a deal when Nirvana signed to Geffen later on. At this time we thought we had a nice cool scene, but it was never gonna get mega-huge. I mean, that was just assured. That was self evident, there was never any question about that."

"At the time," adds Nils Bernstein, "the most exciting thing was Screaming Trees getting signed to SST and then, of course, Soundgarden, but it was like, 'Wow that's huge.' So people were excited, but only on that scale, and no one knew how big the scale would get."

AUGUST 29, 1988:
Nirvana plays another show at the Vogue in Seattle. "This was the first time I saw Kurt smash a guitar," says Slim Moon, even though many (including Kurt himself) have cited the Halloween show at Evergreen later this year as the first time Kurt smashed a guitar.

"Those early shows, they were crazy and that's why they were so much fun. They were crazy," says Sub Pop's Megan Jasper, who went to a lot of early shows but can't really recall which show was which. "I can't remember any that sucked. The clubs were smaller and you were also watching this kid smash up his guitars. He didn't have a lot of money, in fact, I remember so many times watching him smash his guitars and thinking that he rules for doing that because I know he can't have that many more." Sub Pop couldn't afford to pay for smashed gear, so Kurt would either patch it up or buy a new, cheap guitar at a thrift store.

AUGUST / SEPTEMBER 1988:
Alice Wheeler, a friend of the band's, does a photo shoot for the cover sleeve of the "Love Buzz" single in Tacoma. "They wanted to go out to Never Never Land – a public park near the Tacoma Narrows Bridge, and so off we went," Alice tells *Goldmine*. "I was having technical difficulties; I didn't have a very good camera at the time. The pictures are infrared so they're kind of fuzzy. One of them's really underexposed and the other one's really overexposed."

● Never *Nevermind...* ●

" I HONESTLY BELIEVE THAT WITH ENOUGH PRACTICE, NIRVANA COULD BECOME... BETTER THAN THE MELVINS! "

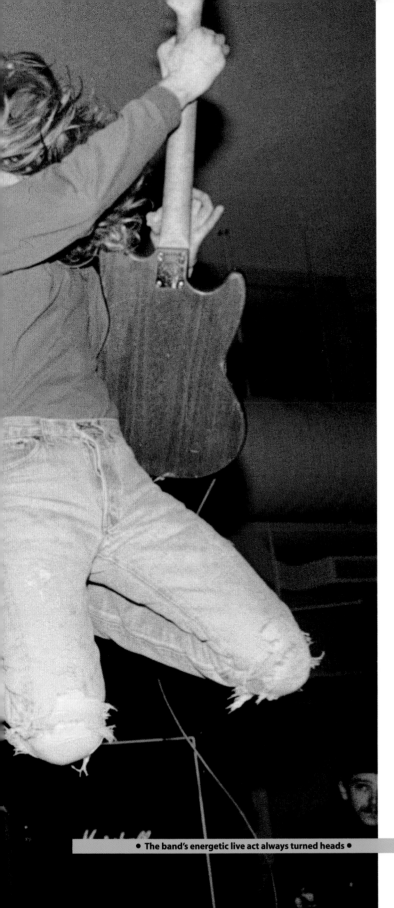

SEPTEMBER 27, 1988:

With "Love Buzz" and "Big Cheese" on their way to the pressing plant by now, a Reciprocal session on this day is used for finishing up and mixing "Spank Thru" for the *Sub Pop 200* box set that Jack Endino was assembling at the time, according to Jack. Kurt told *Melody Maker* that "Spank Thru" was the "most complex thing we've ever done. We're moving towards simplicity and better songwriting at the time."

As one would expect, Kurt was in charge in the studio and band decisions were made by Kurt and Chris. "I basically hadn't anything to say," says Chad Channing of his place in the group. "In a nutshell, I didn't have an opinion on anything because it wasn't an opinion that would've been valid anyway. I didn't really mind at first because it was all just kind of new to me, none of us had ever put out a record before, so I didn't care. Like if Bruce and Poneman ever got together with the band and talked about any important stuff, you can bet it wasn't with me. It was always with Kurt and Chris. It was like any important decisions or anything that had to do with anything regarding the band had nothing to do with me at all. Even if my opinion wasn't taken or valid, it still would've been fine, but it was just I wasn't even an option."

OCTOBER 28, 1988:

Nirvana plays Union Station with the Butthole Surfers and Blood Circus. "I think there were only two shows here," says Slim. "A promoter would find a new place and either it'll go well and become a regular venue or the owner will freak out and not do shows there." The owner apparently freaked this time.

OCTOBER 30, 1988:

Nirvana performs at a Halloween party at the K dorms (the K dorms were the designated loud, party dorms) at Evergreen State College in Olympia, Washington. This is the show that most believe marked the first time Kurt smashed his guitar. However, both Chad Channing and Slim Moon remember Kurt trashing his gear at shows earlier than this one, though not completely destroying his guitar as he did at this show.

"It was mayhem," says Slim Moon, whose band Lush opened the show. "I remember believing that night that the reason they smashed up their stuff was because Kurt just could not bear to be upstaged. My band went on first and we got into a fight about halfway through our set and I kicked over the drummer's kit and he punched me in the face. I felt like, if the band before them did a really good job, then he was gonna do more, and it sort or reminded me of Pete Townshend's comments on the Monterey Pop Festival that they had to go really crazy and smash up their stuff because Jimi Hendrix set his guitar on fire." And, yes, Nirvana did outdo Lush this night. "Yeah, they did," admits Slim.

NOVEMBER 23, 1988:

The band plays Speedy O'Tubbs in Bellingham, Washington.

NOVEMBER 1988:

Nirvana's first single, "Love Buzz" backed with "Big Cheese" is released (only 1,000 copies) as the first offering from the Sub Pop Single of the Month Club, which cost subscribers about $35 a year and they would receive whatever single – limited-edition, of course – Sub Pop released each month. It's Sub Pop single No. 23.

● Kurt gets medieval on the equipment – not for the first time ●

"When we put out the single," says Jonathan Poneman, "we realized that people were reacting like, 'Yeah, this is really, *really* great.' But I don't think Bruce and I realized that the band was going to be as big as they ended up being."

WINTER 1988:

The "Love Buzz" release caused quite a stir in the industry. Prior to the release, Craig Montgomery, who would soon become the band's sound man for the next five years, says that the impression a lot of people had in Seattle at this time was that "they were just these hicks from the woods. But the thing that first made the impression was Kurt's voice. It was like, 'Wow it's this Creedence Clearwater kind of voice from these hick guys from Aberdeen'."

"There was a lot of buzz around 'Love Buzz'," says Charles R. Cross. "What people forget about early Nirvana is that for the first several years of Nirvana's existence they were always the kind of poor stepbrothers to Mudhoney in the scene and that was also true in Sub Pop. Sup Pop always treated Nirvana like they were not as big a deal. It wasn't exactly a Beatles vs. Rolling Stones thing, but they were the B team, and that eventually changed."

Nils Bernstein can't recall much serious talk about Nirvana before the release of the single. "I think it was a little bit after that, but I think it went pretty fast," he says. "People might say that the buzz started and then Sub Pop put out the single, but I think Sub Pop created the buzz with the single. I think a lot of people would *like* to say they were blown away by one of those early shows, but for most people it took the single for them to pay any real attention."

DECEMBER 7, 1988:

Nirvana's listing in the *1988 Rocket Music Directory* reads: "Nirvana: Gunka, gunka, clank, ahh, plunk, deedle, deedle, wah, eeak, unk. 726.9115. 352.0992. 1502 E. Olive Way, 509, Seattle, WA 98102."

DECEMBER 21, 1988:

Nirvana covers Led Zeppelin's "Immigrant Song" and Smack's "Run Rabbit Run" at the Hoquiam Eagles Lodge to a crowd of about 50 in Hoquiam, Washington. Chris plays in his underwear; Kurt painted his neck red, according to *Come As You Are*.

DECEMBER 23, 1988:

It's the night before Nirvana enters the studio to record their debut album, *Bleach*, for Sub Pop. "With *Bleach*," Kurt says in *Spin* years later, "I didn't give a flying fuck what the lyrics were about. 80 percent were written the night before recording. It was like 'I'm pissed off. Don't know what about. Let's just scream negative lyrics and as long as they're not sexist and don't get too embarrassing it'll be OK.' I don't hold any of those lyrics dear to me."

DECEMBER 24, 1988:

This is Nirvana's first of six recording sessions to record *Bleach*. The album cost $606.17 on loan from Chad Channing's friend since fifth grade, Jason Everman, who is credited on the album for playing guitar, but didn't actually work on it. (Chad and Jason are still friends today.)

Kurt would later explain to *Hits* magazine's Roy Trakin: "He was just a person we got into the band to go on tour and play rhythm guitar. We thought he would be a permanent member, which is why we put his picture and his name on the album. It was just to welcome him aboard. But it just didn't work out."

● Kurt in more peaceful mood ●

● Kurt, pleased to be making records ●

DECEMBER 25, 1988:
Kurt gives copies of his band's first single, "Love Buzz," to relatives for Christmas, according to Gillian G. Gaar's *Goldmine* article.

DECEMBER 28, 1988:
Nirvana performs at the album release party for *Sub Pop 200*, released this month, at the Underground in the U-District of Seattle. Seattle poet Steven Jesse Bernstein, who committed suicide in 1991, introduces the band, saying, "And now, the mystery guest...with the freeze-dried music... Nir-VANA!"

"I remember the place was packed," says Chad. "I think it was the one and only time that we played this place. That was a lot of fun. The whole crowd was into it. The energy was totally there." John Troutman, a former roommate of Jason Everman's and employee at Seattle's Peaches Records at the time, says, "They went over massively at this show. Unquestionably the best."

Sub Pop 200, which features Nirvana's "Spank Thru," as well as songs from Tad, Screaming Trees, the Fluid, Soundgarden, Green River, the Fastbacks, and others, lands on the desk of influential British DJ John Peel, who begins talking it up on his radio show, thus starting the buzz on the label, Seattle, and soon Nirvana.

DECEMBER 29–31, 1988:
Three more recording sessions for *Bleach* at Reciprocal. "*Bleach* was pretty easy," says Chad. "We just kind of went in there, we might have had a couple takes on some stuff, but it was pretty straightforward. We set it up, rolled in there, and recorded. Some songs were kind of new, like 'Swap Meet' that didn't really have lyrics yet until we were going into the studio. I recall him finishing up or writing the lyrics on the way to the studio so he could sing that."

These sessions were recorded on an 8-track – four tracks for the drums (kick, snare, and a stereo submix of the rest of the drum kit), track five

NIRVANA

"BLEACH"

● The debut album ●

would be used for either vocal doubling or harmonies (as on "About a Girl" and "Paper Cuts") or for a solo, as on "Sifting," according to Jack. "Floyd the Barber" and "Paper Cuts" from the "Dale Demo" were remixed "with somewhat more care than on that first day in January," says Jack, "and 'Love Buzz' was remixed at [Bruce] Pavitt's request for the album."

There aren't a lot of outtakes from the sessions because if a take wasn't good, they would simply erase it and record over until a good take was captured. "Big Long Now," which later appeared on *Incesticide*, is the only completed outtake from the sessions. The band usually got the take they liked in one or two takes. "A few took longer because Chad was just learning the drum parts," says Jack. "Many of them had not been played live yet."

Explaining why they re-recorded over bad takes, Jack says, "Indie bands cannot afford to keep every take, and doing so is pretty pointless. If it sucked, you go over it. If I thought it was good, but the band wanted to do it again, we would keep the first take and do another one. If the second one was better, we might later on record some other song over the first take, getting maximum usage out of the reel. Tape was expensive and the recording budget was infinitesimally small. Only in La-La Land do they keep every take." (Thus the reason "Blandest" no

THIRD. 1989:

RIGHTEOUS HEAVINESS FROM OLYMPIA

January 1, 1989:

At the insistence of Chris Novoselic, Nirvana and Sub Pop enter into a recording contract that goes into effect officially on this day. A one-year contract with an option for two more records is signed. It's the label's first formal, long-term recording contract, according to Jonathan Poneman, who admits that the label didn't quite know what they were doing when they drew up the document.

"Chris Novoselic was insistent that we have a contract and I thought it was great," says Jonathan. "I thought, damn we have to have contracts. We did have one with Soundgarden for *Screaming Life*, but it was just for one album. So, I kind of pieced together something that was basically taken out of one of those music business primer books and then kind of adapted it to something I thought the band would feel comfortable with.

"I didn't know what I was doing. All I wanted to do was satisfy the band," he continues. "And, yeah, in retrospect I wanted to protect myself, that sort of thing was going through my head to a certain degree because I thought these bands were really hot. But, on the other hand, contracts weren't really part of the culture. Touch and Go, to the best of

my knowledge, didn't do it. SST, to the best of my knowledge, didn't do it. Homestead barely did it. We just didn't really think in those terms. I could've spent $4,000–5,000 to have a lawyer come up with a boilerplate contract that was meaningful, or I can try in my haphazard, ignorant way to put something together that would make the bands feel comfortable. I figured in my own naïveté that the bands would stick by us as long as we had open communication and tried.

"But then the media spotlight turned on Seattle and [we're conditioned] to want the same things, you know, material success and to be pop stars and to follow in the footsteps of our heroes and there's nothing wrong with that whatsoever. But when Nirvana's manager says 'You didn't pay the band!' it's not that black and white. Yeah, I didn't have a royalty system together. I didn't have a lawyer-produced boilerplate contract. I was winging it. But the spirit of taking care of the bands, to this day, I will staunchly defend my record for having put myself out there for every single one of my artists. Have I made mistakes? Hell, yes. A bunch of them... I don't think those guys were using us, or being dishonest. They wanted to do bigger and better things. Until you realize that bigger and better itself has a price and a cost attached to it."

JANUARY 14, 1989:

Session No. 5 for *Bleach* at Reciprocal. "There's nothing too memorable about the sessions. 'Blew' is the only song with a story behind it," says Chad. By now, everyone knows this one: "They thought they would tune down a couple of half-steps to be heavier and to make the singing easier," says Jack Endino. "What they didn't realize was that they were already tuned down. So, it came out real sludgy and mostly kind of out of tune. When they realized their mistake, they opted to re-record most of it. I think we kept 'Blew' though." "We didn't know until after we were done and we listened to it and Jack was like, 'You know, I think you guys were tuned down to C,'" says Chad. "And we listened, and sure enough it was completely low."

Of his two years in the band, Chad Channing says the making of *Bleach* was one of the happiest times. "It's because it was fresh to all of us," he says. "We were really excited about it. We thought it was so cool when it came out on vinyl. Or even when the single first came out, we were very up, very amped and optimistic. Everything was going the way we wanted it to – it was cool. I think those were the best times – may have been for them too, I don't know."

JANUARY 21, 1989:

Nirvana open for the Dharma Bums at the Satyricon club in Portland, Oregon. It's this show where Courtney, who lived in Eugene, Oregon, first saw the band perform. She's quoted in a 1992 *Sassy* story that she saw them play in Portland in 1988, but the band never played that town in that year. Of her first impression of Kurt, she told *Sassy*, "I thought he was really passionate and cute, but I couldn't tell if he was smart or had any integrity." Kurt's first impression: "I thought she looked like Nancy Spungen," he told Michael Azerrad in *Come As You Are*. ". . . Probably wanted to fuck her that night, but she left."

JANUARY 24, 1989:

This is the final recording session for *Bleach* with Jack at Reciprocal. According to Chad and Jack, these sessions have been misrepresented in a biography of Kurt Cobain which quotes a source who claims that Kurt was pouring beer on the mixing board and taking pills during the sessions. After reading those excerpts, Jack contacted the only other two people who worked at the studio and says, "Their recollections are the same as mine: completely routine sessions, and no one else assisted me."

JANUARY 31, 1989:

Chad Channing turns 22 years old.

FEBRUARY 8, 1989:

Nirvana plays another show at Community World Center in Tacoma on this date, and another K dorm party at Evergreen State College in Olympia this month.

Chad Channing says the K dorm parties were his favorite shows to play, though he admits those shows all blur together. "It was some guys' house, some guys' dorm, and we set up in his living room and it was crammed with people," says Chad of the parties. "The floor was literally, you could feel the floor was moving – really, really moving. It was going up and down three inches at least. I thought it was gonna cave in once.

Those photographs where we're covered in blood were taken from there. It gives you an idea of what it was like."

Two other memorable shows around this time – though the dates are unclear – were the gigs the band played at the Reko Muse in Olympia. Slim Moon remembers one of the shows (he believes the band only played two shows at this club): "One of the times was Industrial Nirvana. That was a really weird show," he says. "I think Tobi Vail joined them for a little bit and they borrowed my drum machine and played repetitive beats. And then made noise. It was more like Kurt and Chris and their friends making a whole bunch of racket."

Chad remembers another show at the club, somewhere between early 1989 and June 1989: "I think it was with Treehouse," he says. "At the end, we were playing and Chris threw his bass up in the air, this is the photograph taken for the *Bleach* album – the bass came down, hit me on the head and knocked me out. I didn't need stitches, but I just had a good-sized lump. I was out for I guess 20– 25 seconds. It was all in fun to me. It was just the nature of the way they were."

• February 25, 1989 •

FEBRUARY 1–15, 1989:

Interest grows in the Seattle music scene and the February 1–15 issue of the *SF* (San Francisco) *Weekly* (then called *Calendar* magazine) runs an article with the premature, but prophetic headline of "Screaming North: Seattle Bands Conquer the World." "Just as a joke, I gave it that headline," says the story's author Gillian G. Gaar. "I was surprised when they used it – it was just a joke. It was hysterical. At this time, there was never any expectation that things were gonna get big, so bands were free to just follow their hearts, so to speak, or just do what they wanted to do because it wasn't gonna matter. No one outside of the Northwest was gonna care about it anyway."

FEBRUARY 10–17, 1989:

Nirvana heads out for some West Coast dates, starting February 10 in San Francisco at the Covered Wagon with the Melvins, then opening for Mudhoney at Marsugi's in San Jose, California on February 11, and back to San Francisco at Chatterbox on February 17. Bruce Pavitt told Michael Azerrad in *Come As You Are* that he recalls Steve Turner, Mudhoney's guitarist, "raving that 'Kurt Cobain played guitar standing on his head!'" at the San Jose show.

FEBRUARY 25, 1989:

Jason Everman plays his first show with Nirvana at the HUB Ballroom at the University of Washington, featuring Skin Yard, Girl Trouble, and the Fluid on the bill (four bands for $4).

"Kurt said, 'Hey I've got a surprise for you' [speaking about Jason], because I had told him that I thought they needed to do something to fill their sound out, maybe think about getting another guitar player," says Jonathan Poneman. "I thought they were awesome [with Jason].

● Kurt and Chris on stage at the almost empty Hub Ballroom, Seattle ●

● Two of these men were about to become very famous indeed ●

I know he later came to regret the decision, but I think a lot of it was personality conflicts, but I thought they were colossal. Those three looked kind of goofy. They were three odd-looking guys and Jason was like the band fox, I guess. But it just sort of worked in a weird way. It wasn't slick by any means. It was just another personality in a band full of distinct personalities."

"Most of us were busy watching and listening to see what difference Jason made," recalls John Troutman, part of the Seattle music crowd and a former roommate of Jason's. "And Jason just kicked up a hell of a racket. I can see why they were looking for something maybe *like* him, but I would also see why maybe he didn't last very long. Jason was into the most insane heavy metal you'd ever heard. The guitar he played at the show, and I don't know if you can see it on the poster that came out in the second pressing of *Bleach*, but [on his guitar] he had a pick guard made out of a Venom album. And you walk into his room and it was like walking into *Hellraiser*. He could pull out scary Norwegian death metal albums long before they started setting fire to churches. And he was a metal guitarist onstage too – all over the place and the hair was everywhere and he'd play power chords that were just huge and sustaining. It was a more full sound, but it was definitely sort of edging on too hard a guitar sound for them. It wasn't organic enough. It just wasn't quite right."

Mike Musburger of the Posies was also at this show, and this being his first time seeing the band, he was surprised at how "comical" they looked "with Chris being so tall and Chad was playing this funny drum set and Kurt being left-handed."

"But I was just amazed at how hard they rocked and how melodic they were at the same time," continues Mike. "And then they trashed their instruments and at first I think some of their peers, people like me who played music in Seattle, thought it was a bit of a cliché. But there was such a vengeance and violence to it that it seemed kind of comical also. It had this strange combination of scariness and funniness at the same time. I remember going back to the Posies after saying, 'Oh my God. I just saw the greatest band.'"

MARCH 18, 1989:

You can almost mark the beginning of the Sub Pop hype machine on this date with the publication of the cover story on the Seattle scene by Everett True in *Melody Maker*. The article focused more on Mudhoney, which was the band all thought was destined for super-stardom and Sub Pop's top priority at the time. Sub Pop scrounged up enough money to fly the writer to Seattle for the piece. Some would say it was an extravagant expense, others say it was a stroke of marketing genius.

"It wasn't genius, it was just connecting the dots," explains Jonathan. "The thing is, there was really a lot of learning on the spot, a lot of going with hunches, and a lot of the stuff came through and worked. But in retrospect it's easy to say that we knew what we were doing, but it really wasn't that. The whole flying the journalist over thing was a deal made by Anton Brookes, the UK publicist at Southern, our distributor in England at the time. He said he could get us a tear-away cover of *Melody Maker* with Mudhoney if you flew a journalist over and he'll throw in an article on Sub Pop on top of it. So, I heard that and went, great, sounds good to me."

MARCH 28, 1989:

Kurt, his best friend Dylan Carlson, and Slim Moon go to the Tesla/Cinderella/Poison show at the Tacoma Dome. It wasn't Kurt's idea. "Kurt really hated it," laughs Slim. "Me and Dylan thought it was funny. We even sort of liked Tesla, but Kurt pretty much was bummed. We did it spur of the moment on the day of the show because we were bored."

SPRING 1989:

Kurt records with the Go Team in Olympia with Tobi Vail (his girlfriend after Tracy Marander, and she was once Bikini Kill's drummer) and K Records' Calvin Johnson. Kurt plays guitar on the song "Bikini Twilight," which was released as a 7-inch on K. He never performed live with the group, though he is said to have performed live with Tobi as part of Bathtub Isreal at the Reko Muse.

Also this spring, Nirvana records "Dive" and the Kiss cover "Do You Love Me?" (used later on C/Z's *Hard to Believe* Kiss tribute album) at the 16-track studio at Evergreen State College. It's Jason Everman's only recording as part of the group. Greg Babior, who was also once a member of Dylan Carlson's band Earth with Slim Moon, recorded the session.

"It was my school project," says Greg, who says many aspiring bands recorded at the college which was an "alternative" college where there were no grades or majors. "They needed a recording and I needed to record someone, so we got together and did it. I don't remember if it was a one-day or two-day session, but it went pretty smoothly. With the Kiss song, it didn't seem like something they gave a hell of a lot of thought to, but the other song ['Dive'] they seemed relatively serious about. Jason didn't know what key it was in and he was having a hard time playing the solo. He just couldn't figure it out. He was playing a lot by scales rather than by ear, so he wasn't quite able to hook in."

Greg Babior also recorded the band around this time for another school project at Evergreen. "They came in specifically to do a video shoot," he says. "A guy named John Schneider had a school project to do, so they did this thing with Nirvana. There was a small TV studio at Evergreen and they performed and we recorded them. They did 'Big Cheese.' Kurt had all this footage – stuff he collected from TV – they shot against a blue screen. So they projected this montage against the screen. He had some spooky black-and-white horror film clips with all these flying monkeys, and there was this group of Body Builders For Christ or something weird like that. I don't know if they had a specific goal in mind, other than, 'We're in a band, let's make a video.' It was a two- or three-camera shoot. All the effects went live."

APRIL 7, 1989:

Nirvana plays the Annex Theater in Seattle with Love Battery on the bill. "I remember Kurt had a brown wood Fender Mustang guitar with a Soundgarden sticker – their logo on *Screaming Life* – on it," says John Troutman. "Kurt just smashed the shit out of it at that show. The Annex was tiny. I just remember walking in there and it took me a while to even get in because I ran into everyone – the core group of the Seattle scene was there."

"They were going crazy," notes Jonathan Poneman of the show. "I think it was the first time that Kurt had been lifted up in the air, which at the time was really [a big deal]. There's a real tribal ritual quality – it's sort of like being embraced by the audience. Like you are worthy to be lifted into the air. That was a great show."

APRIL 14, 1989:

Nirvana plays the Hal Holmes Center in Ellensburg, Washington, which is about two hours from Seattle over the Cascade Mountains. "The scene didn't really interact much with Seattle because of the mountains. It's where Screaming Trees are from too," says John Troutman.

APRIL 26, 1989:

Nirvana plays the Vogue in Seattle with the Flaming Lips. "They demolished the Vogue," recalls Tom Phalen, a former freelance writer for the *Seattle Times*. "There was a lot of shit getting trashed; people throwing stuff everywhere. I just remember a lot of stuff flying. It was wild. Everyone was talking about it for a week, and the buzz was really starting to grow on Nirvana."

Flaming Lips singer Wayne Coyne says that when Jonathan Poneman told him that out of all the Sub Pop bands, Nirvana were the ones destined to break out, he thought he was crazy at first. "It was more the metal stuff that they were doing, but they had a couple good songs. I remember thinking Cobain looked like he should be in Lynyrd Skynyrd 'cause he had really long hair and he kind of had a beard. We

were like, 'God this is fucked up.' A lot of the music was kind of this dirge metal stuff that didn't seem that far removed from a lot of the crap metal that was going on. But then they'd have these occasional riffs in songs and we thought, 'Damn, those are some good tunes.' I remember 'School' and 'Negative Creep' especially. We always liked that heavy rock and we liked the punk rock at the same time, everyone talked about the fusion of classic rock and punk rock, you could walk away singing 'I'm a negative creep! I'm a negative creep!' In the end, it just floored us."

MAY 9, 1989:

Nirvana plays another show at the Central Tavern in Seattle.

MAY 16, 1989:

Chris Novoselic turns 24.

MAY 26, 1989:

Nirvana plays the Lindbloom Student Center at the Green River Community College in Auburn, Washington. "It was a great show. Jason gelled a little bit better because he'd been playing with them a little longer, but it still wasn't quite right," says John Troutman. "At the time it seemed right, though. They had this beautiful Nirvana banner in the back: the classic banner tapestry of Elvis painted with Alice Cooper make-up."

● Hoboken, New Jersey. ●

• Seattle, 1989 •

"WE'D BE ON THE MIKE GOING, 'WE NEED A PLACE TO SLEEP. IF ANYONE HAS ANY ROOM FOR US...'

notes, and I screamed a lot," Kurt says in *Nevermind: It's an Interview*. "But, at the same time that we were recording, we had a lot more songs like 'About a Girl.' In fact, 'Polly' was written at that time too. It's just that we chose to put more abrasive songs on the *Bleach* album."

Sub Pop's expectations were understandably low for the release. "We really didn't have any," says Jonathan matter-of-factly. "We didn't. We thought it was just another good record from another band in the area and that it would be great if we sold 5,000 copies. But 'About a Girl' was obviously the song where you go, 'Woah.' It's a pretty standard verse, chorus, verse with really pretty vocals and clever lyrics. We were excited about the band's future because they were a great band. But, it wasn't like 'Oh boy, we're sitting on a gold mine.' We'd joke to a certain degree – but with the same kind of tongue-in-cheek tomfoolery that we always used to talk about things – about taking over the world. At the time, the world wasn't being taken over by rock bands."

Even though the band's performances were getting better with each show, none of the core group of friends or fans interviewed had any inkling of what was to come. "I thought they were the greatest thing ever, but at the time we were so isolated up here that nobody in the scene at the time had any delusion of fame and fortune," explains John. "We didn't think anyone else would get it because we were all from a punk background but we worshipped Led Zeppelin and Black Sabbath. We were just shameless about our love for rock."

JUNE 9, 1989:
Nirvana plays the Sub Pop Lame Fest at the Moore Theater with Tad, Mudhoney, and Blood Circus. "The one show of this tour that really sticks in my mind was the Lame Fest at the Moore Theater because Jason put on this Mickey Mouse outfit just because he wanted to," says Chad. "It was pretty comical, actually. There's the band, and then there's Jason as Mickey Mouse with all this long hair."

While Chad definitely recalls Jason wearing the Mickey Mouse get-up at this show, the review of the gig in *Backlash* and the item in the *Rocket* didn't mention the costume at all, leading us to believe maybe Chad got the date wrong.

JUNE 11, 1989:
The Seattle scene is the subject of yet another Northwest trend piece in the *Tacoma News Tribune*, touting Mudhoney, Mother Love Bone, the Posies, and Sir Mix-a-Lot as the next big things in an article titled "Sound Invasion: Rappers, Popsters Join the Troupes from the Northwest Infiltrating the World of Big Time Music."

JUNE 15, 1989:
Nirvana's debut album, *Bleach*, is released in the US. The first 1,000 copies were printed on white vinyl. The second 2,000 copies included a limited-edition poster. The album's title was inspired from a sign the band saw in San Francisco that said, "Bleach Your Works," urging drug users to bleach their needles as a way to stop the spread of AIDS.

"*Bleach* is seen to be really one dimensional. It has the same format, all the songs are slow, and grungy, and they're tuned down to really low

• More from the Hoboken photo shoot •

● July 13, 1989. Maxwell's, Hoboken ●

Sub Pop described the band's music in their promotional copy for *Bleach* as, "Hypnotic and righteous heaviness from these Olympia pop stars. They're young, they own their own van, and they're going to make us rich."

JUNE 21, 1989:

Nirvana plays the Vogue in Seattle before launching their first US tour to promote *Bleach* the following day. Kurt, Chris, Chad, and Jason hit the road in their white Dodge van right after the show and headed to San Francisco.

JUNE 22, 1989:

Nirvana's first of 26 shows on the tour is at the Covered Wagon in San Francisco. Sub Pop, still the fledgling indie rock label, didn't have a lot of money to provide tour support for Nirvana and, at the time, the band wasn't getting paid a lot from the club owners either.

"We'd be on the mike going, 'We need a place to sleep. If anyone has any room for us...' And we always did find someone to take us in," says Chad. "Mostly, we had enough money to get to the next town. It was almost always that way. But it was our idea. We wanted to go out and tour. We realized it was going to be tough, but it's what we wanted to do." Chad says they usually made $150 a show, but some gigs paid only $50 or even as low as $25. "But, we always seemed to have enough to get gas in the van and get us on the road. Most of our eating on the road was at like Jiffy Marts [a convenience store chain]."

JUNE 23-JULY 5, 1989:

Nirvana performs at Rhino Records in Westwood, California on this date. While in California, they also play at Al's Bar in Los Angeles and Bogart's in Long Beach. From California the tour heads east to Santa Fe, New Mexico where the band plays the Rockin' TP on the 27th, and then through Texas in July. The Texas shows included Axiom in Houston, Axis in Forth Worth, and Concrete Jungle in Dallas.

Kurt relays an often told tale of this tour in the January 1992 issue of *Musician*: "We stayed at this one place in Texas, out in the woods, next to a lake where there were signs all over the grass that said, 'Beware of Alligators.' We slept with baseball bats at our sides."

JULY 6, 1989:

Nirvana plays the Uptown Bar in Minneapolis, and they party at Babes in Toyland's Lori Barbero's house after the show.

JULY 7, 1989:

Nirvana plays Club Dreamerz in Chicago. Kurt bought a large crucifix at a yard sale in Chicago and brought it with him on the tour, according to *Come As You Are*. Along with this find, the band also bought a lot of records with the money they made. "We were totally poor, but God, we were seeing the United States for the first time," says Kurt in the book.

Around this time, the band played the O'Cayz Corral in Madison, Wisconsin. It's here where they noticed a change in Jason's attitude. According to Chad, Jason had become very quiet and wouldn't talk to his band members about what was bothering him. "They asked me what's up with Jason," recalls Chad. "And I wasn't really sure. He was being really quiet and stuff. We tried to talk to him and ask him, 'What's

● Broken in Hoboken ●

up? What's bothering you?' And he just was very tight-lipped. He didn't want to say anything. And we just kind of let it go like that."

Even with the attitude, Chad says the shows were going well and everyone seemed to get along. "Jason was into the mingling thing. We'd crack open a drink of some kind – with Jason it was a Mountain Dew. We'd hang out after shows and things seemed pretty cherry," he says. "It wasn't like show's over, head to the van, shut the fuck up. It wasn't anything gloomy at all."

JULY 9, 1989:

Kurt smashes his Fender Mustang guitar at their show at the Sonic Temple in Wilkinsburg, just outside of Pittsburgh, Pennsylvania. The trashing of the gear is a regular part of the show by now, and without a lot of expendable income, Kurt had to make do with what he could. "He'd patch the stuff up," says Chad. "He'd get another neck made or a body and give them these horrible paint jobs, these pastel colors."

JULY 12-17, 1989:

On the 12th, the band plays the under-attended J.C. Dobbs in Philadelphia with Napalm Sunday opening up. The next night was Maxwell's in Hoboken, New Jersey. Around this time, there is also a show in Jamaica Plain, Massachusetts at the Green Street Station.

● Threesome Again: Kurt , Chris, and Chad ●

● The Screaming Trees ●

JULY 18, 1989:

Jason plays his final show with Nirvana at the New Music Seminar at the Pyramid Club in New York. Leading up to this show, Jason's attitude changed a lot; he became withdrawn and quiet and didn't communicate with his band mates. Fed up, they decided to cancel the rest of the tour dates and drive home. Jason isn't officially fired until after they return to Washington.

"I remember them coming to me, because I booked this tour," says Danny Bland, "and saying that they didn't want to finish it with Jason. I thought it was odd that they would rather kick the guy out and drive home with him, than just finish the tour then boot him out… It was just another day to me; I didn't think it would be history."

"We just decided to drive straight home and bag the rest of the shows," says Chad. "We probably had four or five more shows. But there wasn't really a lot behind [Jason's departure]. There wasn't any discussion about it. We did not say anything about it the entire trip home. We got home, dropped him off, said, 'Alright man, we'll see you later.' And we parted there, then I went home. Kurt and Chris had decided that obviously Jason wasn't happy, something was going on, and they wanted to let him go."

Chad, who was closest to Jason, believes the reason for Jason distancing himself was because he wasn't satisfied just being a guitar player in the band and, like Chad, not being part of any of the decision-making or the creative process. "Later on I realized that the reasons I ended up leaving were the same reasons that happened with Jason," he says.

JULY 22, 1989:

Courtney Love marries husband number one: Falling James (full name James Moreland), lead singer of the LA punk band the Leaving Trains. James says that although it has been reported that they were only married for a day or two, he says they were "officially married for two years, although we only lived together for the first year."

JULY 1989:

K Records releases the "Bikini Twilight"/"Scratch it Out" 7-inch by the Go Team. "Bikini Twilight" features Kurdt Kobain, Calvin Johnson, and Tobi Vail. More than a year later, Kurt gets a homemade tattoo of the K symbol on his arm.

Also this month, a review of *Bleach* by Gillian G. Gaar runs in the *Rocket* that says, "Nirvana careens from one end of the thrash spectrum to the other, giving a nod towards garage grunge, alternative noise, and hell-raising metal without swearing allegiance to any of them."

The Posies' Mike Musburger notes that while grunge was going pretty strong in Seattle at the time, not many bands were doing it as melodically as Nirvana had done on *Bleach*. "The whole idea of the loud/soft distorted guitars and the really chunky guitars, I'd already heard that," he says. "But mostly without melody over the top of it, with no real decent songs. It was just riffs strung together with some words on top of it. And it was powerful, but Nirvana was the first band that really took that idea and wrote pop songs with it."

AUGUST 11, 1989:

CMJ New Music Report runs a review of *Bleach* that declares: "Nirvana could become the coolest thing since toast."

AUGUST 12, 1989:

Nirvana's *Bleach* is released on vinyl in the UK on Tupelo. Also this month, the album is issued on CD/cassette in the US on Sub Pop.

AUGUST 20 AND 28, 1989:

Kurt Cobain, Chris Novoselic, Screaming Trees' singer Mark Lanegan, and Trees' drummer Mark Pickerel record together at Reciprocal with Jack Endino for what was to be a side project called The Jury.

● **Kurt – Flat out and flying, Seattle** ●

They record Leadbelly's "Ain't It a Shame," a song that Jack describes as a "traditional tune done in a style sort of like Creedence Clearwater Revival's 'Lookin' Out My Back Door,' and 'Where Did You Sleep Last Night?'." Leadbelly (born Huddie Ledbetter in 1888) was a Louisiana folk/blues artist, who was incarcerated for 30 years for murder in Texas. This recording of "Where Did You Sleep Last Night?" ended up on Mark Lanegan's 1990 solo album, *The Winding Sheet*.

"An EP was planned," recalls Jack Endino. "Supposedly Kurt and Mark Lanegan got together and wrote a bunch of songs and got everybody excited. When the time came to go into the studio, they had forgotten them all." On "Where Did You Sleep Last Night?" (a song Nirvana would later perform live many times and record on *MTV Unplugged in New York*), Mark Lanegan sang lead vocals, Kurt played guitar, and Chris played bass. "Ain't It a Shame" featured Kurt on vocals/guitar, Chris on bass, and Mark Pickerel on drums.

Slim Moon, Kurt's next-door neighbor, says he turned Kurt on to Leadbelly's music. "When I loaned my Leadbelly records to Kurt, he was really blown away," recalls Slim. "Lanegan had liked Leadbelly for a really long time." One of the first recordings Kurt was turned on to was Leadbelly's *Last Sessions*.

AUGUST 26, 1989:
Nirvana plays their first Seattle show in months at a Sub Pop show at COCA (Center on Contemporary Arts). Cat Butt and Mudhoney are also on the bill. By this time, Nils Bernstein says that it was hard to get a ticket for any of the band's Seattle shows.

AUGUST 1989:
With Steve Fisk producing, Nirvana records "Been a Son," "Stain," "Even in His Youth," "Polly," and "Token Eastern Song" for the *Blew* EP at Music Source in Seattle. From this session, "Been a Son" and "Stain" end up on the EP. The other three songs were unfinished. The nighttime sessions lasted two or three days.

"We were all familiar with the stuff he'd done in Pell Mell and we had a lot of respect for the guy," says Chad. "We had a pretty good time with him. Fisk is a little more technical, a little more of a perfectionist maybe. His approach was different, so it seemed like it took a little longer than normal, but we liked how it turned out."

"The songs were together," Steve Fisk, also a part of Pigeonhed, tells Gillian in *Goldmine*. "They didn't record 'em quick, they did a lot of trying it again. There was sort of medium tension, talking to each other in between takes. I just tried to help; I didn't really have any great ideas. Though if I would've explained that not saying 'fuck' so much in 'Stain,' that song could've been a hit. But I didn't have the forethought then as a record producer to say, 'Kurt, you can't say fuck that many times. It just won't fly on the radio.'"

SUMMER 1989:

Nirvana plays a lot of home state shows this summer in such cities outside of the Seattle circuit as Huquiam, Bellvue, and Olympia.

"They kind of did the 'everything but Seattle circuit' for a while, where they played Tacoma and Olympia and other towns a lot more than they played Seattle," explains Charles R. Cross. "At the start, Nirvana was not a Seattle band. None of the members lived in Seattle until later. The perception is that Nirvana broke by playing clubs in Seattle, and that is patently not true. They broke because of the success of the record and they broke because of the success of them touring nationwide, and eventually indeed their Northwest fans grew to be a larger part of it. They were outsiders and it was indeed very cliquey, and they were outsiders even when they became successful. Eventually, they became insiders, but that was a long time coming."

Kurt confirms this theory in an interview he did with *Melody Maker*: "Both Chris and I thought of ourselves as outsiders – we wrote that song, 'School,' about the crazy Seattle scene, how it reminded us of high school."

SEPTEMBER 1, 1989:

Nirvana plays Iguana's in Tijuana, Mexico.

SEPTEMBER 9–22, 1989

Nirvana kicks off a mini Mid-West tour to make up the handful of dates canceled due to Jason Everman's departure in June. This time around, they have a tour manager, a sound man (Craig Montgomery), a U-Haul truck for their gear, and are earning about $100–$200 a gig.

The first show, on September 9, is at the Cabaret Metro in Chicago, opening for Sonic Youth. The scheduled dates for the tour are said to have included shows in Louisville, Kentucky; Toledo, Ohio; and Denver, Colorado, among many others.

Of the Chicago show, Chad recalls, "Kurt came crashing into my kit, and then these bottles started whizzing by us and we just kind of looked at each other and ran underneath the stage, or the drum riser. I left my drum stool at that show."

SEPTEMBER 23, 1989:

When asked what his favorite tour moment was, Chad says it was in Milwaukee when they bought Pixel Visions, Fisher Price's $100 video camera. "We were driving somewhere in the evening. Chris was driving and me and Kurt were in the back seat and we put a blanket between the back seats of Chris and the passenger side and we turned the light on to use our Pixel Visions, filming each other doing weird stuff. We had a bottle of something, too, Jim Beam, or something. It was totally fun." The show this night was at the Unicorn.

OCTOBER 3, 1989:

Oblivious to the fact that Kurt's microphone is not working, Nirvana open their show with "School" and play through the entire song with the audience unable to hear what he's singing. They're on a bill sandwiched between Steel Pole Bathtub and the Flaming Lips at the Blind Pig in Ann Arbor, Michigan.

"Cobain never looked up, and the other guys were just banging away, so they didn't know his mike wasn't on," says Flaming Lips' singer Wayne Coyne. "So they get done with the song and it's like, hold on, they fixed the mike and he just sang the song again." Backstage, Kurt was quiet as usual. "Cobain didn't talk. He wasn't necessarily mean or nice, he was just quiet. And Novoselic was the bouncy, 'Hey dudes, what's up?' kind of guy. Chad, I liked Chad. Even though he's not technically the Dave Grohl sort of drummer, I always liked him better than Grohl. He had a lot of personality and was fun."

OCTOBER 6–8, 1989:

More Mid-West dates: October 6, Murphy's Pub, Cincinnati, Ohio; October 7, the Outhouse in Lawrence, Kansas; and October 8, the Lift Ticket Lounge in Omaha, Nebraska. Of this period, Chris Novoselic wrote in the liner notes for *From the Muddy Banks of Wishkah*, "At the time, live shows were our bread and butter. We'd hit the road for months at a time... coming back with one or two grand... to be split three ways. In those days, that was about as much 'success' as we thought possible."

OCTOBER 12, 1989:

On this day, Kurt buys an acoustic guitar – a 12-string Stella costing $31.21, according to *Guitar World*. He recorded some of the Butch Vig demos in April 1990 on this guitar.

OCTOBER 20, 1989:

Nirvana takes off for Europe for their first tour overseas. It's a co-headlining tour with Tad, with an entourage of nine (including sound man Craig Montgomery and tour manager Edwin Heath) traveling in a nine-seat mini-van with the gear in the back (and a 300lb Tad Doyle and the 6'7" Chris Novoselic taking up a lot of room). Kurt described the tour as "grueling" in *Route 666*.

● Nirvana + Tad = Sub Pop Tour ●

● Kurt with mid-air solo ●

The band usually earned about $100 or more a show, but it was mostly a "break-even tour." Craig recalls everyone getting a $10 per diem, and they were fed by the promoter at the show at night and usually breakfast was included in their hotel in the morning. Of the tour Jonathan Poneman says, "None of us really knew what we were doing. There was just the basic raw desire to get the band over there, and they wanted to tour Europe, and they went over there and it's a first tour by an unknown rock band, the two of them. There was a lot of hoopla [over the bands] but hoopla on a real grass roots level. They didn't have any money."

OCTOBER 21, 1989:

The *Melody Maker* runs the article, "Nirvana: Bleached Wails," by Everett True, in which Chris Novoselic comments on the hype surrounding Sub Pop and the Seattle scene: "We're definitely not ground-breaking. If there were no Sub Pop sound, we'd still be doing this. If there's anything we're really close to, it's the Stooges – the momentum and the energy." The band spend the night in London before heading to Newcastle for their show the next night.

OCTOBER 23, 1989:

The first show of the 36-date tour is at the Riverside Theater in Newcastle, England. The tour got off to a rocky start. "We had amps breaking and equipment problems," says Chad. "It was chaotic. But it was all right. I think someone threw a beer bottle and it hit Chris in the head. I remember when we got our equipment, a lot of it wasn't the right equipment, such as the drums. Me and Steve [Wiederhold] from Tad were sharing the drums, and I was used to playing on my more powerful North drums. I don't know, they just didn't quite cut it, but we kept it through the whole tour."

"The very first show Chris got drunk and out of control and he would smash a bass amp and it was expensive," says Craig of the show. "We had this Dutch guy for a tour manager named Edwin Heath and I could see this look in his eyes. Like 'Oh God, what am I in for?' It's the very first night, they destroyed some equipment. We had rental stuff that was supposed to last for the whole tour. The agency and the label would have been responsible for the stuff we broke. So we ended up using an extra guitar amp to power the bass cabinets and switching

some stuff around. That was the other thing, Nirvana and Tad were sharing this gear and the Tad guys aren't really gear smashers, so the Tad guys would be like, 'Come on you assholes, we have to play on this stuff too!'"

OCTOBER 24, 1989:

The second show is at Manchester Polytechnic, in Manchester, England. "The shows all sort of blur together, but the second night was better," recalls Craig Montgomery. "We sort of fell into a routine a little bit; kind of figured it out. These European tours that they did are kind of what got the ball rolling because the crowds were just going nuts. People were jumping off stuff."

OCTOBER 25, 1989:

Many of the shows on this tour were at universities, but some were at tiny pubs like this one in Leeds, England called the Duchess of York public house. "The room is maybe 25 feet from front to back and it holds just a couple hundred people. Beer-soaked floor, very packed. It was very English," says Craig.

OCTOBER 26, 1989:

Nirvana perform "About a Girl," "Love Buzz," "Polly," and "Spank Thru" on their first John Peel session at Maida Vale Studios in London. The bands were taken care of on the tour, but the accommodation and meals weren't exactly to everyone's liking. "We would stay in these really budget kind of hotels," explains Craig. "In England it would be these little bed and breakfast kind of places with two of us to a room on these little hard twin beds. English breakfast for breakfast. It would be a couple of fried eggs, a stewed tomato, and baked beans and coffee. But not what we're used to and not very much of it either. So those guys started having a hard time because none of the food was what they were used to. The novelty of being in Europe sort of wore off pretty quickly."

Adapting was pretty easy for Chad, though, who moved around a lot as a child. "It was my first time in Europe and I was having fun," says Chad. "I had a blast on the tour, but I might be the only one that did. Tad got sick all the time, but Tad's problem was he wouldn't chew his food more than a couple bites before he'd swallow. And Kurt had a hard time with the food because of his stomach." Craig adds, "Kurt's problem was, the kid grew up in Aberdeen and he hadn't been exposed to anything in his whole life, so he's really picky about what he'll eat, and the food is different."

OCTOBER 27, 1989:

Nirvana and Tad perform at the School of Oriental and African Studies, which is part of the University of London. "Fans were jumping off the speaker stacks; I'd never seen anything like it," says Craig. "I ended up seeing it with Nirvana all the time, though. They would play this stuff and it was like a tornado hit. People would completely lose control of their bodies. What people don't realize about Nirvana is in the midst of all this chaos going on around them, they are actually a pretty consistent band. They knew how to play their stuff, they knew how to make it sound good. Once in a while there would be a show that was really bad because they were in a bad mood or the monitors weren't working, external stuff. But as far as their playing goes, they were consistent."

● Tad on stage on the Sub Pop European tour ●

OCTOBER 28, 1989:

The next show is in Portsmouth at the Entertainments Hall. The band and crew had trouble finding the place, so they arrived at the show a little late – hungry and cranky, says Craig. Craig agrees that the tour was grueling, due to logistics mostly, but it wasn't the nightmare tour that many have made it out to be – at least not for him.

"I think everyone was optimistic in the beginning, but that may just be my own perception," he says. "For myself, I was excited that I got to go to Europe. I didn't care if we got paid or not, as long as we were getting fed. And we were working with this promoter called Paper Clip, who when we started we were pretty impressed with 'cause they had a van for us and hotel rooms all arranged. It was a pretty self-contained package it seemed at the time. They had two months' worth of gigs for us, they had it all figured out."

OCTOBER 29, 1989:

The next show is upstairs in the pub Edward's No. 8 in Birmingham. Chad points out that there were no signs of drug use on these early tours at all. "If Kurt had some kind of a hardcore drug problem he must have hid it extremely well because he never did [have a problem] when I was in the band," says Chad. "Because we didn't have connections and stuff like that; we didn't have people. Whether he was doing anything or not in the down time, I wouldn't know, but when we were on tour we'd drink a lot, and Kurt, he didn't – I mean, you can tell when people are fucked up, you can totally tell, their attitude changes and they're almost not even there sometimes. And there just weren't any of those kind of problems at all."

OCTOBER 30, 1989:

Like most of the shows on this tour, the Norwich Arts Centre gig in Norwich wasn't "desperately different from the last show I saw," says UK journalist Kevan Roberts. "It was a lot more passive, less people there. It wasn't empty, but it wasn't as packed as the London show."

NOVEMBER 1, 1989:

Nirvana perform "About a Girl," "Dive," and "Love Buzz" and are interviewed on VPRO Radio in Hilversum, Holland. This evening, the band plays Nighttown in Rotterdam, Holland. "Holland was fun for a lot of reasons. One, our booking agent, Paper Clip, was from Holland. So the gigs got better – they were in bigger places, kind of nicer, really good food, we got treated really well," says Craig. "I remember being pretty comfortable in Holland. It was a big deal to be there, because they did this big radio show. Audiences were a little more reserved in Holland. They weren't going nuts like the English."

NOVEMBER 2-5, 1989:

Nirvana and Tad play four more shows in Holland at, in order: Vera in Groningen; Tivoli in Utrecht; Gigant in Apeldoorn; and Melkweg in Amsterdam. The gig at Melkweg ended with Kurt smashing his guitar to the ground and then screaming into the mike as the band jammed. "The monitor was right next to my ear and he was at a higher volume than I'd ever heard. My ears haven't been the same since," laughs Chad.

"The pot smokers [in the band and crew] were really big into the hash bars and looking around the red-light district, all the usual

• Chad , Chris, and Kurt •

Amsterdam stuff," says Craig. "The Bull Dog, it's the big touristy bar, some of the guys went in there and bought some hash. They were all excited about the fact that you could buy it and it wasn't illegal."

NOVEMBER 7, 1989:

Probably the worst sounding show of the tour was at B-52 in Mönchengladbach, West Germany. "Sound-wise, the show was an abortion," says Craig. "It was a shitty little place; they barely had a sound system. It was crappy, and we were supposed to stay at someone's house, but it got pretty sketchy. I don't remember a lot about the actual shows; I remember stuff around the shows. But the shows themselves are kind of fuzzy. People ask me all the time, 'What was the best show?' But, for me, a great show was when they get through the song and stuff didn't fuck up."

NOVEMBER 8, 1989:

Nirvana throws in a bit of the Ventures' "Walk, Don't Run" at their show in Köln, West Germany at the Rose Club.

NOVEMBER 9, 1989:

While in Hanover, West Germany for a show at Schwimmbad, the world is witnessing the fall of the Berlin wall. "We didn't even know what was going on until a little before we got to the border and there were all these little cars crammed full of people offering us fruit," Chris Novoselic says in the December 1989 *Rocket* cover story, "Berlin Is Just a State of Mind" by Nils Bernstein.

"It was incredibly exciting," says Craig about the history they were witnessing. "On our way to Berlin, there are two highways that you can take to get to Berlin from West Germany, they're called corridors, so you have to pass through this big border checkpoint and when you're on the corridor you can't get off the freeway, so there was lots of traffic. We were in line for a long time 'cause what was happening was all the East Germans were driving out to go shopping in West Germany for the first time they could do this since World War II. The amazing thing was the line to get out of East Germany was, like, 80 kilometers long, like 50 miles of cars parked on the freeway waiting to get out, in their little German cars like you see in that U2 video. It was a crazy time to be there."

NOVEMBER 10, 1989:

Another West Germany show at the Forum in Enger, a small town out in the countryside. "It was way out in the country and it was like, 'What the fuck are we doing out here?' There wouldn't even be a hotel in the town, we'd have to drive to the next town to stay somewhere," says Craig.

NOVEMBER 11, 1989:

Kurt smashes his guitar during "Breed" and walks off stage early at the Ecstasy Club in Berlin. "Well, he was having a lot of trouble; his guitars were getting smashed and it would make weird noises all the time or stop working," says Craig Montgomery. "You're in Europe and you don't really have time to get it repaired. We only got one new guitar on this tour via Jonathan [in Switzerland]. They didn't completely destroy stuff every night. The stupid thing is, they would try to fix it. They would try to get another cheap guitar and cobble together parts and make it work."

This night, the band and crew slept upstairs in the dressing rooms and offices at the club. "There weren't any beds and I think some people were squatting," says Craig. "I slept on a hard wood floor; that was pretty rugged. Then we had to get up and drive a long way to Oldenburg."

NOVEMBER 12, 1989:

The band plays at Alhambra in Oldenburg, West Germany. "Nerves were starting to grate a bit from having to pile into this cramped van and just drive," says Craig. "Tad was like throwing up every day for some reason, and he is also the loudest snorer ever, so no one would want to room with him. I would get stuck rooming with him a lot – a take one for the team type thing. It was loud, loud snoring."

NOVEMBER 13, 1989:

The next show is in Hamburg, West Germany at Fabrik. "Hamburg was a neat place, though it took forever to get there. We got there late again. We'd heard about Hamburg with the whole Beatles thing and the Reeperbahn and we went and saw that and walked around," recalls Craig. Other than a few days, like this one, the band members and crew didn't have time to do much sightseeing during the day on this tour, because they were either traveling or tired from traveling, according to Craig.

NOVEMBER 15-19, 1989:

Five more shows in West Germany at: Schwimmbad in Heidelberg; Trust in Nürnberg; Negativ in Frankfurt; Ka-Ba Club in Hanau; and Gammelsdorf Circus in Gammelsdorf.

NOVEMBER 20, 1989:

Nirvana and Tad head to Austria for four shows, starting in Linz, Austria at the Kapu Club. When Gina Arnold asked the group what the highlight of their early European touring was, Kurt joked, "Oh! That place in Austria! Up in the mountains, with all the trolls? The troll village." Chris added, "Oh yeah! A bunch of inbred villagers going, 'Play some rock and roll, bay-bee.'"

Of the first show in Austria, Craig says the only thing that sticks in his mind is Tad, once again, throwing up on the side of the road. "I don't know what his problem was. Everybody was getting sick on this tour. As you can imagine, it was winter; and for the guys who have to sing it was magnified." When asked how the two groups were getting along, Craig said, "They're all friends from back in Seattle, but they weren't the closest of friends. There would be some tension and it would kind of come and go."

NOVEMBER 21, 1989:

The bands play Kozos Rendezvenye, a heavy metal club according to the tour poster, in Budapest, Hungary. "We actually had time to drive around and look around. We went to the center of the city where there was a big plaza and all this really beautiful, sweeping old architecture," says Craig. "But getting across the border was bizarre. It was still a Communist country and it was harder getting through passport control."

NOVEMBER 22-24, 1989:

The tour heads back to Austria for one show in Vienna at U4 on the 22nd, another in Graz at Forum Stadtpark on the 23rd, and the last gig in the country in the small town of Hohenems at Konkret on the 24th.

NOVEMBER 25, 1989:

Frison in Fribourg, Switzerland is the next scheduled stop.

NOVEMBER 26, 1989:

Kurt joins Tad onstage to sing "High on the Hog" and "Loser" at the Bloom in Mezzago, Italy. "It was really hot in there and a really small room. I think Tad passed out or something, so Kurt got onstage," recalls Craig. "At the end of the show, there wasn't much security and people were trying to steal stuff off the stage. Some kid was trying to steal Chris's shoes or something, then I terrified this kid and he backed off, but he was trying to steal shoes!"

NOVEMBER 27, 1989:

Stressed from the tour and missing home, Kurt climbs atop a rafter on the side of the stage during their show at the Piper Club in Rome and threatens to jump. Sub Pop's Jonathan Poneman and Bruce Pavitt were here for this show – they flew out to check on the guys and, as Jonathan puts it, to "prop up the spirits of the bands, be some familiar faces, buy them dinner, do whatever little thing we could because we knew they were roughing it."

Jonathan recalls the moment of Kurt's big onstage freak-out: "I was up in the wings watching. Now, they had started quite regularly smashing up their gear onstage and then methodically re-piece it together after each show, but he was getting frustrated with that. He just wanted another guitar and his guitar was fucking up and everything was just being done on a shoestring budget, in a haphazard way. And I remember his guitar went out, a string broke or something like that, and that was it. He was so pissed off. He climbed up on the frontal mains [mains are the huge speakers in the front of the stage] and he was going to jump, which would have, if it didn't kill him, it would have injured some people below him and he was serious about it. He climbed on these speakers and he *was* going to jump. I was just like, 'What are you doing?' Then the bouncers pulled him off; he was in the air when they pulled him."

Jonathan then walked around the venue with Kurt multiple times to cool him off and Kurt told him that he just wanted to go home. "It was the first time I heard him say, 'I see all these people in the crowd and they're fucking idiots.' And he says, 'I don't know what I'm doing this for. I miss my home. I just want to go back to Olympia. I can't stand riding in the van with those guys; they're making me crazy. My guitar is fucking up. I don't have any money.' He was gonna basically quit. He just had it with this. That was the first time I heard him say anything along the lines of 'I'm playing for a bunch of bumpkins.'"

To calm Kurt down, Jonathan says he promised to buy him a new guitar once they got to Switzerland and he bought Kurt a train ticket so he could travel more comfortably to the next city. "We wanted to get him out of the van. They only had a couple more days left and the London show, so they were almost there. And he was just, 'I want to get out of here. I want to go home.' Then he got a good night's sleep, and the next day we went to the Coliseum and things seemed to chill out a little."

Chad says the only time Kurt seemed depressed was this night in Rome, at which time the singer asked his band mates, "Are you guys having fun any more?" "I didn't really give an answer," says Chad. "I just shrugged. I didn't want to say, 'Yeah I'm having a great time!' Chris just always kind of went the motion with Kurt. If things weren't going well with Kurt and Chris knew it, then obviously they weren't going well [with Chris either.]"

NOVEMBER 28, 1989:

On their day off, some of the guys visited the Coliseum, while others went to the Vatican. When pressed for a fun, light-hearted memory of his time with Kurt, Jonathan says, "The only time I remember anything like that was sandwiched in between two traumatic situations. And that was after the Rome situation when we went to the Coliseum. We had a great time there.

"But then we rode from Rome to Geneva and we got stuck at the border," continues Jonathan. "Kurt fell asleep in the car and got his wallet and passport stolen, so we had to get off the train. That, I'll tell you [pause] that was the picture of unhappiness. So, we got off the

"I WANT TO GET OUT OF HERE. I WANT TO GO HOME."

train, and we had to report the passport stolen; it was a long ordeal. I remember him sitting there with his hood over his head and drinking a cup of hot chocolate or something and he was just in hell. So miserable. He didn't say anything, but you could see he was like, 'What am I doing here?' But even that passed. We did buy another guitar the next day."

NOVEMBER 29, 1989:

Ugdo in Geneva, Switzerland is the next stop on the tour. "This particular show I would *love* to find an audio tape of," says Chad. "It was a really good show and it was the first time we ever played that Leadbelly cover, 'Where Did You Sleep Last Night?' It was just amazing. We had only toyed around with it during sound check, but it wasn't hard to pick up and I had heard the song before because we were big Leadbelly fans anyway. So we just kind of threw it out of the hat and played it. They totally loved it. I loved it."

Jonathan says that even after Kurt's meltdown in Rome, he didn't seem any more depressed that any other person would occasionally get. "I have a problem with depression myself, a different kind I guess, but my whole thing about that was who doesn't have a problem with depression?" asks Jonathan. "I don't mean that in a heartless sense, but when you are a depressive, the whole world appears to be downcast. At the time, I wasn't the happiest camper in the world, so I didn't know the depths of his depression. I did know that he used to get sick pretty regularly before getting on the stage. He did not seem like he was a particularly happy guy, but he also could be very light and fun. He had a great sense of humor. Every single time I hung with him it would just be a matter of time before he'd make a joke. He was a very intelligent, very astute person. And then there were times, I remember seeing him come into the Vogue after *Nevermind* had hit, and he just looked awful. I mean really awful.

"Every biography, every story that I've seen about Nirvana I know there are aspects of this mythologizing, very different from what actually comes out in the portrayal of what Nirvana was and what Kurt Cobain was, but that's showbiz to a large degree. The depressed, whiny person. That's the media," continues Jonathan. "The guy that I knew had such a sense of wonderment, a deep curiosity for the world. There was a certain innocence there. That he became like this cynical junkie, hardened, and I'm sorry, but that wasn't the guy that I knew. He was a very, very sweet person and very kind-hearted. Yeah, there were parts of him from a business standpoint, he told me, 'I think my band can sell millions of records.' He said that to me very early on. I'm going, 'Yeah, yeah.' From that standpoint he had a sense of confidence about his craft and about his talent, whether it was indeed born of naïveté or he was able to look into a crystal ball that none of us mortals had access to, I don't really know and it's almost not even the point. There was a light quality to him when I knew him. That lightness and the sense of wonderment and that sense of innocence get glossed over."

NOVEMBER 30, 1989:

Nirvana and Tad play the Rogue Fabrik in Zurich, Switzerland. "Those were fairly routine shows," says Chad. "Switzerland shows were nicer – better food and better accommodations. It was kind of tense, but it was also kind of business as usual. [The Rome incident] was just a blow-up that passed."

● The Astoria, London, gets a taste of Nirvana ●

● **Portrait of a legend** ●

NOVEMBER 1989:

C/Z releases the compilation EP *Teriyaki Asthma, Vol. 1* featuring Nirvana's "Mexican Seafood" from the January 23, 1988 demo with Dale Crover on drums. The same version of the song also appears on *Teriyaki Asthma Vol. 1–5* and a remastered version is on *Incesticide*.

EARLY DECEMBER 1989:

The *Blew* EP is released in the UK on Tupelo. It was supposed to come out prior to the European tour, but it wasn't ready for release in time.

DECEMBER 1, 1989:

MJC Fahrenheit in Issy Les Moulineaux, France is the next stop on the tour.

DECEMBER 2, 1989:

The last show on the tour before getting on the boat back to England is at Democrazy in Ghent, Belgium.

DECEMBER 3, 1989:

Tad and Nirvana's tour connects with Mudhoney's tour for the only Sub Pop Lame Fest staged in London, at the Astoria. Mudhoney's Dan Peters told Michael Azerrad in *Come As You Are* that Nirvana's set was "pretty fucked up," and Chris Novoselic agreed that "it stunk." The performance couldn't have been that bad, since two songs ("Polly" and "Breed," formerly titled "Imodium") from the show ended up on the live album, *From the Muddy Banks of the Wishkah*, released years later. "They had some gear problems [again], so some of the set was blown off," explains Craig.

Journalist Kevan Roberts says the end-of-tour tension was evident in the band's performance. "They were just all over the place," he says. "Toward the end, I remember Kurt and Chris playing baseball with their guitar. Kurt would throw his guitar up in the air toward Chris and Chris tried hitting it like a baseball. I think they missed a couple of times, so they did it again. And I recall Tad Doyle made as if he was gonna stage dive, he kind of lurched toward the front of the stage and I'd never seen a group of people that were that packed together part so quickly. [Tad weighed about 300lbs, remember.] He didn't do it, but he would've taken out a lot of people if he did. It was pretty riotous really."

In attendance were members of My Bloody Valentine, the Senseless Things, the Faith Healers, and That Petrol Motion, according to Kevan.

DECEMBER 10–20, 1989:

During these 11 days, Mark Lanegan of the Screaming Trees records his solo album, *The Winding Sheet*. It's on one of these days, or possibly January 1, 1990, that Kurt records his backing vocal parts on the song "Down in the Dark," according to *Goldmine*.

DECEMBER 30, 1989:

Chris Novoselic marries his longtime girlfriend Shelli in their Tacoma, Washington apartment. Matt Lukin of Mudhoney was Chris's best man. Matt sums up the wedding in *Come As You Are* as: "They got married and then everybody got drunk."

• A quieter on-stage moment from Kurt •

FOURTH. 1990:

SOMETHING BIGGER ON THE WAY

JANUARY 2, 1990:

Nirvana records "Sappy" (a.k.a. "Verse Chorus Verse") with Jack Endino at Reciprocal Recording. It's not one of Jack's favorite songs. "It should have been 'Verse Verse Verse.' It has barely any chorus and no bridge, and no riff, and hardly any melody, no 'swing' of any kind," says Jack. "It just laid there. I couldn't figure out why they even bothered with it. It seemed like such B-side material next to their other stuff.

"Kurt recorded it at least five times over the ensuing years, so he did not agree," continues Jack. But it never rated being put on one of their albums because there were always better songs... pretty much proving my point. Even Sub Pop was kind of puzzled by it. And there was no reason to record it right then, no single was planned or anything. Going through all that trouble just for one song is not an efficient use of time or recording money."

Jack says they probably spent $400–$500 on this one session. The studio had evolved from an 8-track studio to a 16-track studio in the past two years, and therefore it was slightly more expensive.

JANUARY 3, 1990:

"Sappy" is mixed at Reciprocal. "They also spent almost an *entire* day mixing it with me because they wanted me to get an 'Albini' sound [referring to *In Utero* recorder Steve Albini]," says Jack Endino. "I actually came pretty close, using room mikes extensively (in what was actually a lousy-sounding room) but it didn't magically make it a more interesting song."

JANUARY 6–20, 1990:

Even though Sub Pop isn't actively promoting *Bleach* at the time (it's now eight months past its release), Nirvana plays a string of Washington and Oregon dates before embarking on another tour down the West Coast. The itinerary is: January 6, the HUB Ballroom, Seattle; January 12, Satyricon, Portland; January 19, Rignall Hall, Olympia; January 20, Legends, Tacoma.

"I remember Chris grabbing the mike and singing just a bunch of perverted stuff into it," says Sub Pop's Megan Jasper of the HUB Ballroom show, which also featured Tad, the Gits, and Crunchbird on the bill. "The great thing about their shows was they did whatever the fuck they wanted to and they said whatever the fuck they wanted and they still would play an amazing show. They were everything you kind of want a musician to be. They had that rebellious streak, but they were also super-talented. And when they played, they always seemed like they put everything into every song they were playing. It just felt so much like a party to me. That's what those shows were like."

Chris also grabbed the microphone at the Legends show on January 20, where he sang a bit of the Beatles, including "All You Need is Love" and "If I Fell." "He gets almost all the words to 'If I Fell'," says Gillian G. Gaar upon listening to a bootleg of the show on tape.

JANUARY 31, 1990:

Chad Channing's 23rd birthday.

FEBRUARY 9–19, 1990:

Nirvana embarks on a short West Coast tour opening for Dinosaur Jr., starting at the Pine Street Theater in Portland, Oregon on the 9th. The shows include February 11, Cactus Club, San Jose, California; February 12, Cattle Club, Sacramento, California; February 14, Kennel Club, San Francisco; February 15, Raji's, Los Angeles; February 16, Bogart's, Long Beach, California; February 18, Iguana's, Tijuana, Mexico; and February 19, Mason Jar, Phoenix, Arizona.

The shows that stand out from this trek are the Raji's show (where Charles Peterson took the famous photo of Kurt sprawled across Chad's drums) and the show at Iguana's across the border. Robert Fisher, former art director at Geffen Records, was at the Raji's show: "The highlight was at the end when Kurt was just tearing the place up and doing these dives into the drums. I couldn't believe he didn't walk away from that without a broken back or something. They were all into knocking stuff down, but Kurt was just going for it full force, totally launching himself into the drums. It was a great show. You could tell

● Kurt's drum solo: Raji's, Los Angeles ●

they had something going there."

Nirvana left quite an impression at their Tijuana show too. "[Kurt] came onstage looking very innocent and harmless," recalls Dave Lott, who was a DJ at the radio station at University of California at San Diego's KSDT, which was heavily plugging *Bleach* at the time. "When he launched into the first song with those heavy, harsh chords and his raw throaty voice, people in the pit were taken aback. Just to look at him and hear that was like, *that* sound is coming out of *him*? When he left the stage, everyone stood there kind of dazed. At lot of people left the venue that night saying, 'Mascis [Dinosaur Jr. singer/guitarist J. Mascis] is cool, but *damn* that opening band.'"

FEBRUARY 17, 1990:

"Punk Rock Heaven From Northwest's Nirvana" reads the headline of the *Los Angeles Times'* review of Nirvana's Raji's show. Jonathan Gold writes that Nirvana "sounded for the moment at least like the best punk band you've ever heard in your life: deep-deep metal riffs repeated as relentlessly as beats on a hip-hop record, washes of guitar white noise, singer Kurdt Kobain bellowing punk moans above the din."

FEBRUARY 20, 1990:

Kurt turns 23.

MARCH 12, 1990:

Nirvana and Tad play the Town Pump in Vancouver, British Columbia, Canada. The Bomshells opened. It's during these early '90 tours that Chad says he started losing inspiration because he wasn't a key part of the band.

"I wanted to have a little more input, because I just started feeling like this drum machine," he says. "Kurt, at one point, said, 'Hey, I want you guys to put more input in the band,' and I thought that sounded great, and I was looking forward to it. Finally, I'd have a chance to feel like I'm actually contributing to the band, which, of course, never happened. It just never came about. We just kept going and going.

"That's the whole ultimate demise of me and the band; that's how it started," continues Chad. "The whole thing rests on my shoulders. It was all me. I just wasn't all that happy. I knew after a time that I wasn't going to be anything more than what I was, just this drum machine. And when I felt that happening, I started losing inspiration."

MARCH 19, 1990:

Seattle's increasing heroin problem claims the life of Andrew Wood of the seminal Seattle bands Malfunkshun and Mother Love Bone.

Referring to the overdose deaths of people like Andrew, Sid Vicious, and Janis Joplin, Kurt told Michael Azerrad in *Come As You Are*, "They get drunk and then they get high and then they die. I never drank – I learned that from junkies." Four years later, Kurt washes down 50–60 pills and some champagne in Rome; everyone claims it was an "accident."

"For a long time in Seattle, it seemed like everyone was doing heroin," reveals Nils Bernstein. But Slim Moon notes that it was more taboo in Olympia where he lived than it was in Seattle "among the grunge crowd. Being around punk rock, I'd already had friends die.

I have to say that when people get into heroin there's a part of the

● Jason and Kurt at the Hub, Seattle ●

• Seattle, WA •

brain that just goes, 'OK don't be surprised if they die.' And you just file them in that category from then on. It doesn't mean you quit liking them, but I've had just as many heroin addict friends commit suicide as overdose. So [Kurt's suicide] wasn't that much of a surprise to me either when it happened."

MARCH 1990:

Nirvana rehearses the songs for their upcoming sessions with producer Butch Vig in Madison, Wisconsin for what initially was planned to be their second Sub Pop album, but ends up being demos for their major label debut, *Nevermind*, on DGC. Today, Butch is the founding member of Garbage, but at the time he was known for his work with Tad, Killdozer, and the Fluid. Jonathan Poneman recommended him.

"Before we took off for Madison, we rented a shared jam space in Seattle," recalls Chad Channing. "I think it was called the Dutchman. It's a big warehouse with a lot of rooms that several bands rented out. We shared a spot, maybe, with Mudhoney. I remember the first time we worked on 'In Bloom' there. He brought in the song and it just clicked immediately. What we did that day is exactly what has been on that song. We also worked on 'Lithium,' which I remember hearing that bass line and thinking how cool it was. I think we jammed here about eight or nine times, maybe over three weeks like three times a week or weekends, before we took off for Madison.

"By the time we got to Butch's studio," he continues, "not all the lyrics were done. I can't remember which song, but Kurt was sitting on the bed one night trying to think of rhyming words for a song. It was often that he'd kind of write the lyrics last minute, or he'd have them done but then decide to change them right before we would record."

APRIL 1, 1990:

The night before recording, the band played the Cabaret Metro in Chicago, opening for a popular local band called Eleventh Dream Day. "I went to go see Eleventh Dream Day and I'll never forget what I saw that night. It was like 'Oh my God. [Nirvana] are amazing'," says the *Chicago Tribune*'s Greg Kot. "Here's Kurt, we didn't know who he was, this blonde-haired guy screaming his guts out the whole night for 45 minutes basically. He looked like he was in the jaws of this giant invisible Rottweiler and the Rottweiler was just shaking him back and

forth and back and forth. This scrawny little guy was just flinging his body around the stage with absolutely no regard for the consequences.

"And at the end of the set, he did the whole set-thrashing, drum-trashing routine," continues Greg. "Every instrument onstage was in splinters. The drummer was still playing, still pounding away and Cobain had completely destroyed his drum kit and was lying splayed across it. People just looked at each other, like, 'God, how do you follow that?' Eleventh Dream Day was one of the best bands in Chicago and they just got blown off the stage and they hadn't even played a note yet. To this day, we still talk about that show."

After the show, the band drives through the night to their hotel in Madison, Wisconsin.

APRIL 2-6, 1990:

Kurt, Chris, and Chad record seven songs ("In Bloom," "Dive," "Lithium," "Pay to Play" [later titled "Stay Away"], "Imodium" [later titled "Breed"], "Sappy," and "Polly") at Butch Vig's Smart Studios in Madison, Wisconsin. "Polly" is the only song from these sessions that ended up on *Nevermind*; the rest were re-recorded with Butch the following year. They also recorded "Here She Comes Now" by the Velvet Underground for the *Heaven and Hell, Vol. 1* tribute album on the Communion label.

"When they showed up, they were actually very funny and charming, particularly Chris," recalls Butch Vig in *Goldmine*. "Kurt was always an enigma. He was very charming when he came, and then he would get really moody and sit in the corner and not talk for 45 minutes." Of the sessions, Butch tells the magazine, "I didn't really have to do too much fine tuning in terms of what they were doing. They had been playing most of the songs [live]; the arrangements were pretty solid. I could tell that Kurt wasn't too pleased with Chad's drumming, because he kept going and getting behind the kit showing him how to play things."

APRIL 6, 1990:

Nirvana headlines a sold-out show with Tad and a local band called Victim's Family at the Underground in Madison. Jonathan Poneman had flown in to check out how the recording was going, and to catch the show. "That was the first time I saw them live," says Butch in *Nevermind Nirvana* by Jim Berkenstadt and Charles R. Cross. "It was a

great set, very loose. I remember they were pretty messed up for it."

"We played the new songs at these shows, such as 'In Bloom.' The shows were fun, but it was hard," admits Chad, referring to his growing dissatisfaction with his role in Nirvana. "I don't know. It was pretty hard. It might have been harder on those guys than it was me, in a weird way. There was a feeling like something's gotta be going on. A lot of the books out on them, they said I was burning out on shows [and my timing was off] and stuff, and it's true. I was. I just wasn't getting into it any more."

April 9, 1990:
Nirvana plays 7th Street Entry in Minneapolis.

April 10, 1990:
Kurt jumps into the crowd at the Blind Pig in Ann Arbor, Michigan after "Love Buzz", but this time it's Chris launching himself into Chad's drum set. "The drums came crashing in on that one," says Chad, "and I just happened to fall to the side and drums came down on top of me, and then he's on top of them."

"I just remember walking into the club and it was oddest thing – everybody, including the bartenders, was just transfixed," recalls Gary Graff of the *Detroit Free Press*. "They were just staring at the stage. From the time I came in, the signals had all been there that something really hot was going on, and they did sound really, *really* good."

April 11–13, 1990:
Butch Vig spends these three days mixing the recently recorded batch of songs, though "Here She Comes Now" is mixed a few months later. "We weren't around for the mixing," says Chad. "We had shows to do, so we just got a rough copy and left."

April 14, 1990:
The band plays Shorty's Underground in Cincinnati, Ohio.

April 16, 1990:
Toronto, Ontario, Canada is the next city on the tour. Lee's Palace is the club. "I remember Chris climbing up on these speaker cabinets way up on top and he was standing up there with his bass threatening to jump. There were a lot of beer bottles being thrown up onstage and Chris was barefoot," remembers Chad Channing.

April 17, 1990:
The next stop in Canada is in Montreal at the Foufounes Electrique.

April 18, 1990:
In a room that holds about 300 people, about 75–100 kids showed up for the band's Man Ray show in Cambridge, Massachusetts, just outside of Boston.

"It was unbelievably powerful and heavy. It was heavier than the record was and it kind of reminded me of bands like Black Sabbath," recalls former WFNX Music Director Kurt St. Thomas, who interviews the band for the *Nevermind: It's an Interview* CD in 1991. "I felt that super low-end, heavy vibe and Kurt was totally amazing. It was like, 'Who is this guy, just screaming?' A WFNX DJ, Dwayne Bruce, brought them onstage and introduced them as these 'Fudge-packing, crack-smokin',

Satan-worshipping motherfuckers.' The band seemed not into that intro. [It's actually a slogan from a Nirvana T-shirt.] There was a lot of attitude coming from that stage. They had that total 'Fuck you, we're gonna rock you. Deal with it' attitude. But it seemed totally real. There was not one ounce of fake anything. It came off very sincere."

Also on this day, the band does an interview with Bob Gulla, but the interview isn't published until May 1999 on the online music store www.cdnow.com. In it, Kurt talks about the haphazard way this tour was set up: "I wasn't anticipating going on tour, but I'm having a good time," says Kurt. "You have to psych yourself up. The drives are pretty long, sometimes 12 or 13 hours, like the bookers threw a dart at the map to determine where we'd play. But we sleep, don't show up to sound check if we don't want to. This is what we chose to do, and we always considered rock and roll to be kind of lax. Heck, we may as well not burn ourselves on it."

Kurt goes on to say that they're not looking to move to a major label, even though labels have been knocking on Sub Pop's door. "We're not trying to climb our way to the top and be popular," he tells Bob Gulla. "We're totally comfortable with the level we're on now. It'd be nice to get a little higher so we could pay the rent for sure every month. I mean, we just want people to like our music. We don't want a big multi-million dollar promotional deal to bring us to every high school across the country, to make us into multi-million dollar paper dolls." Later this year, they agree to sign with Geffen's DGC label.

April 22, 1990:
Seattle and Sub Pop get more media coverage when the *Los Angeles Times* runs the story, "The Seattle Sound: Underground Rock Gets a Boost From Sub Pop," written by Jonathan Gold.

In it, Jonathan Poneman describes Sub Pop bands as "all lumberjacks" or "they painted bridges." (Well, Chris did paint *houses*.) The band wasn't too pleased to be portrayed this way. In an article in the *Rocket*, Kurt voices his concerns over this imaging problem: "I feel like we've been tagged as illiterate redneck cousin-fucking kids that have no idea what's going on at all. That's completely untrue."

April 25, 1990:
The band has a photo shoot with Michael Lavine at his studio on 2 Bleecker St. in New York. The photos are used for press and promotional purposes by Sub Pop.

● Kurt gets carried away by his fans ●

> **"WE'RE TOTALLY COMFORTABLE WITH THE LEVEL WE'RE ON NOW. IT'D BE NICE TO GET A LITTLE HIGHER SO WE COULD PAY THE RENT FOR SURE EVERY MONTH."**

APRIL 26, 1990:

By now, there is a huge buzz in the music industry and among "alternative" music fans. In the audience at Nirvana's show at New York's Pyramid Club are Geffen's head of A&R Gary Gersh, Iggy Pop, Sonic Youth, and Helmet.

"I was not impressed. I think they were just kind of sloppy," recalls Page Hamilton of Helmet. "Their sound check was so bad. They were doing 'In Bloom' and I remember thinking that song was so awful, but I later came to love it because they got it down. They were obviously rehearsing it, or working it out or whatever. And they were filming the show for some Sub Pop thing and they trashed all their gear at the end of the show. At that point it seemed like it was completely contrived for the camera. And no offense to Chad, but Dave Grohl [who would join five months from now] is God."

Sub Pop was filming for the compilation *Sub Pop Video Network Program 1*, which features a video of the band's "In Bloom" performance. The compilation was released in 1991 and also featured Mudhoney, Tad, Mark Lanegan, the Fluid, Beat Happening, Afghan Whigs, and others.

APRIL 27, 1990:

Nirvana plays the Saga Dining Rooms at Hampshire College in Amherst, Massachusetts. Kurt calls his girlfriend of three years, Tracy Marander, and tells her that he doesn't want to live together any more, but that he still wants to be boyfriend and girlfriend, according to *Come As You Are*. They soon break up.

APRIL 28, 1990:

The band plays Maxwell's in Hoboken, New Jersey with the Jesus Lizard on the bill. Chris calls Sub Pop the day of this show: "That [Pyramid] show was so bad that Chris called up the next day and I think the shit had just hit the fan, maybe it was van trouble, because they were calling in a lot. And he was going on about how bad their show was: 'You don't understand, it sucked. It was the worst show we ever played.' And so Chris went out afterwards and shaved all his hair off his head," says Sub Pop GM Megan Jasper.

APRIL 29, 1990:

Nirvana plays the 9:30 Club in Washington, DC, where Kurt's guitar amp starts acting up on him.

APRIL 30, 1990:

J.C. Dobbs in Philadelphia is the next stop on the tour. Tom Sheehy, the publicist for the club at the time, remembers the band talking about their frustration at kids not being able to find *Bleach* in the local record store in the town they're playing. "[Chris] and Kurt were sick and tired of being on the road and they'd meet these kids who'd love the band, but couldn't find the records anywhere," says Tom.

SPRING/ SUMMER 1990:

Meanwhile, Dave Grohl, who is in Scream at the time, records a studio side-project under the name Harlingtox AD with Tos Nieuwenhuizen from the Holland band God, Bruce Merkle of 9353, and producer/engineer Barrett Jones of Churn, Bark, and 11th Hour. They

• Kurt gets a little help from his friends •

every now and then I put it out of my mind and felt like giving a rat's ass to play."

A fan with wealthy parents invites the guys to stay at his house in the suburbs on the water."We wake up and nobody is there, and we're in this fancy house," remembers Craig. "So, the guys decide they're gonna go and make this big, huge mess in the kitchen, dump out all this food and crap, and Chris is running around naked in the cul-de-sac. I'm just burying my head in my hands wishing I wasn't there. But they left him a $100 bill on the counter. You really can't stop those guys when they're in that kind of mood because then you're like [their] dad and you're no fun."

MAY 5, 1990:

Nirvana plays Einstein-A-Go-Go in Jacksonville Beach, Florida."That was cool," says Craig."It was this little punk rock club with a record store next door. We stayed in this motel right on the beach... went and jumped in the water. Kurt bought this old record player to play some records and he got some old Beatles records on this tour. In the van, there was always this box of records that we played in hotel rooms – vinyl records, old pop music stuff from the '60s, the Beatles, Shocking Blue, whatever, just any old funky thing they would come across in a record store."

MAY 6–14, 1990:

The next string of dates include May 6, Masquerade, Atlanta, Georgia; May 9, Staches, Columbus, Ohio; May 11, Tulsa Theater, Tulsa, Oklahoma; May 12, Axiom, Houston, Texas; and May 13, Duffy's, Lincoln, Nebraska.

"Usually it'd be a pretty good crowd, once in a while there'd be a show that was kind

record a five-song EP titled *Harlingtox Angel Divine* at Barrett's Laundry Room Studios in Arlington, Virginia. The album is released in 1996 on Barrett's Laundry Room Records.

MAY 1, 1990:

Mark Lanegan's *The Winding Sheet* is released on Sub Pop, featuring Kurt and Chris on guitar and bass, respectively, on the cover of Leadbelly's "Where Did You Sleep Last Night?" Kurt also sings backing vocals on "Down in the Dark."

MAY 1–2, 1990:

Nirvana plays two shows in North Carolina: May 1 is in Chapel Hill and May 2 is at Milestone in Charlotte, where Kurt buys a new guitar amp.

"They were making fairly good money at these shows at this time," says Craig."They were making $600 or $800 or $1000 a night. His guitar amp crapped out and we had enough money to go to a music store and buy him another Mesa Boogie, a fairly nice set-up. He was happier then. He didn't know very much about equipment, so he was asking, 'What can I get to make a good sound?' And there was a lot, so I helped him pick out this stuff and it was kind of the same set-up, basically, that he used the whole rest of the time."

MAY 4, 1990:

Nirvana plays the Masquerade in Tampa, Florida."This was a really good show actually," says Chad. "During this time, I was losing interest, but

• A freshly shaven Chris, post-Pyramid club •

of dead," recalls Craig. "At this time, people were catching on that there was a 'grunge scene' or whatever, but a lot of people's idea of that was like this funk metal, like Chili Peppers-ish, so every show we'd have some horrible local funk metal band open up and we'd always be like, 'Oh, not this crap again.' These guys playing slap bass. It just made you hate the Chili Peppers for what they had spawned."

MAY 16, 1990:
Chris Novoselic's 25th birthday.

MAY 17, 1990:
The last gig of the tour – at the Zoo in Boise, Idaho – is Chad Channing's final show with Nirvana. He didn't realize it at the time, but he felt it coming. For a few months now, he's been mulling over whether he should voice his complaints about his role in the band to Kurt or Chris. He chose to stay quiet. About a week after they return from the tour, Chris and Kurt – without calling first – showed up on Chad's door in Bainbridge Island and gave him the news.

"I was just wondering what I should do – say that I've had enough of this or wait for them to say that to me?" says Chad. "I just figured we'd go back at the end of the tour and I'd spend some time to think about what my next move should be, but then they made that move for me, which was a good thing. They came over, and I respect them for that. But there was no other way they could've done it – we were also really good friends during that time. It was just as intense for them as it was for me. If I had been some kind of an asshole, they could've just called, but we all pretty much were the starting members of the band, first recordings at least... I was glad [the ordeal] was over, but at the same time, it was weird to think that it was over. We'd gone through so much. It was a big head rush."

JUNE 8, 1990:
Butch Vig mixes "Here She Comes Now" from the April sessions.

JULY 7, 1990:
Rumors run rampant about who is going to replace the recently departed Chad Channing on the Nirvana drum stool. A *Sounds* magazine article suggests that J. Macsis of Dinosaur Jr. auditioned for the spot and might get the gig. This, of course, didn't end up happening.

JULY 11, 1990:
Kurt, Chris, and Dan Peters, on loan from Mudhoney, slip into Reciprocal Recording to record one song with Jack Endino. Using Tad's amps and drums, they record "Sliver" for the "Dive"/ "Sliver" single. "It was so spontaneous. That song kind of gelled together in three or four days, then we jumped right in there and recorded it," Chris told Dawn Anderson in *Backlash*.

"They brought their own guitars, and Danny brought his snare drum and kick pedal and they just plugged into Tad's amps, which were already miked and they went for it," recalls Jack Endino. "The song was done in about an hour... while the Tad band took their dinner break. We mixed it at a later session. There were two takes, and we used the second one. I think the first one still exists, but has no vocal."

JULY 24, 1990:
Nirvana has another session for "Sliver" at Reciprocal with Jack Endino. "Likely, he sang it on the second session in about one take and then we mixed," says Jack.

SUMMER 1990:

After Susan Silver, Soundgarden's manager and Chris Cornell's wife, introduced Nirvana to LA-based music attorney Alan Mintz of Ziffren, Brittenham & Branca, the band's demos from the Butch Vig sessions made their way to major labels unbeknownst to Sub Pop. Nearly every major label at the time (Columbia, Island, Capitol, Slash, Charisma, MCA, et al) was interested in the group. Around this time, Sub Pop was also talking to Sony about a distribution deal for the label.

"We were terrified. But we drove down to LA and found an attorney and started talking to these label people. We just gained an education and are comfortable with it now," Chris Novoselic told the *New York Times'* Karen Schoemer in 1991.

Jonathan Poneman and Bruce Pavitt took it pretty hard when they heard the band was looking to get off Sub Pop. "Oh, it was *really* hard," admits Jonathan. "We first heard they were taking meetings with Susan Silver about how to shop themselves." One of the reasons why Nirvana wanted to leave was because of Sub Pop's financial limitations at the time. "I didn't necessarily know what I was doing, but I know that once they started recording for Sub Pop, all these bands that I allegedly didn't pay stopped working [their day jobs.] Sure, if you want to move on in your life and buy houses, then it's probably good to get hooked up with an organization that knows how to do all that stuff. At the time, we didn't."

Nirvana didn't tell Sub Pop themselves what their plans were. "I just don't understand how you're expected to come right out and tell someone something like that," Kurt says in *Come As You Are*.

AUGUST 13, 1990:

Nirvana heads out for eight West Coast dates opening for Sonic Youth. The Melvins' Dale Crover fills in on drums, starting on the 13th at Bogart's in Long Beach, California.

"It was while we were on the Sonic Youth dates that we went and saw Dave Grohl's old band Scream," says Craig Montgomery. "It was before the start of the actual dates, because what we did was went and stayed in San Francisco for a few days at Buzz Osborne's house." Buzz introduced (and suggested) Dave Grohl to the band. Like Kurt and Chris, Dave Grohl has a fond appreciation of the Melvins too. "There is no band that changed my perspective of music like the Melvins. I'm not joking," Dave told *Spin*. "I think they're the future of music." "And, the present and past," added Kurt. "They should get recognized for that."

AUGUST 16, 1990:

Nirvana and Sonic Youth perform at Calamity Jayne's Nashville Nevada (a former whorehouse) in Las Vegas. It's both bands' first time playing Sin City. Sonic Youth's Kim Gordon was so excited to have Nirvana open for them that she watched their set from the dance floor.

"I was standing next to Kim Gordon, who was dancing up a storm," recalls Donna DeChristopher who worked at KUNV, the University of Nevada's radio station, at the time. Donna didn't share Kim's enthusiasm. "Nirvana was unbearable. I couldn't listen to more than a few songs. As I turned to head outside, Kim grabbed my arm and shouted, 'No, you have to stay! They're great!' Who was I to argue with Kim Gordon? I stayed for a few more songs, but Nirvana still sucked. By the end of the set, more people were in the parking lot than inside Calamity's."

AUGUST 17, 1990:

The tour hits the Hollywood Palladium in Hollywood, California. "I was hooked after that show," says LA-based music publicist Josh Mills. "I bought *Bleach* the next day. They were just having fun with being stupid. It seemed like they were so in awe that they were onstage and that people liked their music that they acted stupid as if this whole thing was a house of cards."

AUGUST 19, 1990:

Nirvana and Sonic Youth play to about 150 fans at the Casbah, which only held about 75 people, in San Diego, California. "This is one of the best shows I've ever seen," says Drunk Ted from the indie rock fanzine *Flipside*, an early champion of both Nirvana and Hole.

"The Sub Pop thing was really happening, and it was packed. People didn't leave their spots," he continues. "Back then, Sub Poppers were known for having long hair and playing punkish garage music that was authentic. And it was really weird, 'cause when Nirvana showed up Chris and Kurt had completely short hair, and we were like, 'Woah.' Watching these guys play this totally twisted, hard music with short hair was strange. I'd never seen that up until this point. It was cool, though, 'cause they pulled it off. Another thing that Kurt did that really surprised us was he stood up on this ledge near the side of the stage, and he did a guitar solo. We're looking at him like, 'Who the fuck does he think he is doing a guitar solo in a tiny club?' It's something you do in an arena if you're Eddie Van Halen, but you don't do that if you're in a little punk band."

Kurt also did one of his infamous backward stage dives, with his guitar in hand, and feedback piercing the ears of everyone in attendance. The crowd grabbed him with honor and moved him across their heads back to the front of the stage. "The show was so amazing, nothing could compare to it," adds Ted. "It was like Kurt was possessed."

● ... Hello Dave Grohl ●

AUGUST 20, 1990:

The next tour stop is at the Crest Theater in Sacramento, California.

AUGUST 21, 1990:

Nirvana and Sonic Youth play another impressive show; this night it's the Warfield Theater in San Francisco. "I was in shock that this far away from home, in San Francisco, that this band was that popular," says the Posies' drummer Mike Musburger, who was at the show. "I was really blown away. I think this was one of the first times I had an inkling that something bigger was going to happen. I was just watching the crowd's reaction – people were just really intensely watching them."

AUGUST 23, 1990:

On the way back home, the tour stops at the Melody Ballroom in Portland, Oregon. John Troutman opines, "Dale is an amazing drummer and having that kind of power behind those songs, that's when I starting thing, 'Wow, that is a big step.' These shows were the first time

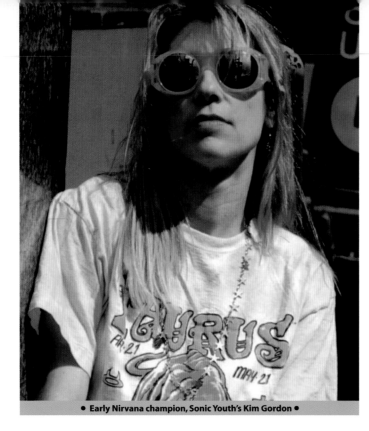

• **Early Nirvana champion, Sonic Youth's Kim Gordon** •

where you could really hear what Nirvana was. They were obviously more confident, but that's more of a natural progression for any band. In retrospect, Nirvana were the best thing of the evening, but that's not to disrespect Sonic Youth because they were great too."

AUGUST 24, 1990:

Nirvana plays a hometown show at the Moore Theater in Seattle. Opening for Nirvana and Sonic Youth is a band called STP (the girl band featuring Julia Cafritz from Pussy Galore and Sally Barry of Honeymoon Killers, not the Stone Temple Pilots).

"The response was real strong," recalls Tom Phalen, a former freelance writer for the *Seattle Times*. "A lot of the shows at the Moore, people would just be outside hanging out, but for this one, everyone was coming in to see Nirvana as much as they were for Sonic Youth. But it always seemed like the bigger the room and the more response, the more withdrawn Kurt got."

AUGUST 25, 1990:

Nirvana opens for Sonic Youth at the New York Theater in Vancouver.

"This performance wowed me far more than any other Nirvana show," says Sub Pop's Megan Jasper of the New York Theater show. "That was the night when, for me, they sort of crossed the line and went from this great local rock band to becoming something more. That was the time I really saw the doors open and I thought, 'My God. These guys really could be huge.' Their performance was great, the sound was amazing, and Kurt's voice, his voice was always great, he always had that crazy scream that no one else could ever do. But something about the way they played that night that was un-*fucking*-real. That show is what every musician wants to have."

AUGUST 1990:

Seattle-based C/Z Records releases the Kiss tribute album, *Hard to Believe*, featuring Nirvana's cover of "Do You Love Me?". Daniel House, president/owner of C/Z and once a member of Skin Yard with Jack Endino, says there are three versions of the album: an Australian double album on Waterfront, a single album European version on Southern, and the single album version on C/Z. "The only difference is I actually added a couple tracks that were not available on the European or the Australian version, like the Melvins, Skin Yard, Coffin Break, and Hullabaloo. Nirvana is on all three versions, though," says Daniel. This release features the only studio recording with Jason Everman in the band.

SEPTEMBER 20, 1990:

Rolling Stone magazine runs a feature story titled "A Seattle Slew" by Dave DiMartino, with a sidebar focusing on the Posies, Alice in Chains, and Mother Love Bone. The article also credits Sub Pop as having "defined the Seattle sound – loud, fast, grungy rock and roll."

Even though Nirvana was part of the "Seattle Sound" or "Sub Pop Sound," there was always something a bit different about them. Nils Bernstein explains, "The reason everyone thought so well of them, why they had their credibility, is they were less polished than other Seattle bands or Sub Pop bands, but at the same time, they were better too. At the time, it really did sound like a sound, as much as we all tried to get away from that and point out to people not from Seattle how different each band was from each other. Nirvana, Skin Yard, Bundle of Hiss, Soundgarden, Feast, and the Melvins had a hell of a lot more in common with each other than they did with other alternative bands at the time, like Hüsker Dü or Dinosaur Jr."

• **Sonic Youth** •

gonna happen." Charles R. Cross agrees: "Things started going crazy for them after this show, and suddenly they were bigger than Mudhoney. At that point, things shifted."

SEPTEMBER 23, 1990:

At Chris and Shelli's place in Tacoma, Kurt, Chris, and Dan Peters are interviewed by Keith Cameron of the British music magazine *Sounds* and the three are photographed for the piece by Ian T. Tilton.

SEPTEMBER 25, 1990:

Dave Grohl auditions for the group at the Dutchman rehearsal space and instantly gets the gig as Nirvana's new drummer. Also on this day, Kurt shows up unannounced and by himself to try out some news songs at Calvin Johnson's KAOS radio show, "Boy Meets Girl," at Evergreen State College in Olympia. He plays a solo show on acoustic guitar, and it's believed that the songs he did were "Lithium," "Dumb," and the Wipers' "D-7," though no one involved remembers exactly. It's on this show that Kurt announces that Dave Grohl is their new drummer.

SEPTEMBER 1990:

"Sliver"/"Dive" single is released on Sub Pop in the US. It's not released until months later in the UK, though the initial intent was for it to help promote the band's upcoming UK tour.

SEPTEMBER 21, 1990:

Dave Grohl, whose band Scream has just broken up, flies to Seattle to audition for Nirvana. Kurt later tells journalist Roy Trakin, "Dave is a fantastic drummer. There's no denying that. And he can sing back up vocals, which has really helped us out in our live sound."

However, at the time, most thought that Dan Peters of Mudhoney would continue playing with Nirvana, according to his friend and former Sub Pop publicist Nils Bernstein. "Danny was really psyched to be in Nirvana and I think basically what Kurt did was hire Dave without telling him, which seemed kind of shitty," says Nils. "But I know Kurt wanted a drummer who could sing."

SEPTEMBER 22, 1990:

Nirvana plays one of their best – and at this point biggest – shows in Seattle, at the Motor Sports International Garage, with Dan Peters from Mudhoney on drums. It's Dan's only show with Nirvana. The Melvins, the Dwarves, and Derelicts are on the bill for the all-ages show as well. Dave Grohl was in the audience of 15,000.

"I just remember walking in and it's this huge cavernous place, all the people there were so excited," says DGC's Northwest promo rep Susie Tennant, who was also friends with the band early on. "You just knew you were witnessing something. There was this feeling that everything was so amazing. Everyone knew that something big was

● The future of rock and roll ●

OCTOBER 11, 1990:

Dave Grohl plays his first show with Nirvana at the North Shore Surf Club in Olympia. "The Surf Club is kind of a large bar and it probably held 300 people. It was just this big empty space, and the kids were going crazy," says Slim Moon. "Something happened after Dave Grohl joined Nirvana. That Geffen record hadn't come out yet or anything, and nothing significantly different had happened, but suddenly they were much bigger."

On what Dave brought musically to the band, sound man Craig Montgomery says, "It was really solid, well it was really solid with Dale too, but Dave's sound was very solid. Chad was a good drummer but he wasn't all that consistent; he would miss a beat. But with Dave, he was like the perfect drummer with the band. Everything really came together then."

OCTOBER 21-27, 1990:

With their new drummer in tow, Nirvana kick off a UK tour, starting with a John Peel session in London on October 21. They do a set of all cover songs, including the Wipers' "D-7," the Vaselines' "Molly's Lips" and "Son of a Gun," and Devo's "Turnaround." The opening band is the Los Angeles-based all-girl punk band L7, featuring Dave Grohl's girlfriend at the time, bassist Jennifer Finch.

The shows include: October 23, Goldwyn's Suite, Birmingham, England; October 24, Astoria, London; October 25, Polytechnic, Leeds, England; October 26, Carlton Studios, Edinburgh, Scotland; and October 27, Trent Polytechnic, Nottingham, England.

"By then, all the shows became a blur," says sound man Craig Montgomery. "The band is really consistent at this time. We're headlining pretty big rooms, we have plenty of gear, we're not worried if we're gonna have enough guitars to finish the shows. And there was hijinks with L7. But that said, they're not as destructive as people think. It would only be every once in a great while [that things got trashed]. It was pretty professional by this point. We had Alex MacLeod tour managing. We had a good crew. We pretty much had it together."

UK journalist Kevan Roberts witnessed the Nottingham show on the 27th. "I remember Dave singing, and thinking how good it sounded. I was almost surprised by it, how it worked between the two of them. It

seemed to make a big difference in their sound," he says. Also on this day, the *Sounds* magazine article by Keith Cameron is published. In it, Kurt says, "All my life my dream has been to be a big rock star."

OCTOBER 1990:

Upon their return from the European tour, Kurt, Chris, and Dave practice nearly every day in their new rehearsal space in Tacoma for the next few months.

EARLY NOVEMBER 1990:

Nirvana signs on with Gold Mountain for management. At the time, Gold Mountain had punk credibility as managers of Sonic Youth and pop sensibilities as managers of Belinda Carlisle. The core management team throughout the years consisted of Danny Goldberg, who was the primary owner and president of the firm until 1992, John Silva, Michael Meisel, and Janet Billig.

"At the first meeting, Kurt was very quiet and Chris did most of the talking," says Danny Goldberg, who was turned on to Nirvana by Sonic Youth's Thurston Moore and Gold Mountain's John Silva. "Over the course of time, later in the relationship, I talked to Kurt all the time and Chris took more of a back seat. Kurt was very quiet and they kind of just wanted to review the idea of protecting where they were in the alternative culture, and we talked about different labels and they were interested in my civil liberties background, they liked that. I was chairman of the ACLU [American Civil Liberties Union] in LA, and I told them about what we did.

"I think there was a tremendous comfort level because of our relationship with Sonic Youth," continues Danny. "And I think Dave Grohl was a Led Zeppelin fanatic – because he asked me about Zeppelin. [Danny had been Led Zeppelin's publicist in the '70s]. It was a relatively short meeting – maybe a half hour. And I think they wanted to come with us anyway because of Sonic Youth and because of whatever they knew about my background, and then they committed to us a few days later. It happened very naturally, very easy."

Danny says his first impression of Kurt was that he was "shy and dark. But he was sardonic and sarcastic about the mainstream culture... He had a beautiful smile that lit up the room."

NOVEMBER 3, 1990:

Nirvana's John Peel session that was taped on October 21 is aired on the BBC.

● Back in the UK: The Astoria again ●

• Kurt with a smile to light up the world •

NOVEMBER 25, 1990:
Lots of A&R scouts flew to Seattle for Nirvana's show at the Off Ramp. This is an infamous Nirvana show, because they played an extra 30–45 minutes after the club cleared the room at closing time.

"It was this little club, and just an incredible show," says Susie Tennant, DGC's Northwest promotional rep. "I've never seen a club do this, because Seattle has really Draconian liquor laws, but the show was done and the promoter had everyone go outside and he put away all the liquor and all the beer under lock and key and then brought everyone back inside and the band continued to play. That never happens. Everyone was so into it, it was just the most amazing night."

Winter 1990: Dave Grohl, who had been staying at Chris and Shelli's house in Tacoma, moves into Kurt's North Pear Street homestead in Olympia and lives with him for about eight months. Also around this time, it's pretty clear that DGC – especially since Sonic Youth was on the label – is the right label to go with, though the deal isn't finalized until April 1991.

"Everybody wanted them," recalls Danny Goldberg. "They were the

'ARREN'T YOU IN NIRVANA? WHAT ARE YOU DOING, DOING YOUR OWN LAUNDRY?'

• Nirvana, as things start to really take off •

treating them more like rock stars, and you could tell they kind of felt uncomfortable with it."

DECEMBER 23, 1990:

Dave Grohl records some demos at Barrett Jones' Laundry Room Studio called *Pocketwatch* (Dave collects antique watches) under the name Late! for the now defunct Simple Machines label. Dave plays everything himself on the tape, but Barrett Jones contributes backing vocals on the song "Petrol CB."

"I'm not sure if it was ever considered a 'band.' I think Dave Grohl played and wrote everything except for a couple of last-minute lyrics by Geoff Turner. Dave wanted to call the tape Late, but he didn't say that it was a 'band name' per se," says Simple Machines' Jenny Toomey. "Back in those days, Dave was a shy and self-deprecating fellow. All of the copies of the Late tape were dubbed in our basement. We did five at a time and sold them for between $3.50 and $5.00 apiece. ($3.50 if you were buying the entire series of tapes)."

DECEMBER 31, 1990:

Nirvana plays the Satyricon Club in Portland, Oregon. "They were getting shopped around to labels at the time, and I remember this show because they couldn't hang out afterwards because they had to hang out with these A&R guys," says Slim Moon. "I think they were actually excited, but they pretended to act like it was this big chore that was really a drag. This was a notable night because I had watched Nirvana get more popular and this was the first time I saw this really attractive girl in the front row making eyes at Kurt the entire time. That signified they had gotten past the point of increased popularity to the point where they now had groupies!"

buzz band of the moment. I was positive we should go with Gary Gersh and Geffen and I think John wanted to meet with a few other people at first... but it was a very quick decision. It was a no-brainer. They offered a decent deal. It wasn't the most money, but it was a lot of money and it was a good royalty rate. It was a top of the line deal at the time for a new act. And in terms of just understanding where they were in the culture, there was no comparison between the team that Geffen at that time had and the other companies."

"In late '90, early '91, they got a lot bigger," says Slim Moon. "I remember Dave Grohl saying something about being at the laundromat doing his laundry, and he was living in Olympia with Kurt, and some kids were like, 'Aren't you in Nirvana? What are you doing, doing your own laundry?' They were pretty down-to-earth guys. After they had management then all of a sudden they had Sonic Youth's guitar tech going on tour with them and they had professional gear. They had their shit together in that way. Someone must have stepped in and helped them out because even when they were getting bigger, they still didn't know what the hell they were doing. And I never felt like there was a big change in their attitude, not at this point. Others started

● Nirvana was here ●

FIFTH. 1991:

CANNONBALLING OFF THE BALCONIES

JANUARY 1, 1991:
Nirvana records at the Music Source in Seattle with their touring sound man, Craig Montgomery, manning the knobs for the first time. It's also the first recording with Dave Grohl on drums. "All Apologies," "On a Plain," "Radio Friendly Unit Shifter," "Token Eastern Song," "Aneurysm," and "Even in His Youth" are recorded. The latter two are used as the B-side to "Smells Like Teen Spirit."

Kurt told *Backlash*'s Dawn Anderson in March 1991 that the sessions didn't turn out very well, and commented that the studio "is good for making Nordstrom commercials." Craig Montgomery agrees. "It sounds OK, at best, sound quality-wise. It doesn't sound like a record."

"They had some songs they wanted to throw down and I had been pestering them to let me record them for some time," says Craig. "Back then I didn't really know what I was doing, and they showed up with their gear sounding like crap and the drums were falling apart. It was all really raw. They would play the songs live and then Kurt would either put a vocal on it or he wouldn't. It was all first take. They hated doing re-

takes." The band recorded for free because Craig's friend, Brian Nelson, worked at the studio.

JANUARY 14, 1991:
Dave Grohl turns 22 years old.

JANUARY 16, 1991:
Nirvana plays at Evergreen State College in Olympia, Washington.

JANUARY 21, 1991:
Some home video footage of Nirvana is taken on this day and used for what would later be the Nirvana documentary home video, *Live! Tonight! Sold Out!!* (If you look closely at the scene in the beginning of

the video with Chris and Kurt looking into the camera, you'll see the January 21, 1991 date in the corner.)

"Kurt spent months and months and months on it," says Danny Goldberg of the video. "We got him the equipment that he had in his various apartments and he worked on every inch of it. That was his statement on what he had accomplished. That was his home video. That was not created by Geffen. I think that really is his self-portrait, and other than the records, it's the thing he spent the most time on. I think that's the best indication of how he felt about [his success] because he documented all that and went to a great deal of trouble to get that footage from all over the world. I think it was something that he was correctly proud of, but that good feeling didn't deal with the other pain that he had."

JANUARY 1991:
"Sliver"/"Dive" single is released in UK on Tupelo. "People thought 'Sliver' was really brilliant, because it was like a weird pop song with this angle, lyrically, that other people hadn't really done. It was a cool idea," says Slim Moon.

FEBRUARY 20, 1991:
Kurt Cobain turns 24 years old.

MARCH 2-8, 1991:
Nirvana plays a handful of shows in Canada, including the Bronx, Edmonton, March 2; Westward Club in Calgary, Alberta, March 4; the Forge in Victoria, Vancouver Island, March 7; and Commodore Ballroom in Vancouver, March 8.

At the Commodore Ballroom show, "Territorial Pissings" is said to have made its debut, and a photo is taken of Kurt seemingly playing guitar on his head that is later used for one of the "Smells Like Teen Spirit" singles. Nirvana was third on a bill featuring the Wongs, Doughboy, and Screaming Trees at this show.

APRIL 17, 1991:
Possibly the most memorable Nirvana show is the OK Hotel gig in Seattle when they perform "Smells Like Teen Spirit" for the first time. Fitz of Depression and Bikini Kill are also on the bill. Kurt addresses the crowd with "Hello, we're major-label corporate rock sell-outs."

"I remember going, 'Wow, God this is a really good song,'" recalls Jonathan Poneman of his first time hearing "Smells Like Teen Spirit." "And it's just cruising along and and it's like, 'Wow this is a really catchy verse.' And then it comes to the chorus and everyone went, 'Oh my God, this is one of the greatest choruses of any song I've ever heard in my life!' And I remember standing in the back of the room looking around and there was this feeling of 'What is this?' The first part of the song was so good, and then it goes into this chorus and takes good and just leaves it in the dust. It's really just one of the all-time great songs."

Nils Bernstein and Susie Tennant were also there and had the same reaction. "I was standing there next to Kurt [Bloch] from the Fastbacks and we just looked at each other like, 'What was that?' I was totally riveted," says Nils. "After the song was over, I could swear there was a two-second pause before everyone just freaked out." "It was all so new," recalls Susie. "Nothing bad had happened yet and it was all so exciting and cool and fun."

"HELLO, WE'RE MAJOR-LABEL CORPORATE ROCK SELL-OUTS."

• Live at the Commodore Ballroom, March 8 •

• Chris indulges in a spot of tour filming •

APRIL 30, 1991:

Impressed by their young, hip, alternative staff, Nirvana formally signs their recording contract with Geffen's DGC label. They receive an advance of approximately $290,000, and Sub Pop receives $75,000 and points on their forthcoming recordings on sales over 100,000 units. Sub Pop is also allowed to release one more Nirvana single ("Molly's Lips").

"We've had more control being on this label than we did on Sub Pop," Kurt later tells *Hits'* Roy Trakin. "Everything is very precise and laid out. I'm totally confident with what they do. They meet demands. They get things done when they're supposed to. They have more than enough money to invest in whatever we want to do. We designed our album cover. We chose what songs [went on the album] and how they would be recorded on the record. If I didn't want to do this interview, I could just call up my manager and say I don't want to do it."

The decision to sign with DGC was an easy one, according to Danny Goldberg. "It was clear to me, although many labels were interested in them, that Geffen was a good place to go. The people at Geffen were tuned into the culture that they cared about; they'd been through the Sonic Youth experience. This guy Ray Farrell had worked at SST Records and Mark Kates was sensitive to the culture at the time. They wanted to feel that who was representing them would have enough confidence in them and enough clout to enforce that... They didn't have the slightest misgivings about trying to get on a big label. I think they had very mixed feelings about Sub Pop and didn't have any particular wish to stay there. There was no ambiguity about it."

That said, the band still voiced their concerns about how people would perceive the move. Dave Grohl told *Spin* magazine, "And now we're snubbed by people who think we're big rock stars. They think that when you get signed to a major label you get all this cash to spend."

APRIL 1991:

Also this month, Sub Pop releases the split single of Nirvana's cover of the Vaselines' "Molly's Lips" and the Fluid's "Candy" as Sub Pop Singles Club No. 27. And Tupelo releases the 12-inch of "Sliver," "Dive," and a live version of "About a Girl" in the UK.

Kurt told *Backlash* that he didn't want that split single to be released: "I called up Jon at Sub Pop and asked him not to do it. It was just a throwaway. I like the song, but the performance just wasn't up to par. But part of the buy-out deal was that single. So we said, 'OK, we'll let you do the single,' and they said, 'Good, because we already have the test pressings.'" Sub Pop, not the band, etched the word 'later' into the vinyl of the single.

LATE APRIL 1991:

Butch Vig, who recorded the April 1990 demos, gets the call to come to LA to produce Nirvana's *Nevermind*, which at one point had the working title of *Sheep*, according to Geffen art director Robert Fisher. Of choosing Butch for the job, Kurt told *Guitar World*, "We think along the same lines, on the same level. So every suggestion he had, there was no conflict at all. A few songs weren't finished, so he helped us with arrangements, cutting them down to the average three-minute pop song."

The band drives down to Los Angeles – Chris in his Volkswagen and Kurt and Dave in the white Dodge van. They stopped in San Francisco to stay at Dale Crover's house for a couple of days, according to *Come As You Are*. Their first stop in LA was Universal Studios. Before beginning recording on May 2, they do three days of pre-production in a rehearsal space in North Hollywood, California.

MAY 2, 1991:

The drums Dave Grohl records *Nevermind* on are rented on this day from the Drum Doctor in LA for 10 days. Total rental cost: $1,542.

MAY–JUNE 1991:

Starting on May 2, 16 studio days are initially booked to record *Nevermind* at Sound City Studios in Van Nuys, California, where Fleetwood Mac, Tom Petty, and the Jacksons have recorded. With Butch Vig at the helm, basic tracks took place on the first five or six days in Studio A. The budget was set at $65,000, but it ended up costing $120,000–$130,000.

"We screwed around," says Chris Novoselic of the recording sessions in Craig Rosen's *The Billboard Book Of Number One Albums*. "We would sleep in every day and then lay on the couch and play pinball all day and then we would stroll in and occasionally lay down a few tracks."

Butch Vig describes what their days were like in Alan di Perna's *Guitar World* article, "Nirvana: The Making Of *Nevermind*": "They were in LA, they'd just signed a record deal with Geffen, they had a bit of cash, so they'd go out and do a little partying. I know they used to go down to Venice and stay up all night... So sometimes I'd get to the studio at one and they wouldn't show up till three 'cause they'd slept in. But basically they showed up when they needed to show up."

Of the sessions, Butch tells *Goldmine* that the songs were basically in "really good shape." He says that he did help out with some arrangements, though: "'Teen Spirit' was longer and the little ad-libs after the chorus were actually at the end of the song. I suggested putting those in at the end of each chorus as a bridge into the next verse."

Once again, the lyrics weren't entirely finished in advance. "We were just standing there with our arms crossed and our feet tapping, just staring at Kurt as he sat there sweating and writing and looking and writing and looking," Chris Novoselic says in the *Rocket* cover story that ran shortly after the release of the album. "*Nevermind* was an accumulation of two years of poetry," Kurt says of the lyrics in a 1993 *Spin* article. "I picked out good lines, cut up things. I'm always skipping back and forth to different themes. A lot of bands are expected to write as a whole. One song is supposed to be as cut and dried as a 'Dragnet' episode."

An additional four or five days are booked at Devonshire Studios in Burbank to complete the overdubbing – one of the last was the cello part on "Something in the Way" by Kirk Canning. "We only did a few backing vocal tracks and rough mixes of all the songs," Butch Vig says in *Nevermind Nirvana*. "I did mix a couple of the songs there with the band, but we weren't happy with them." So the band's A&R guy, Gary Gersh, sent over a list of potential mixers, including Scott Litt, who was best known at the time for his work with R.E.M., but the band shot that idea down. They decided on Andy Wallace because of his work with the metal band Slayer.

MAY 16, 1991:
Chris Novoselic turns 26 years old.

MAY 23, 1991:
Michael Lavine photographs the band for the *Nevermind* publicity at Jay Aaron Studios in Los Angeles. From the music to the artwork, Kurt was very involved in all aspects of the creative process. "He was very serious about doing a good job on the record," says Danny Goldberg. "And he thought incredibly carefully about the artwork and the poster, every detail of it. He had a craftsmanlike concern about it."

MAY 29, 1991:
Nirvana plays a last-minute show at Jabberjaw in Los Angeles with I Own the Sky opening up. In the audience was Iggy Pop and Courtney Love with her good friend Jennifer Finch, L7's bassist and Dave Grohl's girlfriend. Flipside writer Carlos "Cake" Nunez, who's a big collector of Nirvana bootlegs too, has a tape of the show where you can hear Courtney jokingly yelling out, "Jennifer loves you, Kurt!"

"I think it was announced that morning or the evening before that Nirvana was gonna play," says Cake. "Chris was really drunk off his ass and he was spouting off about how stupid the word 'alternative' was and how MTV was stupid. It's really ironic because they didn't know that five months down the line they would be the figureheads of alternative rock. They did like a 45-minute set, or even longer. At one point, Chris or Kurt goes, 'How do you guys know the words?' And somebody yelled out, 'Bootlegs!' Because there were all these 7-inch bootlegs of [*Nevermind*] demos."

● Courtney on stage with Hole ●

● **Water Music: The unsuccessful photo shoot, May** ●

MAY 1991:
Kirk Weddle's photo shoot for the album's cover took place after Kurt and Dave saw a documentary on water-babies. Geffen art director Robert Fisher found Kirk's name in a directory, which listed him as a specialist in "submerged humans." Robert says, "I read that and thought, 'This guy sounds perfect.' We originally had a stock photograph of a baby swimming underwater that I found, that Kurt liked, but for some reason [it was too costly to license the photograph] we couldn't get the rights to use it, which actually worked out better in the end because the shot that we got was way better than that one."

Kirk, his assistants, Robert, and about three or four sets of parents and their children were there for the shoot. Having a penis on the cover, by the way, was not the original intention. "Some of the babies were girls too," says Robert. "At the time, we didn't specifically care if it was a boy or a girl. The penis just in the shot and it just worked out that way. And, if you look closely at the picture, you see a hand print on the

baby's chest – it's kind of red and then white. The parents would take the baby and pass it underwater just a few feet and the dad would catch it. That was the hand print where the mom was holding it and just passed it off to the father." Five-month-old Spencer Elden's photo came out the best and was used for the cover. The fishhook with the dollar was shot afterwards and superimposed on to the photo.

To emulate the album's cover, Robert thought it would be a fun idea to do an underwater photo shoot with the band. The ill-fated session is shot again by Kirk Weddle at a swimming pool in Van Nuys, California. "Everything that could have gone wrong did go wrong," says Robert. "When we got there, it was kind of run down. The weekend before, the pump of the pool broke and it was really windy that weekend so the water was really murky and the pool was kind of cold. And then the band came and Kurt was really like, uh, sick at the time and he was sleeping on the deck. He was curled up with his guitar with a towel over him. We had to get a big heater."

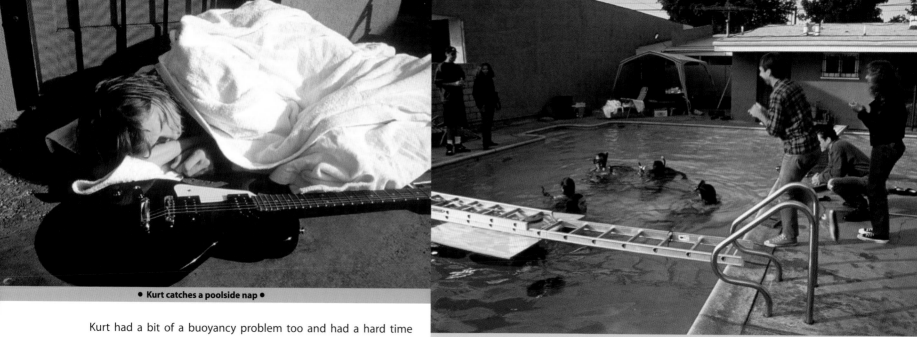

• Kurt catches a poolside nap •

Kurt had a bit of a buoyancy problem too and had a hard time getting and staying under the water, according to Robert. "He'd sit at the top of the water and kick to try to go underwater and he just couldn't do it. At the time, the band was kind of grumpy with it and Kirk Weddle had rented all these guitars and a drum set and he built this elaborate thing so the drum set was underwater upside down. The band kind of warmed up to it after a while and started having fun underwater, but we never really got any great shots. In the end, we took like three solo shots and put them together on the computer to make one good one."

Also this month, Kurt and Courtney meet up again at a Butthole Surfers/Redd Kross/L7 show at the Palladium in LA. Kurt and Courtney later admitted that they had feelings for each other at this time. Courtney (who nick-named Kurt "Pixie Meat" for his small size) punches Kurt in the stomach; he hits back, and they end up wrestling on the floor.

Also around this time, Courtney paid a few visits to Kurt at the Oakwood Apartments where he and the band were temporarily staying while making *Nevermind*. "I really pursued him, not too aggressive, but aggressive enough that some girls would have been embarrassed by it. I'm direct," Courtney later tells *Sassy* magazine. "That can scare a lot of boys. Like, I got Kurt's number when they were on tour, and I would call him."

JuNE 1–9, 1991:

Nevermind is mixed by Andy Wallace at the shabby Scream Studios in Studio City, California. It took nine or ten days to mix. After the album was released, Kurt was quite vocal about his dissatisfaction with how slick the album sounded. "Looking back on the production of *Nevermind*," he says in *Come As You Are*, "I'm embarrassed by it now."

"I think Andy's mixes sound great," the album's producer Butch Vig says in *Goldmine*. "He didn't add too much polish to the songs, but got really good separation between the instruments and vocals, mostly through EQ." Commenting on Kurt's complaints about the slick sound of the record, Butch continues, "I know for a fact that Kurt loved the album when it was finished. But over a period of time I think all artists

"HE'D SIT AT THE TOP OF THE WATER AND KICK TO TRY TO GO UNDERWATER AND HE JUST COULDN'T DO IT..."

become critical of their work. And as a punk, it's not cool to endorse an album that sells in the millions. When Kurt talked to me about working on the first Hole record with Courtney, he told me he wasn't happy with *In Utero* either."

JuNE 10–20, 1991:

Nirvana tour for the second time with Dinosaur Jr. on the West Coast. The scheduled dates included: June 10, Gothic Theater, Denver, Colorado; June 11, Pompadour Rock & Roll Club, Salt Lake City, Utah; June 13, Warfield Theater, San Francisco; June 14, Hollywood Palladium, Hollywood, California; June 15, Iguana's, Tijuana, Mexico; June 18, the Catalyst, Santa Cruz, California; June 19, Crest Theater, Sacramento, California; and June 20, Melody Ballroom, Portland, Oregon. At the San Francisco show, they play "Drain You" in concert for the first time.

Talking about the Palladium show, Danny Goldberg says, "It was really an epiphany. I went from doing it because Thurston [Moore] and John [Silva] were talking about them and everyone was buzzing about it, to realizing I had seen one of the best things I had ever seen in my life... The union of him and the audience was so amazing. I knew I was witnessing history. There was an intimacy he had with this audience that I had just never seen in my life before."

With no disrespect to Dinosaur Jr., many people who saw these shows realized that the opening band was outshining the headliner. "I think Nirvana were kind of on their way past Dinosaur Jr. and I think put on a way better show than Dinosaur Jr.," says Craig Montgomery. Nils Bernstein, who saw the Portland show on this tour, agrees: "That was a big deal, because Dinosaur was huge to us. So it was like, 'Oh my God! Nirvana's bigger than Dinosaur Jr.?!'"

JULY 1, 1991:

Hole's debut album, *Pretty on the Inside*, is released on Caroline Records featuring the future Mrs. Kurt Cobain, Eric Erlandson, Caroline Rue, and Jill Emery. Kim Gordon of Sonic Youth produced it. The *New Yorker* called the album "probably the most compelling album to have been released in 1991." Well, so far.

Also released in June is Sub Pop's *The Grunge Years* compilation featuring Nirvana's "Dive," along with tracks from Tad, L7, Beat Happening, Screaming Trees, Babes in Toyland, and others. And also the Communion Label's Velvet Underground tribute album, *Heaven and Hell, Vol. 1*, featuring Nirvana's cover of "Here She Comes Now." It's also released as a split single with the Melvins' cover of VU's "Venus in Furs."

JULY 9, 1991:

Courtney Love turns 26 years old. In the summer of 1991, she is dating Smashing Pumpkins lead singer Billy Corgan, though she had a crush on Kurt.

JULY 27, 1991:

Along with December 23, 1990, this is the other date listed on Dave Grohl's *Pocketwatch* demo release under the name Late!, though Barrett Jones tells *Goldmine* that the songs were actually recorded in more than these two sessions. The album, released only on cassette, was issued in early 1992. It has since appeared as bootleg CDs.

"Late orders nearly broke the label in half when Dave became famous," says Jenny Toomey of the now-defunct Simple Machines label. "It took endless hours to dub the things, our profit was tiny and after years of use, the master cassette ultimately sounded like it had been recorded on a boom-box wrapped in cotton, set on a concrete floor, duct-taped under an oil drum. Needless to say, we finally took it off the catalog. It's a shame that Dave never let us release the songs on CD. *Pocketwatch* is joyous, intimate and entirely unself-conscious music. It was recorded without a plan and without an audience and that suited the songs perfectly."

AUGUST 2, 1991:

Howie Weinberg masters *Nevermind* at Masterdisk Studios in New York. Four hours after the scheduled start time, the band, mixer Andy Wallace, and DGC's Gary Gersh show up after Howie was practically done mastering. Due to an apparent miscommunication, Howie didn't include "Endless Nameless" in the final sequence.

"In the beginning, it was kind of a verbal thing to put that track at the end," says Howie in *Nevermind Nirvana*. "Maybe I misconstrued their instructions, so you can call it my mistake if you want. Maybe I didn't write it down when Nirvana or the record company said to do it. So, when they pressed the first 20,000 or so CDs, albums and cassettes, it

wasn't there." Chris Novoselic has called "Endless Nameless," which appears 13 minutes and 51 seconds after the last song on *Nevermind*, just another "cool, loud prank."

AUGUST 3, 1991:

Metallica holds a listening party for their self-titled album (referred to as "the black album") at Madison Square Garden in NY. Kurt and Chris were there. "I ran into them outside of the Garden, they were in town mastering the album," says John Troutman, who by this point had moved to NY to work for RCA. "They said the album was sounding great, and just commented on how cool the whole Madison Square Garden thing was."

MID-AUGUST 1991:

Boston alternative station WFNX is the first commercial station in the US to play "Smells Like Teen Spirit." The station's music director Kurt St. Thomas got an early copy of the song and played it even before the label was officially going for adds.

"I met Kurt St. Thomas in June and he said to me, 'This song is gonna change the face of music,'" recalls Ted Volk, who was the Northeast radio representative for DGC at the time. "I said, 'That's a crazy statement to make, don't you think?' But he's like 'You don't understand, you don't understand.' That was my first introduction to what we were about to witness. That was sign number one for me."

"We put it in heavy rotation really quick," says Kurt St. Thomas, who is also author of the 2000 book on the band, *Nirvana: The Chosen Rejects*. "And requests started coming in right away, almost immediately. It was kind of weird, actually." Neither Ted nor Kurt can remember the actual date the song was first aired on the station.

AUGUST 15, 1991:

Some call this the best Nirvana show of all time, others just remember not being able to get into the show at the tiny Roxy on the Sunset Strip in Los Angeles. It was basically a showcase for Geffen/DGC brass to get a peek at what they'll be working soon and to get key members of

● Hole ●

radio, retail, and press excited about the band.

"I was always struck by their passion," says Lisa Gladfelter Bell, the band's Geffen publicist from 1991 to 1993. "It was just very raw and it spoke to everyone for different reasons, and live there was so much feeling in it. Back then, they gave it everything they had. They kind of got that trademark apathy – as obviously anyone who has that kind of fame thrust on them is gonna get – a little later on. But at this show, they were just great."

"The crowd was going bananas," says Cheryl Kovalchik, who was the San Francisco promo rep for Geffen. "There was a big pit, and people were just completely nuts. It was a great show." Says Danny, "All of us at Geffen and management came out for this and I remember saying, 'God, we're gonna remember this for the rest of our lives.'" Also at the show, Geffen's art director Robert Fisher is handing out flyers to fans to be extras in the video for "Smells Like Teen Spirit."

AUGUST 17, 1991:

Nirvana shoots their video for "Smells Like Teen Spirit" at GMT Studios in Culver City, California with director Sam Bayer. The call time was 8:30 a.m.; filming started at 11:30 and went on all day. The video cost just under $50,000, and featured real Nirvana fans as part of the pep rally-in-hell kids.

"At one point when we were making the video," Dave Grohl tells *Newsweek* in June 1999, "the director had a loud bullhorn thing, and he was trying to explain the concept to the crowd, and saying, 'OK, now, in the first verse, you're supposed to look bored and complacent and unhappy. Just sit in your seats and tap your foot and look, you know, distraught, whatever.' And then by the end of the song, they're supposed to be tearing the place to shreds. When they got to the first chorus, the crowd was completely out of control, and the director was screaming at the top of his lungs for everyone to fucking calm down and be cool, or they'll get kicked out. So it was pretty hilarious, actually, seeing this man trying to control these children who just wanted to destroy."

Drunk Ted from *Flipside* magazine didn't just write about the band and was a big fan, but he was also an extra in the video. "All that smoke you saw there was actually chalk dust, so it was hard to breathe," he recalls. "Chris was in the audience talking to people, but Kurt hung out mostly by the drum kit by himself and people weren't allowed to go around there. They played the song on the little concert speakers, which wasn't a very good sound quality, like 50 times, but we still couldn't tell what the lyrics were, so we started to make them up ourselves. We were in the lunch area making sandwiches singing, 'Hold the mayo! And the pickles!' [To the tune of the lyric 'An albino! A mosquito!']. It was pretty funny."

Kurt was pretty vocal afterwards about his distaste for the video, and this was the only time the band worked with director Sam Bayer.

AUGUST 19, 1991:

Nirvana takes off for a European tour with Sonic Youth. Footage of this tour is the meat and potatoes of Dave Markey's video documentary, *1991: The Year Punk Broke*, featuring Nirvana, Sonic Youth, Mudhoney, Dinosaur Jr., Babes in Toyland, Ramones, and Gumball.

"This tour, I mean, the way I see it, this tour to me is like a dare,"

explains Sonic Youth's Thurston Moore in the beginning of the video."... to us and Nirvana and all the other bands that we're gonna be playing with, to us it's like a dare to our parents. It's a dare to the Bush administration. It's a dare to the KGB, who have overthrown [Mikhail] Gorbachev this morning as we speak. God knows what it's gonna be like in the future and the future to us is a dare. So to us, fuck 'em. Fuck 'em all."

Danny Goldberg sees this European tour as an important early milestone for Nirvana: "I think going to Europe and breaking Europe was a big deal. Many American bands don't break Europe. And especially doing well in a place like France, which isn't always susceptible to American success."

AUGUST 20, 1991:
The tour kicks off in Cork, Ireland at Sir Henry's Pub. "Lounge Act" is played live for the first time, and Kurt plays around with "Negative Creep," singing it in falsetto.

AUGUST 21, 1991:
In Ireland, the band plays Dublin's the Point. Back home, Geffen is having their weekly Wednesday marketing meeting where they discuss the plans for each of their upcoming releases. It's the first big meeting since most of the key staff saw the band's show at the Roxy on the 15th.

"When Nirvana was brought up, it was just like, 'Wow,' everyone was blown away by what they had seen," says Lisa Gladfelter Bell. "I think what happened in that first meeting was, the planned initial pressing of 40,000 [copies of *Nevermind*] went up to 80,000," says Bill Bennett, who was just about to become the General Manager of Geffen Records at the time.

Danny Goldberg says that in addition to the label's excitement after seeing Nirvana's live show for the first time, the orders were increased also because of growing interest from key retail stores. "The anticipation was much more than would be typical for an indie band or a new band," says Danny. "So I think as they monitored those orders, they increased it and at this time, the press was coming in. There were a lot of factors driving it."

Also on this date, Slim Moon's Kill Rock Stars label releases the compilation, *Kill Rock Stars*, featuring Nirvana's "Beeswax." Slim and Courtney Love later have some words over whether he had the right to release the song or not, but Slim insists that Chris Novoselic told him the song was "theirs to give me."

"I was a little paranoid, but I just believed him," says Slim. "Later I heard rumors that it really belonged to Sub Pop, but they never sued and I spoke to Bruce [Pavitt] and it was no big deal, except for Kurt's wife posting stuff on the Internet about how I had ripped off Nirvana. I paid their royalties and the publishing, the mechanical publishing got paid."

AUGUST 23, 1991:

They may have only been onstage for about 40 minutes, but Nirvana's performance at the Reading Festival in Reading, England still has fans talking. The band brings Eugenius lead singer Eugene Kelly, formerly of one of Kurt's favorite bands, the Vaselines, up onstage to perform the Vaselines' "Molly's Lips." Nirvana also jams on the Doors' "The End," which was dedicated to MTV's Dave Kendall. The show is infamous for the manic way Kurt threw himself into the drums at the end of the set, which resulted in a dislocated shoulder.

• Kurt at Reading •

Backstage, Chris is seen in a Dinosaur Jr. T-shirt, and Courtney Love is chatting with Babes in Toyland's Kat Bjelland and Sonic Youth's Kim Gordon about Kurt. There, UK scribe Kevan Roberts gets a glimpse of a Courtney not many people see: "The press paints this certain picture of Courtney, but there were times where you'd see her backstage and she just looked completely innocent. Dave [Kendall] was interviewing Dinosaur Jr. for MTV and she just sat there, cross-legged and watched almost in awe." There's also a cute moment from backstage in *1991: The Year Punk Broke* where Courtney says into the camera: "Kurt Cobain makes my heart stop. But he's a shit."

AUGUST 24, 1991:

Nirvana and Sonic Youth play another festival – Monster of Spex Festival in Koln, Germany. Speaking of this tour as a whole, and only partially sarcastically, Kurt tells *Melody Maker*, "You see, no one knows it, but those Sonic Youth kids, they're wild. They were instigating violence and terrorism throughout the entire European festival tour." There was lots of heavy drinking going on too.

AUGUST 25, 1991:

The Pukkelpop Festival in Hasselt, Belgium is the next stop on the tour. Nirvana's slot on the festival is 11 a.m. As told in *Come As You Are*, the band starts drinking in the morning and then decides to have some fun by rearranging the names on the tables in the dining area, starting food fights, and when Black Francis hit the stage early in the evening, Kurt (who'd been wearing Francis's nametag during the day) sprayed the fire extinguisher on him until security came after him.

AUGUST 27, 1991:

Back in the US, "Smells Like Teen Spirit" is sent to radio. And in the UK, various formats of the "Smells Like Teen Spirit" single are released, starting in August with the 7-inch and cassette backed with "Drain You."

"When 'Teen Spirit' went to radio, we thought it was gonna be a tough record," says ex-Geffen GM Bill Bennett. "You have to remember, there was nothing like it at the time. We were working, I think, Whitesnake or Guns, and instead of coming in with 15 stations [playing the song the week it hits radio], the *entire* modern rock panel came in."

The original plan was for "Smells Like Teen Spirit" to be the college radio track, and "Come As You Are" would be the label's big push to alternative (a.k.a. modern rock) radio. "There was no question about it, it was always gonna be 'Smells Like Teen Spirit.' That was bigger than we all thought," says Danny Goldberg. "We thought it was gonna be the college/alternative rock track and the feeling was that 'Come As You Are' was a more melodic song so it would be more of a pop song. In a sense, we all miscalculated and underestimated the mass appeal power of 'Smells Like Teen Spirit.' We had just seen it as a rock song, we didn't know that it would be a pop [radio] song too."

AUGUST 27-30, 1991:

The band plays a stretch of shows in Germany, which include: August 27, Aladdin, Bremen; August 28, Halle; August 29, Longhorn, Stuttgart; and August 30, Serenadenhof, Nuremberg. Bremen is where the now infamous Sonic Youth/MCA story takes place.

"This representative for MCA gave us a gift, a wastepaper basket full

• **Kurt mounts Chris live on stage at Reading** •

of candy and magazines, with a little note welcoming us to Germany," Kurt explains to *Melody Maker* a few months after the incident. "The gift had been in the dressing room for two hours, while we'd been doing our set and eating our dinner. During that time Kim Gordon had written 'Fuck You' underneath the woman's signature on the note. So we saw this and thought, gee, that's kinda peculiar, but we can make good use of the sweets. So we met the rep, thanked her and Chris proceeded to get drunker and drunker. He shot off a fire extinguisher, ripped up the magazines and threw the candy all over the place and destroyed the whole room."

AUGUST 29, 1991:

Kurt St. Thomas at Boston's alternative station WFNX world premieres *Nevermind* from start to finish at 7 p.m. Eastern Standard Time. "This was sign number two for me that something big was happening," says Ted Volk, Northeast radio rep at DGC. "He world-premiered a record for a band that no one ever really heard of."

• **On their way to becoming the biggest thing in rock 'n' roll** •

AUGUST 30, 1991:

The *Seattle Times* runs a piece on Jack Endino where he says that following his success with Sub Pop and Nirvana, he's getting a lot of copycat bands coming through his studio: "I'm getting Melvins imitators and Soundgarden imitators and Mudhoney imitators and Tad imitators, and I'm going, wow, there went the Seattle sound."

SEPTEMBER 1, 1991:

The Nirvana/Sonic Youth trek ends in Rotterdam, Holland at a place called De Doelen. A drunk Chris gets into a fight with a security guard onstage. Wrapping up the tour, Thurston Moore says in *1991: The Year Punk Broke*: "It is the last show of our two-week tour with Nirvana, Sonic Youth, some Gumball action, some Dinosaur action, some Black Frances action, some Ramones action etcetera etcetera and not discounting Iggy Pop and Agnostic Front. It's the end. It feels like we haven't even begun. It's so short. It's sweet. It's to the point."

SEPTEMBER 3, 1991:

Nirvana performs "Dumb," "Drain You," and "Endless Nameless" on the John Peel show at Maida Vale Studios in London.

SEPTEMBER 9, 1991:

"Smells Like Teen Spirit" backed with "Even in His Youth" and "Aneurysm" is released in the UK on DGC.

SEPTEMBER 10, 1991:

"Smells Like Teen Spirit" is released commercially to record stores in the US. The 7-inch and cassette are backed with "Even in His Youth," and another cassette, 12 inch, and CD had that plus "Aneurysm." Both B-sides are from the Craig Montgomery session on January 1, 1991.

"The first time I heard 'Teen Spirit,' I remember feeling a little angry that the song was doing so well because I thought it was essentially an angry version of Boston's 'More Than a Feeling,'" says Dave Navarro, formerly of Jane's Addiction and Red Hot Chili Peppers. "But there was something about the vocals that were really just undeniably captivating. There was such an honest gut-wrenching sadness to the sound of his voice that I was astonished that he had any motivation to lay down a vocal track. If you sound that sad how can you bring yourself to the studio to sing it? If I felt as sad as he sounds I wouldn't want to sing. But at the same time, I can relate to having that instrument being your only avenue of release."

SEPTEMBER 13, 1991:

Nirvana gets thrown out of their own record release party at Re-bar in Seattle for starting a food fight.

"The story goes that Chris started throwing guacamole dip, but it was actually Green Goddess dip for vegetables, which is much more slimy," quips former Sub Pop publicist Nils Bernstein, who had a catering company on the side that catered this event. "And of course, the legend is that they are the only band to get thrown out of their own record release party... The party then moved to Jeff Ross's house [Ross made Nirvana's T-shirts] and then about 20 of us ended up at Susie Tennant's house where things got out of hand. Chris and Kurt went into her bedroom and started putting on dresses, and then people started wrestling and pig piling on each other. It lasted for hours."

"It was super fun," says Susie, whose roommate at the time was Kim Warnick of the Fastbacks. "Kurt wore this little green and white dress that I got in San Francisco, this little Holly Hobby summer dress. He looked sweet in it. And Dave put on this really dumb dress with big polka dots. They just did stuff like that. Another time, they took all my CDs out of my office and made these huge mazes of CDs and 'dink' – like dominos, they go down. And I have this Nelson plaque on my wall that they completely defaced. Kurt would come over and we'd dye his hair at the house, or we'd get out eggs and start throwing them at people."

● **Kurt goes acoustic** ●

SEPTEMBER 16, 1991:

The band does an in-store performance at Beehive Records in Seattle. The set list includes "Drain You," "Breed," "Floyd the Barber," "Smells Like Teen Spirit," "Come As You Are," "School," "Territorial Pissings," "Blew," "Negative Creep," "Been a Son," "Something in the Way," "Stain," and a jam on Kiss's "Love Gun."

"They said they were only going to play three songs, but I don't think they knew how cool it was going to be," says Jamie Brown, the marketing and promotions director at Beehive (formerly Peaches) Records. "We cleared away the bins to make room for a mosh pit, the band played an electric set, and about 300 kids were inside the store, while another few hundred were watching from outside, and this was before they really got much radio or MTV play. Kurt came up to me afterwards and said it was really cool and asked if I could sell some of his friend from Olympia's comic books on consignment."

When some members of Soundgarden showed up, they turned around because it was too crowded. But Mike Musburger of the Posies was there: "I went downstairs, met Chris and Dave, and Kurt was sitting on the floor intensely writing out a set list and no one was talking to him. People were milling around him, but while I was there people just left him alone. He didn't seem unapproachable; he just seemed really shy and like he didn't want to be bugged, so no one did."

SEPTEMBER 20, 1991:

Nirvana kicks off their first North American tour for *Nevermind* in Toronto at the Opera House and debut "Pennyroyal Tea" there. Their good friends the Melvins open for them on the East Coast and in Canada, while Das Damen and Urge Overkill got the South and Mid-West opening slot, and Sister Double Happiness were on the West Coast dates.

Kurt told *Rolling Stone* magazine's David Fricke that this period was the happiest time for the band. "The best times were right when *Nevermind* was coming out and we went on that American tour where we were playing clubs. They were totally sold out, and the record was breaking big, and there was this massive feeling in the air, this vibe of energy."

SEPTEMBER 21, 1991:

"Smells Like Teen Spirit" debuts at No. 27 on *Billboard*'s Modern Rock Tracks chart. This night, the band plays Foufounes Electrique in Montreal, Canada.

SEPTEMBER 22, 1991:

Nirvana has dinner at Division 16 in Boston with WFNX's Kurt St. Thomas, DGC head of alternative music Mark Kates, DGC radio rep Ted Volk, and others. "They threw ribs and stuff at each other. They were having fun. That was by far the best dinner I've ever been at in my life," says Ted. "Kurt was very quiet, but you just couldn't take your eyes off him. Dave Grohl was always the same, sarcastically goofy. And Chris was pretty goofy as well."

After dinner, Dave remembered that the Melvins had a club show at the Rat in town, so they went over to see them, but when they get there they find that their names aren't on the guest list as expected. "Kurt goes, 'No, no, I'm on the list. My name is Kurt Cobain and I'm on the list,'"

• Surfing the crowd •

remembers Ted. "So then out of nowhere this blonde grabs the bouncer's hand and says, 'Don't you know who this is?' Now, remember, the album hasn't even come out yet. The guy goes, 'No.' And she goes, 'This is Jesus Christ and you gotta let him in this club right now.' I turn around and say to my girlfriend, 'Now that's fucked up.' And the girl was Mary Lou Lord. We get into the club, and there aren't more than 20 or 30 people there, but three of them were wearing Nirvana shirts and they walked up to him like they found the Holy Grail, or Moses just walked into the room. It was fucking weird."

Kurt and the diminutive indie rock diva Mary Lou Lord dated for a brief time, before Courtney came back into the picture a month later.

SEPTEMBER 23, 1991:
Nirvana plays WFNX's birthday bash at Axis in Boston. The shows are held at multiple clubs on Lansdowne Street near Fenway Park. Nirvana headlined the show at Axis, with none other than Smashing Pumpkins opening, along with Bullet La Volta.

Before the show, Kurt St. Thomas interviews the band on 'FNX. After the interview, MTV taped a silly segment with Chris Novoselic playing Twister in Crisco oil with the Smashing Pumpkins and Bullet La Volta and he used the American flag to wipe himself off. "These jocks came up and were really bad-vibing me. Like, 'Hey, you don't do that to our American flag.' So I ended up having some kind of bodyguard go with me to the club," Chris tells *Spin*.

"They opened the show with 'Aneurysm,'" recalls Kurt St. Thomas.

"The reaction was insane, way over the top. You could feel that there was something intense going on."

SEPTEMBER 24, 1991:
Nevermind, the album that changed the face of the music industry and brought the underground to the mainstream, is released. Because the 'FNX show the night before was at a 21-and-over club, the band schedules a last-minute, all-ages show on this night at the Axis once again. "They did a sound check and normally when a band sound checks everyone goes their separate ways, but when Nirvana sound checked, you know those E.F. Hutton commercials? Everybody just stopped what they were doing to watch this, because again, it was like nothing you'd ever seen before," says Ted Volk.

SEPTEMBER 25, 1991:
Nirvana plays Club Babyhead in Providence, Rhode Island with the Melvins opening. That morning Kurt did an interview with the local alternative station WBRU; it would be his last US radio interview.

Ted Volk says the on-air interview went well, but afterwards he took Kurt out to lunch at a place called Amsterdam's. "He said, 'You know...' (Now, we had learned at this point that the midnight sales were outselling the Chili Peppers or something.) And he leans over to me and said, 'You know, I just wanted to be as successful as Sonic Youth.' And then about 10 minutes later, he leaned over to me again, and said, 'You know what? I've decided, I'm never going to do another radio interview again.' And I asked 'Why's that?' And he goes, 'You know, I'm just not interested in talking about myself,'" recalls Ted.

This night, the band performs to yet another rabid audience. "I've never to this day remembered seeing a show where people were that over-the-top crazy," notes Ted. "It was like you were seeing something really magical; something that I'll never witness again."

SEPTEMBER 26, 1991:
Sound problems always seemed to plague Nirvana – obviously due to the fact that they smashed their gear often only to play on the same gear again. At their New Haven, Connecticut show at The Moon, Chris and Dave jam on "Blew" while Kurt fiddles with his guitar to get a better sound. Of his guitar smashing, Kurt once told *Guitar World*, "I guess I've never considered musical equipment very sacred."

SEPTEMBER 27, 1991:
The City Gardens in Trenton, New Jersey is the next stop on the tour. "I remember what struck me wasn't even so much the music, but how many New Yorkers that were down in Trenton to see the show. There were a lot of industry people, which was weird. It was not an easy club to get to," says Jim Merlis, who becomes Nirvana's third Geffen publicist in 1993.

SEPTEMBER 28, 1991:
Nirvana plays the Marquee Club in New York and does an in-store at Tower Records during the day. And just four days after the release of their major label debut, they have a top 20 hit when "Smells Like Teen Spirit" bolts up 10 positions on *Billboard*'s Modern Rock Tracks chart to No. 17.

"KURT WAS VERY QUIET, BUT YOU JUST COULDN'T TAKE YOUR EYES OFF HIM. DAVE GROHL WAS ALWAYS THE SAME, SARCASTICALLY GOOFY. AND CHRIS WAS PRETTY GOOFY AS WELL."

"A bunch of us went out to dinner before the show – the band, John Silva, Julia Cafritz from STP (the girl band, not Stone Temple Pilots), and Everett True. And by the time we got back to the club for sound check, the place was already packed and buzzing," says John Troutman. "The performance was just absolutely perfect."

At the Tower Records in-store, the band played about four or five songs acoustically, remembers John. "That was pretty packed too. It was the whole East Village scene." When a deli tray was set out for them with roast beef sandwiches, the band joked, "I thought these guys were an alternative band, but they're eating meat."

SEPTEMBER 30, 1991:

Nirvana plays Graffiti's in Pittsburgh, Pennsylvania. Kurt smashes his guitar into Dave's snare drum. By this time, Kurt doesn't need to find cheap thrift store guitars to mend his broken axes. The band now has a $750-a-week equipment allowance while on tour, according to *Melody Maker*.

After their show, a couch gets set on fire in a dressing room and the finger is pointed at the Nirvana entourage by the Pittsburgh police and the club. Kurt Cobain explains what really happened in *Melody Maker*: "That was a classic case of coked-out Pittsburgh Mafioso promotion. That club was the type of place that would have John Cafferty and the

Beaver Brown Band, Huey Lewis and the News, and all those other professional bar bands. What's rock and roll to them?"

OCTOBER 1, 1991:

The day of Nirvana's show at J.C. Dobbs in Philadelphia, the club gets a call from the band's road manager saying they might have to cancel the show because Kurt is sick. "[The tour manager Monty Lee Wilkes] called back saying that they really, really want to do the show, but Kurt's stomach is really bothering him. This the first time I heard about the legendary stomach problems," says Tom Sheehy, the publicist for the club at the time.

Marci Cohen, a writer in town, described the audience as "full of jarheads" – something that didn't go unnoticed by Kurt Cobain. In *Come As You Are*, he complains that there were "more average people coming into our shows and I didn't want them there." But, when questioned about his attitude to Nirvana's new audience this month by Roy Trakin, Kurt offers a different story, saying, "There's no mixed feelings between us and the audience. We love and respect our audience."

Of contradictions like this, and like Kurt's conflicting feelings toward fame and success, Danny Goldberg offers, "He obviously had many feelings, some of which contradicted each other, like many people both healthy and disturbed."

OCTOBER 2, 1991:

The band plays the 9:30 Club in Dave Grohl's old stomping grounds of Washington, DC. Dave's mom is in attendance and hangs out with the band eating pizza backstage after the show.

OCTOBER 4-7, 1991:

The tour heads down the coast for the Southeast dates starting October 4 at Cat's Cradle in Carrboro, North Carolina. The shows include: October 5, 40 Watt Club, Athens, Georgia; October 6, Masquerade, Atlanta, Georgia and October 7, Omni New Daisy Theater, Memphis.

OCTOBER 5, 1991:

As Nirvana is playing one amazing show after another, the band's album sales and radio airplay are reaching new heights. On *Billboard*'s Modern Rock Tracks chart, "Smells Like Teen Spirit" moves up six more positions from No. 17 to No. 11.

OCTOBER 8, 1991:

As *Nevermind Nirvana* points out, the certificate of registration for "Smells Like Teen Spirit" that is filed with the United States Copyright Office on this day credits the song's words and music to all three members of Nirvana, but on *Nevermind* itself, only Kurt Cobain is credited with writing the lyrics.

An early lyric sheet of "Smells Like Teen Spirit" was published in *Come As You Are*, revealing Kurt's aborted attempt at lyrics for the song that read, in part: "Take off your clothes. I'll see you in court/We know we'll lose, but we won't be bored." Another line that didn't get used: "Who will be the King and Queen of the outcasted teens?".

And of course, the title of the song comes from a moment spent in Kurt's room with his friend Kathleen Hanna of Bikini Kill who wrote on his wall, "Kurt smells like teen spirit." "When I wrote the song, I had no idea what I was writing about," Kurt told journalist Roy Trakin. "The majority of the lyrics are just pieces of poetry that I had written that I threw together. It's more of a personal idea, mainly just me dealing with my own apathy rather than attacking my generation and accusing them of being apathetic."

OCTOBER 9, 1991:

Staches in Columbus, Ohio is the next stop on the tour. While in town, Kurt Cobain is interviewed via phone by Roy Trakin for *Hits* magazine.

When asked if he can feel the excitement over *Nevermind* and the buzz yet, Kurt responds, "I try to keep myself as insulated as possible, but the other night I was talking to a friend on the phone and gazing on MTV and saw a Metallica video and after that our video came on, so that made me realize that maybe we're a bit more popular than I realized... I don't know what to think of it. Going from no attention to a whole bunch of attention immediately is pretty overwhelming."

OCTOBER 10, 1991:

Nirvana plays the Empire in Cleveland, Ohio.

OCTOBER 11, 1991:

St. Andrews Hall in Detroit, Michigan is the next tour stop. *Detroit Free*

Press's Gary Graff, who had seen their Blind Pig show in nearby Ann Arbor, Michigan in 1990, noticed what a big difference Dave Grohl made to the band. "It was like, yeah, now they got it. Now they got a guy who kicks ass on the drum kit. They definitely sold the audience," says Gary. "The people who were coming to see them on the strength of one song ['Smells Like Teen Spirit'], I think left feeling like this was really a good band."

OCTOBER 12, 1991:

Dave Grohl's drum set is completely destroyed at the Cabaret Metro in Chicago; *Nevermind* debuts on The Billboard 200 at No. 144; and Kurt and Courtney – who finagled a free plane ticket to Chicago from a hungry record executive eager to please her – finally hook up.

"It was right at the Metro when they first got together and they were pretty much together after that," says Danny Goldberg. "She was there with Lori [Barbero] from Babes in Toyland and someone else and she worked her way through the dressing room, and when I looked back she was sitting on his lap and it was pretty much from then on they were together." Later that night, according to *Come As You Are*, Kurt and Courtney, fresh from a break-up with Billy Corgan that evening, came back to the hotel room Kurt shared with Dave and made love for the first time. Dave quickly left the room.

• **Lori Barbero from Babes in Toyland** •

The show was yet another stellar performance, and in each city fans and critics continued to comment on Dave Grohl's presence. Greg Kot of the *Chicago Tribune* remembers the show as "phenomenal" and that Dave "transformed the band into this incredible powerhouse."

On the charts, "Smells Like Teen Spirit" officially becomes a bona fide hit when it moves up another six positions from No. 11 to No. 5. The song remains in the top 5 of the chart for 14 consecutive weeks, and in the top 10 for 16 consecutive weeks.

OCTOBER 14, 1991:

In Minneapolis, Nirvana does an in-store performance at Let It Be Records and then plays First Avenue at night. Meanwhile, the video for "Smells Like Teen Spirit" gets an added boost at MTV when the powerful network places the clip in their Buzz Bin rotation for nine weeks straight.

"It's not that great being on MTV 20 times a day," Kurt says in *Spin*'s December 1992 issue. "It's great for record sales, but I wish there was some kind of contract you could draw up where there was only a certain amount of time they could play you in a week."

"The first time I saw that video, my 20-year-old son and I looked at each other and went, '*That's* important.' I can't think of many times in the last year I've said that," says Michael Greene, president/CEO of the National Association of Recording Arts and Sciences. "It had an immediate effect on anyone who heard Nirvana or saw Nirvana for the first time."

OCTOBER 16, 1991:

Nirvana plays Mississippi Nights in St. Louis, Missouri. Nirvana jokes onstage about the riot that happened at a Guns N' Roses show a few days earlier and mockingly stages their own riot onstage with Kurt encouraging fans to stage dive. They also invited hundreds of fans onstage to get away from the aggressive bouncers down front.

OCTOBER 17, 1991:

While in Lawrence, Kansas for their show at the Bottleneck that night, Kurt met one of his idols – beat poet and former heroin user William S. Burroughs. The two would soon record a 10-inch together called "The 'Priest' They Called Him."

Burroughs describes the meeting in the self-titled biography on Kurt: "I waited and Kurt got out with another man. Cobain was very shy, very polite, and obviously enjoyed the fact that I wasn't awestruck at meeting him. There was something about him, fragile and engagingly lost. He smoked cigarettes but didn't drink. There were no drugs. I never showed him my gun collection."

The two exchanged presents – Burroughs gave him a painting, while Cobain gave him a Leadbelly biography that he signed. Kurt and music video director Kevin Kerslake originally wanted Burroughs to appear in the video for "In Bloom."

OCTOBER 18, 1991:

Sub Pop releases Earth's *Bureaucratic Desire for Revenge* EP, which features Kurt on guitar and backing vocals. Kurt is credited on the album as a "specialist."

● Rock 'n' roll couple #1: Kurt and Courtney ●

● Rock 'n' roll couple #2: Patti (Smith) and William (Burroughs) ●

OCTOBER 19–21, 1991:

Nirvana plays three shows in Texas. The first one, at Tree's in Dallas on the 19th, is another one of the band's most infamous moments.

The incident starts nine songs into the set, after "Polly," when Kurt notices the security guards pushing kids back, so he waves the fans on in a sarcastic motion to come up onstage. Three songs later, during "Love Buzz," Kurt jumps into the crowd and is being pushed back to the front of the stage and you can clearly see on the tape of the show that, during the fracas, the bouncer pushes Kurt in the face. The bouncer then gets clocked in the head with Kurt's guitar.

The bouncer, who's bleeding from his head, then punches Kurt in the back of his head and kicks him when he's down on the stage. Chris and Dave jump in to break it up, and meanwhile the crowd is chanting "Bullshit! Bullshit!" Kurt storms off stage, but then returns to finish the set. Kurt chalked up the incident to having the flu and "feeling the results of the antibiotics and heavy booze" in a *Melody Maker* story.

The next two Texas shows are October 20, Houston, the Vatican and October 21, Austin, Liberty Lunch. The band also plays an in-store at Waterloo Records in Austin. Meanwhile, *Nevermind* makes a significant jump from 144 to 109 on The Billboard 200.

OCTOBER 22, 1991:

Greg Watermann photographs Nirvana for the cover of *Spin* magazine (January 1992) at a photography studio he rented in Phoenix, Arizona. The shoot lasts for about five hours, during which the band makes it pretty clear that they're weary of having their faces splashed all over the cover of a major magazine.

"Kurt dyed his hair blue that morning to be rebellious about being photographed for the magazine," says Greg. "He filled his buthtub in his hotel with the blue dye and then stuck his head in the tub, so he was blue from the neck up, and his hands were blue. [Nirvana's publicist Lisa Gladfelter Bell described Kurt as looking like a 'Smurf.'] Fortunately, I had a make-up artist there to give him a normal skin tone. I didn't want the photos to look like he was a floater – when he showed up, he looked dead."

● As you want us to be: Nirvana at the *Spin* photo shoot, October ●

● **Courtney and Rickenbacker** ●

OCTOBER 23, 1991:
Nirvana performs at After the Goldrush in Phoenix, Arizona.

OCTOBER 24, 1991:
"Well, at least nobody died." John Godfrey's assessment of Nirvana's show at Iguana's in Tijuana, Mexico in the *San Diego Union-Tribune* pretty much sums up the show. "A sold-out crowd explored the limits of sanity (and safety) in what was the most violent pop show this critic has ever witnessed," wrote John in the review, which ran two days later. "Crazed music fans leaped from 18-foot balconies on to other, similarly crazed music fans below, countless people fell in the slam pits and were trampled by fellow moshers; the security guards didn't even try to prevent more than a hundred people from diving headlong off the stage."

Kurt questioned the fans: "Why in the world are you screaming for me?" Chris's parting words to the crowd were, "Thanks for having a good attitude and for having a little fun." Hole and Sister Double Happiness were on the bill. "It was insane," recalls Scott Becker, publisher of the alternative music magazine *Option* at the time. "The whole vibe was almost bordering on a riot. It was hard to tell who was more out of control, the band or the crowd. People were cannonballing off the balconies."

OCTOBER 25, 1991:
Nirvana plays the first Rock For Choice benefit concert at the Palace in Hollywood, California with L7, Hole, and Sister Double Happiness on the bill. Rock For Choice is a non-profit abortion rights organization that was founded this month by L7 to benefit the Feminist Majority Foundation.

"That was the buzz show in LA," says Danny Goldberg. "I remember Axl [Rose] was there with [Geffen president] Eddie Rosenblatt and Kurt had left the dressing room because he didn't want to say hello to Axl. And no one knew what Kurt looked like then, so he was just standing against the wall with all these people milling about and they didn't know he was the guy they just saw onstage. He called me over and wanted to discuss rewriting the bio because the articles were making him seem too political and not like they had a sense of humor. I was impressed that he had the insight to know that there was one sentence in the bio that was skewing some of the questions wrong. It was unusual clarity for anybody in the business, especially an artist in the middle of the hurricane."

Also on this day, dressed in a yellow gown, Kurt ("Wearing a dress shows I can be as feminine as I want," he once told the *LA Times*) and Chris tape an interview with MTV's long-gone late-night metal show, *Headbanger's Ball*. Kurt said he wore the dress because, well, it was a ball.

OCTOBER 26, 1991:
At the Warfield Theater in San Francisco, L.A. Kanter's review in *Guitar Player* describes Kurt as appearing "unimpressed, even bored."

"He turns his back on the audience and tears into a blistering, out of key solo, ending with a passage of noisy sustained feedback that pushes the crowd even higher," writes Kanter. "All night long Cobain remains aloof, ambivalent."

● Rehearsals continue ●

In the audience was Nils Bernstein, who drove down from Seattle with Kurt's former girlfriend Tracy Marander and Wade Neal from the band Seaweed (Tracy and Wade were dating at the time, but Wade was friends with Kurt so Nils says it wasn't an uncomfortable situation.) "It was the day after [legendary music promoter] Bill Graham died, and one of the last things he did was got them these red and black velour or terry robes with their names and the Nirvana logo on the back," recalls Nils. "They went onstage wearing these robes."

Meanwhile, copies of *Nevermind* are flying out the doors of record stores nationwide. The album jumps an astonishing 44 spaces up The *Billboard* 200 from No. 109 to No. 65. "This week, it was clear to me that they were gonna be the biggest band in the world," says Danny Goldberg. "In that one moment it had gone outside the cult of that indie rock scene. But, honestly, we – Gary Gersh, myself, John Silva, – always thought there was a chance that they were going to be the biggest band. We played it down that we thought they would sell as well as the Pixies, but by the time the record came out a lot of us had this tingly feeling and it took a while to convince the rest of the record company, but we knew this was something that was very special."

OCTOBER 27, 1991:
Nirvana plays the Palace in LA again, but this time it's with Portland's own Greg Sage and the Wipers and Hole on the bill.

OCTOBER 29, 1991:
Nirvana is told by DGC's Northwest promotional rep, Susie Tennant, that *Nevermind* has gone gold (sales of 500,000 copies) at their Portland show at the Fox Theater.

"Since I knew it went gold and the company or Silva had told me, I just thought they knew too," says Susie. "So I said to Chris, just off the cuff, 'Congratulations.' And, he's like, 'For what?' 'Well, your record went

gold.' They didn't know so it was like, 'Oh my God.' He was really surprised and really happy." Nils adds, "Everyone portrays the whole band as this anti-success, anti-whatever, especially Kurt. But that didn't mean that he didn't want to be successful. Chris was elated they sold this many records. They just didn't want the assholes coming to shows and people coming up to him all the time, but he wanted to do good."

Danny Goldberg also notes that there were times when Kurt celebrated – or at least embraced – his commercial success. "He was not successful by accident," he says. "He was a complicated fellow. But, yeah, there were times where he got pleasure out of it both here and around the world." Kurt later tells the *LA Times* that he couldn't comprehend what was happening in the beginning and "we didn't handle things very well."

Meanwhile, the *Hollywood Reporter*'s Marc Pollack declares, "Nirvana is destined to be 'the next big thing'" in his review of the band's October 25 show, which was published on this day. In it, Nirvana is described as a Seattle band whose "songwriting flair surpasses anything that has come out from there before, including such critical favorites as Soundgarden and Alice in Chains."

OCTOBER 30, 1991:
Nirvana plays the Commodore Ballroom in Vancouver.

OCTOBER 31, 1991:
After two months on the road and with a gold record and a top 5 single under their belts, Nirvana plays a triumphant homecoming show at the Paramount in Seattle with Mudhoney and Bikini Kill opening up.

Some of the footage from this show is later used in the "Lithium" video, and their performance of "Negative Creep" this night is later included on *From the Muddy Banks of the Wishkah*. TV crews and other members of the press (among them *Spin* and *Rolling Stone*, which only gave *Nevermind* a three out of five star review at the time) swarmed the place. Chris commented during the show: "There's more cameras in here than a 7-Eleven.")

The show almost signified the end of an era for Nirvana and the start of a new one. "That was a real event. That was *the* event," says Seattle writer Tom Phalen. "Everybody just knew that this was the last time we'd see them at the Paramount, let alone at a club." "This one felt celebratory," says Sub Pop's Megan Jasper. "There was still a fun feeling to it, and I think that was the last time I ever felt that. The shows later on, they were great shows, but it was a bummer."

Joining the band onstage were a few go-go dancers, who danced throughout the show. "They were hardly professional dancers – one skinny white boy with horn-rimmed glasses and he was as non-glamorous as you could possibly be, really kind of a geeky dude doing very '60s go-go moves," says Tom. "It was kind of incongruous with what was going on. Kurt seemed to be amused."

"I remember the total chaos and the excitement, but I remember specifically going backstage and Chris Novoselic's parents were there and there was this huge party going on backstage," says Bill Bennett, who was among the many LA-based label and management folks who flew up for the show. "And Kurt was curled up on a rug with blue hair and was so pained to see all these people back there."

Tom has a similar memory of Kurt backstage at the show: "Sitting in the center of the room was Cobain and he was sitting in a folding chair knee to knee with a girl across from him and they were huddled and really intensely talking as all these people around him were sort of watching. He just put up this wall. I remember a few people walking up to him to say hello and comment on the show and you could see that he wasn't having any fun with that."

OCTOBER 1991:

Also this month, the first battle over Nirvana's name results in the Seattle Nirvana having to pay $50,000 to an LA-based group also named Nirvana, according to an article in *Billboard* magazine. The magazine reported, "[In 1991], the more famous Nirvana, from Seattle, slapped a trademark infringement suit on the Los Angeles-based Nirvana. As it turned out, however, the locally popular LA band Nirvana was the original holder of the Nirvana name. The case was settled in court in October 1991 when the Seattle outfit agreed to pay the LA crew $50,000." A ruling was also later made in April 1992 that both bands would have the legal right to use the name Nirvana.

Elsewhere this month, Nirvana is featured on the cover of their hometown music paper, the *Rocket*, with an article written by their former Sub Pop publicist Jennie Boddy.

NOVEMBER 1, 1991:

The *Seattle Times* review of Nirvana's Halloween show echoes what fans have been saying about the band for the last two months: "The set included many songs Nirvana has been doing live here for years, but they were tighter and more condensed, and delivered with a new sense of confidence and style. A good deal of credit has to go to Dave Grohl, the sixth in a long line of Nirvana drummers, who held it all together with his powerful rhythms."

NOVEMBER 2, 1991:

The band departs for Europe. *Nevermind* cracks the top 40 of The *Billboard* 200, moving from No. 63 to No. 35 on the chart this week.

NOVEMBER 3, 1991:

Nirvana-mania is setting in and Kurt Cobain is a bit uneasy with it. In a story in the *Chicago Tribune* on this day, Kurt says, "All this attention is getting to be a bit unrealistic. I hardly have any time for my life anymore. I don't have a life. It's Nirvana, Nirvana, Nirvana. It's a bit exaggerated. We just want to play music."

NOVEMBER 4-9, 1991:

The band kicks off a six-week European tour starting in Bristol, England at Bierkeller on the 4th and playing a week's worth of shows in England, including November 5, Astoria, London; November 6, Wulfrun Hall, Wolverhampton; November 8, "The Word" television show, London; and November 9, Mark Goodier's BBC radio show, London.

The highlight of these English dates would have to be the band's performance on "The Word," where Kurt declares to the audience, "I just want everyone in this room to know that Courtney Love, of the pop group Hole, is the best fuck in the world!"

A review of the Astoria show runs in the *Independent* on November 7 that describes Nirvana's sound as a mixture of the Beatles and Black Sabbath – "heavy metal you can whistle to." Kurt described it similarly in *Guitar World*: "We sound like the Bay City Rollers after an assault by Black Sabbath."

At the Astoria, the band opened with "Jesus Doesn't Want Me For A Sunbeam" by the Vaselines. Eugene Kelly of the Vaselines opened the show with his new band, which was called Captain America before Marvel Comics made them change the name. Eugene soon changed it to Eugenius.

And on the 9th, at their Mark Goodier taping, Nirvana performs "Something in the Way," "Been a Son," "Aneurysm," and "(New Wave) Polly" (a faster, electric take on "Polly"). "Been a Son" is later used on a "Blew" 12-inch.

NOVEMBER 9, 1991:

Nevermind cracks the top 20 on The Billboard 200, moving from 35 to 17 in this issue of the magazine. The album remains in the top 20 for 30 weeks, and in the top 10 for 28 of those 30 weeks. Meanwhile, "Smells Like Teen Spirit" debuts at No. 27 on *Billboard*'s Mainstream Rock Tracks chart. The success of *Nevermind* puts the once-flailing Sub Pop in the black.

NOVEMBER 10-13, 1991:

The next four dates on the tour are in Germany: November 10, the Loft, Berlin; November 11, Markhalle, Hamburg; November 12, Batschkapp, Frankfurt; and November 13, Nachtwerk, Munich. Of the tour, sound man Craig Montgomery says, "They were pretty chaotic shows. It was cold. Nothing too out of the ordinary. It was a pretty hectic trip."

● Rock 'n' roll becomes serious business ●

NOVEMBER 14, 1991:

Jack Endino's Skin Yard opens for Nirvana at the Arena in Vienna, Austria. "Kurt was okay in Vienna," Jack tells *Goldmine*. "They seemed to be having fun."

NOVEMBER 16–20, 1991:

Nirvana is in Italy during this week, with Urge Overkill opening the shows. The first Italian gig is on the 16th at Sala Verdi in Trieste, and then the Bloom in Mezzago (near Milan) on the 17th; Castle Theater in Rome on the 19th (the recording of "Spank Thru" from this show is on *From the Muddy Banks of the Wishkah*); and Kriptonite in Bologna on the 20th.

NOVEMBER 16, 1991:

Back home, *Nevermind* breaks into the top 10 of The Billboard 200 at No. 9. It remains in the top 10 for 28 consecutive weeks. "It was all relative. Once we got into top 10, it could've been No. 1, 2, or 3. It didn't matter," says Bill Bennett. "It was great that it went No. 1 [in January 1992], but being No. 1 has a lot to do with what's going on around you."

"People tell us, 'Oh you guys are number nine in the *Billboard* charts in America!' We don't jump around and laugh or jump for joy. We just sort of say, 'oh.' But when someone says 'Rush want you to tour with them!' we bust out laughing and roll on the floor," Dave Grohl later commented to Australian journalist Murray Engleheart.

Craig Montgomery says the reaction from the band and the crew on the US success was that "it was bizarre. It was freaky and heady and crazy. No one knew what to do... That's the crazy thing. While we were over there screwing around in Europe, *Nevermind* was blowing up in the States. We shouldn't have even been in Europe [at this time] really."

"We thought we'd sell a couple hundred thousand at the most, and that would be fine. Next thing you know, we go top 10. I wish we could have a time machine and go back two months. I'd tell people to get lost," Chris Novoselic tells *Rolling Stone*.

NOVEMBER 23, 1991:

Nirvana plays to 900 fans at Vooruit in Ghent, Belgium. During Leadbelly's "Where Did You Sleep Last Night?" Dave switched to bass – playing it laying on his back on the stage, Chris to drums, and Kurt wielded his guitar into the drum kit. The instruments end up in splinters on the stage floor at the set's end.

Rolling Stone's Chris Mundy was there to capture the mayhem: "Blood is pouring on to the floor of Nirvana's dressing room. To make matters worse, the source of the bleeding – a fan with a hole in his mouth where his front tooth used to be – has gone into shock and is convulsing uncontrollably," begins the article. "Backstage, Novoselic is kneeling next to the convulsing fan, trying to console him, as paramedics strap him to a chair and wheel him away. The band's tour manager is shrieking about finding equipment for the rest of the tour." Chris later admits that it was a low point of the tour and "what happened had a lot to do with alcohol and with some really weird tension in the air."

Back home, *Nevermind* jumps from No. 9 to No. 4 on The *Billboard* 200 and "Smells Like Teen Spirit" hits the No. 1 spot on the Modern Rock Tracks chart. In just eight weeks, *Nevermind* has sold 1.2 million copies in the US.

NOVEMBER 24, 1991:

Nirvana perform Leadbelly's "Where Did You Sleep Last Night?" and the Velvet Underground's "Here She Comes Now" on VARA Radio in Hilversium, Holland.

Nirvana performed on several European radio stations, but back in the States they chose not to make any radio appearances. "There's no reason, really. Just probably too busy," explains Danny Goldberg. "And I think there was a certain feeling of not wanting to screw alternative and college radio. I don't think they wanted to turn their back on the alternative culture that spawned them. There was a time when there was a little competition between more mainstream radio and the more alternative radio. There might have been a feeling of not wanting to diss alternative media, and to try to keep a sense of proportion.

"Something like MTV was so big, they did what they could to keep MTV involved with them, but I think there was a feeling of not wanting to betray them," continues Danny. "Sometimes if you don't have time to do three interviews, it's better to do none. It's nothing about radio, just time management. But there was definitely a concern to keep the respect of the alternative media. And that was where the credibility and the long-term career would be based."

NOVEMBER 25, 1991:

Nirvana – with Kurt's guitar sporting the "Vandalism: Beautiful As a Rock in a Cop's Face" sticker – plays the Paradiso in Amsterdam, Holland. VPRO-TV taped the show and "Lithium," "Been a Son," "School," and "Blew" are later included on *From the Muddy Banks of the Wishkah*. In the book *Come As You Are*, Kurt admits to taking heroin with Courtney while in Amsterdam. He says it was his idea, but Courtney was the one who actually went out to find it. Courtney would later say the two "bonded over pharmaceuticals."

"In Amsterdam, he wasn't doing too good. It was a really weird show," says Jack Endino in *Goldmine*. "Kurt was really pissed off; there

• Dave and Chris – the rhythm section •

● Grinning and bearing it ●

were all these people with cameras and movie cameras on the stage, and he was a little out of tune and he was very angry at these cameras – 'Get the hell off my stat!' and backstage he was really uneasy, he looked really pale. Everybody seemed to be really uneasy and very unhappy. Like suddenly the success was starting to bother them because people were starting to come at them. Suddenly people wouldn't leave them alone."

NOVEMBER 26, 1991:

Nirvana plays Bradford University in Bradford, England. The UK dates at this time feature Shonen Knife as the opening act. Nirvana has a long history of being generous with their opening band slots – giving them to bands they love and admire. "Since our record has done so well, we can open doors for other bands, from where we come from, like Sonic Youth or Mudhoney or the Melvins or L7 or Dinosaur Jr.," Chris says in *Nevermind: It's an Interview* in 1992.

NOVEMBER 27, 1991:

The Hummingbird in Birmingham, England is the next stop on the tour. In the US, the Recording Industry Association of America (RIAA) officially certifies *Nevermind* gold (500,000 copies sold) and platinum (1 million copies) at the same time. And in Canada, Mike Jastremsky and Kevin Shea of Geffen's distributor MCA – dressed in a nightgown, slippers, a shower cap and a diaper – picketed radio station CHOM-FM in Montreal's offices from 8 a.m. until 1:30 p.m. because the station wouldn't play Nirvana's "Smells Like Teen Spirit." The stunt worked and the station added the song.

NOVEMBER 28, 1991:

Nirvana performs at the Octagon Center in Sheffield, England at night, and earlier, they appear on the London TV show "Top of the Pops." When asked to lip-sync "Smells Like Teen Spirit" to a pre-recorded tape of the song, the band protested by delivering what is arguably one of the funniest TV musical moments in recent memory. Kurt sings in a gothic, loungey voice (he even mouths the mike at one point), and Chris and Dave don't even try to mime their parts to the recorded song.

It's humorous moments like this that Craig Montgomery feels are more indicative of Nirvana than the angst-ridden image that most fans conjure up of the band today. "The image of Nirvana now is all this angst and drugs and grunge and anger," he says. "And it really wasn't about that at all. It was the most hilarious thing you ever saw. Kurt had a great sense of humor. A Nirvana show was just this unbridled joy. It was this craziness and they were totally taking the piss out of rock and roll. If they played a festival with serious bands they would just make the serious bands look silly. Every show it was what could we do that'll be funny and hilarious and make fun of how stupid stuff is."

NOVEMBER 29 – DECEMBER 1, 1991:

Nirvana has three engagements in Scotland, starting in Edinburgh at Carlton Studios on November 29, then QMU in Glasgow on November 30, and an acoustic set at the Southern in Edinburgh on December 1. Kurt's stomach was really acting up by this time, and he tried medicating it with lots of cough syrup and alcohol.

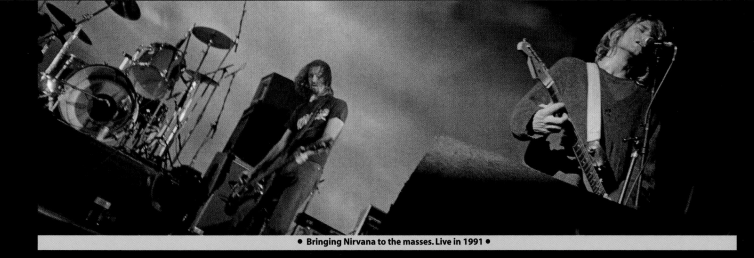

NOVEMBER 1991:

"Smells Like Teen Spirit" with "Even in His Youth," ""Aneurysm," and "Drain You" is issued as a CD-5 in the UK. And, in the US, C/Z Records releases *Teriyaki Asthma, Vol. 1-5* compilation, which included Nirvana's "Mexican Seafood" from 1989's *Teriyaki Asthma, Vol. 1*.

DECEMBER 2-5, 1991:

Nirvana heads back to England for a few more gigs: December 2, Mayfair, Newcastle; December 3, Rock City, Nottingham; December 4, Manchester Academy, Manchester; and December 5, Kilburn National, London.

DECEMBER 5, 1991:

Lying in bed, Kurt and Courtney decide to get married. Her engagement ring is from the early 1900s with a ruby stone. Of the engagement, Kurt tells *Sassy* in early '92, "I've gotten engaged and my attitude has changed drastically, and I can't believe how much happier I am. At times I even forget that I'm in a band, I'm so blinded by love. I know that sounds embarrassing, but it's true. I could give up the band right now. It doesn't matter, but I'm under contract."

DECEMBER 6, 1991:

Jonathan Ross of London's "The Jonathan Ross Show" announces that Nirvana is going to play "Lithium," but the band – much to everyone's surprise – performs "Territorial Pissings" instead. The band once again knocks their equipment over at the end of their performance. Kurt once told *Melody Maker*, "I don't do it nearly as much as everyone thinks I do. I just wait for a good time to do it – like when I'm pissed off or I want to show off in front of Courtney. Or, if I'm appearing on TV, just to piss the TV people off."

DECEMBER 7, 1991:

During the day, Chris and Dave represent the band at a press conference in Rennes, France. That night, the band plays the TransMusicale Festival and they decide to bag the rest of the tour due to stress, too much drinking, and Kurt's stomach problems. Back home, "Smells Like Teen Spirit" debuts on the top 40 chart, The Billboard Hot 100, at No. 40 and on the Hot 100 Singles Sales chart at No. 19. On the album chart, *Nevermind* moves up one notch to No. 4.

"IF SOMEONE IS A HEROIN ADDICT, YOU CAN'T MAKE THEM WANT TO GET CLEAN."

Upon returning from the European tour, Kurt and Courtney move in together in Los Angeles and continue to do heroin together, as they admit in *Come As You Are*. The band has said that they didn't know what to say to Kurt – if anything – about the drug issue at the time.

Craig Montgomery felt the same way. "If someone is a heroin addict, you can't make them want to get clean," says Craig. "They have to want it for themselves and if they don't there's nothing anyone can do. [I was thinking] he'll either figure it out or he won't, but you can't make him. Life is hard enough even if you're not a drug addict. Life, a lot of the time, is sad and hard and you don't see how things are going to work out, and it's like you just have to find the place in the world where your mind can live, and it was hard for him. That's my take on it. But in the last couple years I really wasn't that close to him. In the earlier years, we were fairly close and we would hang out and do stuff together sometimes. I was never into heroin. I never did it, so when he got more into that we had less to talk about, obviously."

DECEMBER 9-14, 1991:

Nirvana cancels the tour of Ireland and Scandinavia. The dates were supposed to be: December 9, Conor Hall, Belfast, Ireland; December 10, McGonagles, Dublin, Ireland; December 11, Lepakko, Helsinki, Finland; December 12, La Garage, Bergen, Norway; December 13, Alaska, Oslo, Norway; and December 14, Melody, Stockholm, Sweden.

DECEMBER 17, 1991:

The nominations for the 19th annual American Music Awards are announced and Nirvana is up for Best New Artist in the Heavy Metal category. At night, Kurt attends the Hole/Smashing Pumpkins show at the Whisky-a-Go-Go in Hollywood, California. Courtney ends her set by hurling her guitar to the ground.

DECEMBER 21, 1991:

"Smells Like Teen Spirit" debuts on another one of *Billboard*'s top 10 charts, the Hot 100 Airplay chart, which monitors only top 40 (a.k.a. pop) radio stations. The song was a tough sell on pop radio because Mariah Carey, Michael Bolton, and Bryan Adams were the format's core artists at the time.

"The first time I brought up working ['Teen Spirit'] to pop radio to Geffen, I think some were horrified because pop radio was Paula Abdul at the time," notes Danny Goldberg. "But there was this record by Jesus Jones ["Right Here, Right Now"] that got some pop play – it didn't go all the way, but it showed there was some pop audience for modern rock. And it seemed to me it was worth trying to get it played on the stations that played Jesus Jones, and of course within 10 days it was much bigger than Jesus Jones, but it was a turning point in radio. It's true that prior to that, this whole type of music wasn't mass appeal music. Nirvana helped shift the whole thing."

DECEMBER 25, 1991:

Chris visits his mother back home in Aberdeen for Christmas. "He couldn't even go to the store, because people just make such a big fuss over him," Chris's mother Maria Novoselic says to the *Seattle Times'* Patrick MacDonald a few months later. "And Chris is a very down-to-earth kid, he doesn't want all this fuss."

DECEMBER 27, 1991:

Nirvana, Pearl Jam, and the Red Hot Chili Peppers play the Los Angeles Sports Arena. The venue sold out of their 16,000 seats in one day. The three groups play the next five shows together, with Nirvana as the

middle band. During sound check, Jerry McCulley of the now-defunct LA-based music magazine *Bam* interviews Kurt. The article, which runs the next month, hints at Kurt's drug use.

Onstage, the band's 35-minute set includes the Who's "Baba O'Riley," in which they jokingly do the infamous Pete Townshend windmills as if to mock the fact that they are playing a big arena "rock show." They also played rousing renditions of "Smells Like Teen Spirit," "Lithium," "Come As You Are," "Breed," and "Territorial Pissings."

Backstage, Kurt remained aloof. "When people would come up to him that he didn't want to talk to, he would just transform himself somehow," says Susie Tennant. "This look would come over him and just emanating off his body was, 'Don't talk to me.' It was just the coolest thing; it was like, look at him go! But he wasn't an intimidating person. That was really the amazing thing about it. It was just a protective thing. He wasn't gloom and doom. And when I saw that happen, I realized at the time that this was certainly a self-protective thing. It wasn't like he was being an asshole. I just saw that and thought, that poor guy. At the same time, I thought it was awesome that he found this way, without being mean to anybody, to show people that he wanted them to stay away and people respected that."

DECEMBER 28, 1991:

Nirvana, Pearl Jam, and the Chili Peppers play the O'Brien Pavilion at Del Mar Fairgrounds in Del Mar, California, outside of San Diego. Their performances of "Drain You," "Aneurysm," and "Smells Like Teen Spirit" are included on *From the Muddy Banks of the Wishkah*.

DECEMBER 29, 1991:

Nirvana, Pearl Jam, and the Chili Peppers play the Arizona State University in Tempe, Arizona.

DECEMBER 31, 1991:

At the Cow Palace show in San Francisco, Pearl Jam, who was first on the bill, plays the intro of "Smells Like Teen Spirit" then stops and says, "We played it first!" Nirvana's crew wasn't amused.

Nirvana once again delivered another explosive performance with the entire pit jumping up and down in unison. "When they came out, it was a solid thud. It just kicked ass. They sounded great, they looked great, it was just a thick rock sound," says Mike Musburger. "They smashed their gear at the end better than I'd ever seen them do before ... and they did it forever. They smashed their gear for like 10 minutes and they kept coming out and throwing stuff around. It was funny. It was like a circus act in a lot of ways. There would be silence and then you hear the welling of the crowd and someone would pick something up to smash it and the crowd would just go, 'YEAH!'"

Backstage, it was the scene of all scenes. Bill Graham Presents created a festive atmosphere in the VIP area for the New Year's holiday. Each band had their own tent and between the tents was a jukebox where Dave Grohl and Chris Novoselic were playing Beatles songs, according to John Troutman, who was there. Keanu Reeves and the late River Phoenix were also backstage. Steffan Chirazi was there doing an article for the now-defunct metal magazine *Rip*. Someone had changed Nirvana's name card on their dressing room to Thee Nirvana (like Thee Headcoats). Inside their trailer, recalls Mike, it was completely trashed.

• Kurt in a quiet moment during the *In Utero* sessions •

"THEY SMASHED THEIR GEAR AT THE END BETTER THAN I'D EVER SEEN THEM DO BEFORE ...AND THEY DID IT FOREVER."

TOTALLY VIOLATED

JANUARY 1, 1992:
"I quit drinking New Year's," Chris Novoselic tells the *Seattle Times*.

JANUARY 2, 1992:
At the Pearl Jam/Nirvana/Red Hot Chili Peppers gig at the Salem Armory in Salem, Oregon, Nirvana finds out from DGC's Susie Tennant that *Nevermind* will be No. 1 in the next issue of *Billboard*.

"Monqui, the promoters, bought a bunch of champagne and after the show we told them they went No. 1," says Susie. "I was shocked, because the underground world of music just never crossed over. These were the days of hair bands. It was like this unbelievable ride that you were on and it just kept going. That was the amazing thing, it just kept going. I certainly know that I'll never have the highs or the lows like I did working with Nirvana; it was such a personal thing to me because they were my friends."

JANUARY 3, 1992:
Chris Novoselic and Dave Grohl hang out at the Crocodile Café in

Seattle until closing. Coincidentally, KIRO-TV in town aired a news segment on Nirvana's success from the Crocodile that day. Soon the club was deluged with calls from fans asking if Nirvana would be playing there, to which co-owner Stephanie Dorgan, Peter Buck's wife, gave a firm "No." And then, without prior notice, Chris and Dave actually did show up at the club around 11:30 p.m., but not to perform, just to hang out. "They were very nice," Stephanie told the *Seattle Times*. "Dave asked me if it was OK to put his cigarette out on the floor before he actually did it."

JANUARY 4, 1992:
Interest in *Nevermind* brings new fans out to buy the band's first album, *Bleach*, which debuts on this day at No. 185 on The Billboard 200.

JANUARY 7, 1992:
Just four months after its release, the RIAA confirms *Nevermind* is certified for 2 million copies sold. The band initially thought they'd be lucky if they sold a quarter of that. "You know, whatever's happened, is,

was surely out of our control, and I'm glad it's happened," Chris says in *Nevermind: It's an Interview*. "You know, it's nice to sell that many records. It's nice to turn on people to something different. People are telling me... 'I think you guys are gonna go platinum.' And, we're like 'Oh, man, come on. You know, if we get a gold record out of this, that'll be amazing.'"

JANUARY 8, 1992:
The National Academy of Recording Arts and Sciences (NARAS) announce the 34th annual Grammy Awards nominations, and Nirvana is nominated for Best Alternative Music Album for *Nevermind*. Their competition is Jesus Jones' *Doubt*, Elvis Costello's *Mighty Like a Rose*, R.E.M.'s *Out of Time*, and Richard Thompson's *Rumor and Sigh*.

"The thing I first admired the most, and the thing to this day that makes me the saddest about Kurt not being with us anymore, was his songwriting," says Michael Greene, President/CEO of NARAS. "I truly believe that Kurt Cobain was – and had he lived – would have continued to be, the most important songwriter of the '90s. I don't see anybody who really comes close."

JANUARY 9, 1992:
Nirvana rehearses at NBC Studios in New York for their first appearance on "Saturday Night Live." The band is supposed to run through their performance exactly as they would do it live on the show.

"We ran through the two songs they did a couple of times," says Lisa Gladfelter Bell, the band's publicist at the time, who was with them for SNL. "You're supposed to do exactly what you're going to do on Saturday – any movements, you jump over your drum kit or switch places or go upstage – so they can block the shot. I remember saying, 'If you're gonna break an instrument or something like that, at least go through the motions.' And of course, they didn't."

After rehearsal, Chris and Dave went to watch a taping of "Late Show with David Letterman" in the same building and Kurt went back to the hotel. "Fans came out of the woodwork for this; it was scary," recalls Lisa, who escorted Kurt to his hotel. "I remember I grabbed the back of Kurt's sweater, he signed a few things, then I pushed him through the door into a cab. He was pretty low-key about it. He was cool with the fans."

JANUARY 10, 1992:
While in New York, the band also tapes a live performance for MTV. The set list includes "On a Plain," "Stain," "Drain You," "Polly," "Smells Like Teen Spirit," "Territorial Pissings," "Aneurysm," "School," and "Molly's Lips." During sound check, the band also jams on the Breeders' "Hellbound" from *Pod*. Some clips from this taping have been aired on MTV, but never the entire nine-song set.

"That one experience of working with Kurt showed me how sensitive he was as a person," MTV's Alex Coletti, who was on hand for the taping and would later produce Nirvana's "MTV Unplugged", says in *Guitar World*.

Kurt's mother was one of the 100 or so people at the taping. "She's attractive and she didn't look like what I thought she was gonna look like. I thought she'd be more like Aberdeen and she was totally not," recalls WFNX's Kurt St. Thomas. Later this night, Kurt St. Thomas

• Kurt in mock shock •

interviews Dave and Chris – separately, actually – for the interview CD *Nevermind: It's an Interview* at the Rihga Royal Hotel. Kurt was scheduled to be interviewed this night too, but he blew it off. Chris later goes to see a Mike Watt show.

Also on this date, one of the first articles to mention Kurt's drug problem is published in the Los Angeles music paper, *Bam*. The interview was conducted after the band's LA Sports Arena show on December 27, 1991 and the author, Jerry McCulley, wrote that Kurt was "nodding off occasionally in mid-sentence... He's had but an hour's sleep, he says blearily. But the pinned pupils; sunken cheeks; and scabbed, sallow skin suggest something more serious than mere fatigue."

"[The drug rumors] all started with just one article in one of the shittiest, cock rock-oriented LA magazines, where this guy assumed I was on heroin because he noticed that I was tired," Kurt said in *Melody Maker* in July 1992, around which time his heroin habit reportedly rose from $100 a day to $400 a day, he would later admit. "Since then the rumors have spread like wildfire. I can't deny that I have taken drugs and I still do, every once in a while. But I'm not a fucking heroin addict."

For damage control, the band's publicist, Lisa Gladfelter Bell, says the label's stance was to simply tell reporters that Kurt was "tired from being on the road and that [*Bam*] had the wrong take on it." When asked about his reaction to the *Bam* story today, Danny Goldberg says, "There were about 500 articles written about Nirvana at that time. We didn't need articles to tell us what was going on [because] we were in the middle of it."

January 11, 1992:

The infamous first "Saturday Night Live" performance – Kurt is high on heroin and sick. The performances of "Smells Like Teen Spirit" and "Territorial Pissings" are OK. Chris French-kisses both Kurt and Dave during the goodbyes. NBC brass apparently isn't too thrilled.

"This was a nightmare," says Lisa Gladfelter Bell of the day. "Kurt was an hour and a half late when I went to pick him up in his hotel lobby [a limo was offered by SNL, but the band refused to take it]. He finally came down and then we're on the way in the cab going to the show and he's like, '*Ohhhh*, my breakfast didn't agree with me. I have to vomit.' And he starts vomiting. So, we pull over."

"The head of NBC wanted autographs for his kids, and they said 'Fuck it.' It was bad. And Rob Morrow, the host of the show, came over to say hi and they were kind of rude to him. That was horrible. That SNL, Kurt was so fucked up, him and Courtney went into the bathroom for like an hour... Before the taping, Kurt was asleep on the couch and I was told to wake him up five minutes before he goes on and try to get him to drink tea with honey. It was obvious to me, but no one was copping to the fact [that there was a problem] at that point and I don't think he admitted it at that point either. I know when someone is about to go on a huge appearance on national television, that is not the time to confront them, but...."

During the day, the band does a photo shoot with Michael Lavine at his studio on Bleecker St. – Kurt nods out in front of the camera. After the show, Kurt is finally interviewed for his part in *Nevermind: It's an Interview* with Kurt St. Thomas, who says that Kurt didn't appear messed up during the interview – in fact, he was "totally right on in the interview, but you don't need to be a rocket scientist to figure it out."

Kurt's interview lasted from 1 a.m. until about 4:30 a.m., according to St. Thomas.

While all this is going on, *Nevermind* takes the No. 1 slot on The Billboard 200 by selling 373,520 copies this week. It outsells Garth Brooks, Hammer, and U2 this week and knocks Michael Jackson's *Dangerous* out of the top spot. The album, last week's No. 6, also hits No. 1 in France, Ireland, Spain, Sweden, Canada, and Belgium among other countries. "Smells Like Teen Spirit" continues its ascent up the charts from No. 13 to No. 6 on *Billboard*'s Hot 100 Singles chart. On going No. 1, Danny Goldberg says, "It's nice that it happened, but it wasn't a big milestone. The milestone was just to reach a lot of people – to get it to the millions and there are records that sell millions that never go to No. 1. So that was a

• Live, early 1992 •

● **Courtney and Kurt get cuddly, 1992** ●

nice surprise actually... But, it seemed to me [Kurt] liked being No. 1."

JANUARY 12, 1992:

Kurt and Courtney do a photo shoot together for *Sassy*'s April issue with Michael Lavine back at his studio on Bleecker. Michael described the two as "totally in love" in *Come As You Are*. They are also interviewed for the article with Christina Kelly at a restaurant in the East Village while in NY. It's around this time that Courtney says she found out she's pregnant.

"Somewhere around "Saturday Night Live" is when it started to become clear that there was a drug problem," admits Danny Goldberg. "Between that time and the time he died, it was a constant series of discussions and meetings and ups and downs with a series of different people. I think we were all focused on the drug problem because that was the visible problem. And in retrospect, I wished that we had also focused on the psychological issues, but there was so much pressure in just dealing with the drug problem. So we talked to everybody we could talk to, and there were five or six different people that I met with

and that other people in his life met with."

Craig Montgomery, the band's sound man, also says that SNL was the point where everyone realized just how serious Kurt's problem was. "Everybody knew. And it was scary. You didn't want to think about it," he says. "I never felt like it was my place [to speak to Kurt about the drug issue]. I mean, I tried to make myself available to him, if he ever just wanted to talk or hang out. It was something that I really couldn't relate to, even the simple fact of being a heroin addict, I couldn't relate to, or the fact of what he was going through in his career and stuff. I started to feel more like an employee. There was always that whole drama going on."

JANUARY 13, 1992:

With a No. 1 record approaching double platinum sales, Nirvana piques the interest of not just the music press, but the business media as well. The *New York Times* business section features a story on the phenomenal success of *Nevermind*, quoting DGC president Ed Rosenblatt humbly stating, "We didn't do anything. It was just one of those 'Get out of the way and duck' records." Charles R. Cross, editor of the *Rocket*, notes, "The only genius involved here was Kurt Cobain, and the other people [involved in their careers] were either lucky, dumb, or just by sheer chance ended up associated with this band."

Also on this day, Washington State Governor Booth Gardner gives his "State of the State Address" and says he's proud to be the Governor of the State with the most popular band in the country: Nirvana. Around this time, Nirvana can be seen on the cover of *Option*, *Details*, *Rip*, and *Kerrang!*

Between SNL and the Pacific Rim tour, Kurt and Courtney detox together at a Holiday Inn. Courtney also consults a doctor who informs her that heroin use in the first trimester isn't harmful to the fetus, and who puts her on Methadone, a prescription heroin substitute that eliminates cravings for the drug, to help kick her habit. Detoxing isn't pretty. Severe withdrawal symptoms include restlessness, diarrhea, insomnia, vomiting, muscle spasms, and mood swings. Methadone, usually taken once a day, "stimulates the same brain mechanisms as heroin, but their effects are not as severe as heroin so a user can function normally," according to onHealth.com.

January 14, 1992:
Dave Grohl turns 23 years old.

January 15, 1992:
Chris and Dave join the Melvins onstage in Seattle at the Crocodile Café for what was billed as Melvana. The one-time group featured Chris on bass, Dave on drums, and the Melvins' Buzz Osborne on guitar and vocals. They opened for Churn and Bliss (Bliss was also a name that Nirvana used years back). They perform Flipper's "Sacrifice" and "Way of the World."

"Hey, we've only had about 45 minutes of rehearsal and then some asshole calls the End [KNDD, the station which leaked the news of the show earlier in the day]. Just don't take this seriously," Chris warns from the stage.

"During sound check, Grohl came in," recalls Tom Phalen, who was there. "And the guy who was setting up his drums asked if there was an extra snare drum or an extra drum head. And, we're like, 'Why?' 'Because he's gonna break it. He always does.' And, everyone's like 'Yeah, right.'" Dave comes in and hits the drum once and puts his stick right through it." After the show, Dave drank beer at the bar, Buzz hung out, and Chris went to the Vogue to see Tad play.

January 18, 1992:
Garth Brooks' *Ropin' the Wind* knocks Nirvana's *Nevermind* out of the top spot and down to No. 4, but not for long. And the second single from *Nevermind*, "Come As You Are," debuts at No. 20 on *Billboard*'s Modern Rock Tracks chart.

Danny Goldberg says that Kurt was hesitant to release "Come As You Are" as the second single from *Nevermind* because it sounded like the Killing Joke song, "Eighties" from 1985's *Night Time*. "We had had a meeting at Jerry's Deli on Ventura, I think it was Silva, Gary, myself, and the band, and we met to discuss what the second single would be," says Danny. "We couldn't decide between 'Come As You Are' and 'In Bloom.' Kurt was nervous about 'Come As You Are' because it was too similar to

a Killing Joke song, but we all thought it was still the better song to go with. And he was right, Killing Joke later did complain about it. I felt it was not a good reason to disqualify it as a single."

Though it has been reported that Killing Joke filed a copyright infringement lawsuit over the song, Killing Joke's bassist Paul Raven says that the band actually never did sue Nirvana. They did have their music publishers consult two different musicologists to determine if there was indeed enough of an infringement to sue for, but due to band problems and money issues at the time, the band never thoroughly pursued this.

January 19-22, 1992:
For three days during this time frame, music video director Kevin Kerslake (whose credits at this time included Hole, Iggy Pop, and Mazzy Star) shoots the "Come As You Are" video in Los Angeles. Kevin was introduced to the band through Courtney because Kevin had directed Hole's "Garbage Man" video and they were friends at the time.

The shoot was spread over three days in three different locations: Wattles Garden Park in Hollywood was the first location. The background footage that was projected on the wall in the video was shot there and "they were interviewing dogs for the video in the park, well, meeting dog trainers there," says former Geffen Art Director Robert Fisher. The next two shoots were at Kurt's house in L.A. and the Van Nuys Airport hanger, which was where the set was built featuring the house that was in ruins. Growing tired of seeing his face everywhere, Kurt was shot through plexi glass with water running over it to distort him.

January 22, 1992:
The RIAA certifies the "Smells Like Teen Spirit" single gold for 500,000 units sold. Bill Bennett says he doesn't ever remember the band celebrating their commercial success. "All I remember is, at the time, them saying, 'All we want to do is open for Sonic Youth.' In the very early days, there was still that kind of guilt over the commercial success and that kind of innocence, and they really believed in punk music."

January 23, 1992:
Nirvana arrives in Australia for their tour Down Under. Australian journalist Murray Engleheart reports that Kurt Cobain had mutated his "Please Do Not Disturb" sign on his hotel room door at Sydney's Hotel Newhampshire to read "Please Burn Down My Room." The label holds a reception in their Sydney offices to mark the sales of *Nevermind*, but only Dave and Chris showed up, while Kurt's stomach illness kept him in his hotel room.

January 24, 1992:
The first show of the tour is at the Phoenician Club in Sydney with Tumbleweed and the Meanies opening up. "The place, both on the upper levels and on the floor, was packed," says Murray Engleheart of the Phoenician show. "Due to his stomach agonies, Kurt, for the most part even at this point, kept to himself, thus unwittingly creating and accentuating his own mystique." The band also performs on JJJ radio in town. Back home, the *Rocket* announces Kurt and Courtney's engagement.

"THE ONLY GENIUS INVOLVED HERE WAS KURT COBAIN, AND THE OTHER PEOPLE (INVOLVED IN THEIR CAREERS) WERE EITHER LUCKY, DUMB, OR JUST BY SHEER CHANCE ENDED UP ASSOCIATED WITH THIS BAND."

● Kurt gets a Messiah complex ●

● The performances continue. Kurt with Telecaster ●

JANUARY 25, 1992:

Nirvana plays the inaugural Big Day Out festival in Sydney at the 6,000-seat Hordern Pavilion. "There was an amazing sense of community, but for some the manic attraction also made for an event that ranked as one of their most frightening gig experiences," wrote Murray about the show. "The fine line between fun and pure unbridled fear came close to being breached on many occasions. The huge curtains that sealed off the backstage area from the view of punters never looked so ominous."

Back in the US, "Smells Like Teen Spirit" hits No. 1 on *Billboard*'s Hot 100 Singles Sales chart. The single fared better on the top 40 sales chart than on the top 40 radio chart, because many top 40 program directors didn't find the song appropriate for their stations. One pop program director even told *Billboard*, "Personally, I think it sucks."

JANUARY 26, 1992:

Nirvana performs at Fisherman's Wharf in Gold Coast, Australia.

JANUARY 27, 1992:

The show at Brisbane Festival Hall in Brisbane, Australia is cut short due to Kurt's illness. In Los Angeles, the 19th annual American Music Awards are held at the Shrine Auditorium. Nirvana loses to Firehouse, a hair band whose biggest hit was the power ballad, "Love of a Lifetime," for the Best New Artist award in the Heavy Metal category.

JANUARY 29, 1992:

The band's show in Freemantle (which is part of Perth), Australia is cancelled due to Kurt's problems. "There was some bad shit," remembers Craig Montgomery. "Canceling the show in Perth, that was pretty bad news." When asked how Chris and Dave reacted to this, Craig says, "There was tension because of that. So yeah, they'd be pissed off at having to miss shows. Days that we would cancel a show would be bad."

JANUARY 30, 1992:

The band is back on their feet after three days off and perform at the Thebarton Theater in Adelaide, Australia.

JANUARY 31, 1992:

Next stop: the Palace in Melbourne, Australia.

JANUARY 1992:

Also in January, Nirvana appears on the cover of *Spin* magazine. It's their first major magazine cover. Also, buried deep in an article in *Musician* is the first public dig against Pearl Jam by Kurt. He says that bands like Pearl Jam are "responsible for this corporate, alternative, and cock-rock fusion."

In this month, Kurt's father tries contacting his record label, management, and even "Saturday Night Live" to re-connect with his son. And Danny Goldberg leaves Gold Mountain for Atlantic Records, but stays on as a consultant to work with Nirvana and Hole as co-manager. (He is currently head of Artemis Records.)

Meanwhile, the six-song *Hormoaning* EP is released in Australia and Japan. It features "Even in His Youth" and "Aneurysm" from the "Smells Like Teen Spirit" single and "Molly's Lips," "D-7," "Turnaround," and "Son of a Gun" from the 1990 John Peel session. The EP was issued as a 12-inch, CD, and cassette in Australia, but only on CD in Japan.

FEBRUARY 1, 1992:

Powered by the exposure from Nirvana's "Saturday Night Live" appearance, *Nevermind* returns to the No. 1 spot on The Billboard 200. "They sold almost another million records in just the two weeks after the SNL appearance, then it was like a rocket," says Lisa Gladfelter Bell. Of their success, John Lydon, of Sex Pistols fame, told the *Seattle Times*, "Nirvana has done what the Pistols, the Clash, and all those could never do. They've taken punk to the top of the charts."

Meanwhile, on *Billboard*'s Mainstream Rock Tracks chart, "Come As You Are" debuts at No. 37 and "Teen Spirit" reaches its peak position at No. 7. Back in Australia, the band plays an all-ages show in the afternoon at the Palace in Melbourne, which Murray Engleheart says was the high point of the tour.

FEBRUARY 2, 1992:

The band plays their third show at the Palace in Melbourne.

FEBRUARY 3, 1992:

Nevermind is certified for 3 million units by the RIAA.

FEBRUARY 4, 1992:

Another Australian show is cancelled – this time it's the Sydney gig at the Dee Why Hotel. According to journalist Murray Engleheart, who wrote about the tour in *Kerrang!*, this show was just penciled in, but later scrapped for two shows at Selina's Coogee Bay Hotel instead.

FEBRUARY 5, 1992:

The band performs at the ANU Bar in Canberra, Australia, which is the country's capital city.

FEBRUARY 6, 1992:

Guns N' Roses singer Axl Rose turns 30 years old and had asked Nirvana to perform at his birthday party. They declined. "[Guns N' Roses' camp] kept calling me and calling me, and my boss is like 'You have to get me an answer.' I didn't even want to ask the band – they hated him, they despised him," says former Nirvana publicist Lisa Gladfelter Bell. "Plus, you don't ask a band that's gold to play at your birthday party. Then he's calling me and I'm getting these messages on my personal answering machine from Axl Rose. It was awful."

Axl – who was genuinely a fan at first and even wore a Nirvana cap in the Guns' "Don't Cry" video as a show of support – also asked the band to tour with them and Metallica. They once again declined.

FEBRUARY 6–7, 1992:

Nirvana performs at Selina's Coogee Bay Hotel.

FEBRUARY 8, 1992:

Though the single hasn't been commercially released yet, radio airplay lands "Lithium" at No. 25 on *Billboard*'s Modern Rock Tracks. That's the highest position the song reaches on this chart.

Kurt explained the song's meaning to *Hits* in an interview conducted in late 1991: "It's not necessarily about religion, it's about depression and resorting to religion. As a last resort. [Are you religious?, the interviewer asks.] No I wasn't. I've always avoided religion. I don't

see any use for it. I wasn't born anything. I was born white trash, working blue-collar class family."

In addition to dominating the *major* televised awards shows, behind-the-scenes honors from the music industry are racking up as well. On this day, the National Association of Recording Merchandisers (NARM) announces the nominations for their 1991 Best Seller Awards. Nirvana's *Nevermind* is up for Best-Selling Recording by a New Artist against Color Me Badd (*CMB*), Boyz II Men (*Cooleyhighharmony*), C&C Music Factory (*Gonna Make You Sweat*), and the Black Crowes (*Shake Your Money Maker*). *Nevermind* is also nominated for Best-Selling Alternative Music Recording against Red Hot Chili Peppers (*Blood Sugar Sex Magik*), Jesus Jones (*Doubt*), R.E.M. (*Out of Time*), and EMF (*Schubert Dip*).

FEBRUARY 9, 1992:

The band plays in Auckland, New Zealand at the Logan Campbell Center.

FEBRUARY 11, 1992:

Tori Amos' piano version of "Smells Like Teen Spirit" is released on her five-song *Crucify* EP on Atlantic Records. Due to Nirvana's success and a heightened interest in all things alternative, Hole's show at the Whisky-A-Go-Go in LA this night packs in hoards of major-label A&R scouts looking to sign the group. The guest list is said to have outnumbered the paying guests.

● Axl Rose, Nirvana fan ●

FEBRUARY 12, 1992:

Nirvana press day in Singapore.

FEBRUARY 14, 1992:

The band plays their first of five shows in Japan, starting in Osaka at Orakuan Hall. "The shows were all pretty consistent," says sound man Craig Montgomery. Shonen Knife came and visited, but they didn't play. They had a really bad time in Australia, drug-wise, Kurt and Courtney, so I was just grooving on being in Japan now. I barely saw Kurt except for the shows, and he wasn't doing sound checks at this time."

While in Japan, Nirvana does an ID (where they say something like "Hi, we're Nirvana") for a Japanese TV station with a silly name. Kurt starts, "You're watching Space Shower TV"; not able to pass this one up, Chris chimes in "You're watching Golden Shower TV." No one seemed to get the joke.

FEBRUARY 15, 1992:

"Come As You Are" reaches its peak position at No. 32 on *Billboard*'s Modern Rock Tracks chart. In Japan, the band plays a second night in Osaka.

FEBRUARY 16, 1992:

Nirvana plays Club Quattro in Nagoya, Japan. Craig says the Japanese fans were pretty polite on this tour. "They hadn't learned yet that you could go nuts at a rock show."

FEBRUARY 17, 1992:
Next stop: Club Citta in Kawasaki, Japan.

FEBRUARY 18, 1992:
"Come As You Are" is released on CD and cassette in the US with the bonus tracks "Endless Nameless" and live versions of "Drain You" and "School" from the 1991 Halloween Paramount show.

Meanwhile, the press catches wind of "grunge" fashion: flannels, the ripped jeans, thermal shirts and leggings. On this day, the *Boston Globe* runs an article on this so-called fashion trend that says, "Check out the jacket of the next homeless man you see waking up on the street. Look in old wartime photos at the boots on prisoners of war. There! You've captured the fashion essence of the typical rock band, epitomized by the group Nirvana."

"That was nauseating," says Lisa. "The kind of magazines that never call you, like *Vogue*, were calling and would want a press kit on the band or color photos or just want a comment. A lot of times they'd want a quote from me on why the band's dressing like this, and I'm like, 'It's just what they wore. It's cold in Seattle. End of story.' They didn't try to start a fashion trend, it just happened."

● Punk rock... in bathrobes ●

FEBRUARY 19, 1992:
Chris sings part of Queen's "We Will Rock You" before Kurt kicks into "Smells Like Teen Spirit" at their Sun Plaza Hotel show in Tokyo, Japan.

FEBRUARY 20, 1992:
Kurt Cobain turns 25 years old. In the UK, the "Come As You Are" single is released.

FEBRUARY 21–22, 1992:
Nirvana plays two shows at Pink's Garage in Honolulu, Hawaii. "It was really packed and insane, people were going nuts," notes Craig.

"[The club] was very small, smaller than they were playing in the US for years," says Gina Arnold, author of *Route 666: On the Road to Nirvana*, who attended both shows. "Those were the best shows I'd seen in a really, really long time. It was very intense. I don't think it had to do with them, it had to do with the audience being so psyched to see them because those were the only shows they played in America since they had become No. 1."

"IT WAS REALLY PACKED AND INSANE, PEOPLE WERE GOING NUTS"

Also on February 22, *Bleach* reaches its peak position on The Billboard 200 at No. 89.

FEBRUARY 24, 1992:
Kurt Cobain and Courtney Love are married in Waikiki overlooking the beach by a non-denominational female minister found from the Hawaii wedding bureau. The bride wore a white vintage dress worn by Frances Farmer, the Seattle actress who, like the Cobains, was persecuted by the media. The groom wore bluish green and white plaid pajamas, a knit purse, and was high on heroin. Everyone wore leis and the couple carried matching flowers. He cried. She didn't.

Craig Montgomery says, "Most of us went home by the time of the wedding. They were keeping it very, very private. There was a lot of tension within the band." Kurt and Courtney's drug use drove a wedge between them and Chris and Shelli, who weren't welcome at the wedding. In attendance were Dylan Carlson, who served as best man, Dylan's girlfriend, Dave Grohl, tour manager Alex MacLeod, and two crew guys, Nick Close and Ian Beveridge. Kurt and Courtney have a pre-nuptial agreement made up, which she has claimed was her idea.

FEBRUARY 25, 1992:
The 34th annual Grammy Awards are held in New York at Radio City Music Hall. Nirvana loses out to R.E.M.'s *Out of Time* for the Best Alternative Music Album award. Nirvana was asked to perform on the show, but the band made that impossible.

"They had it in their minds that they were gonna come up from the pit and they wanted to come up with absolutely no clothes on. Out of nowhere, they wanted to appear," says NARAS' Michael Greene. "And we kept trying to find a median ground to get that accomplished. I remember them telling us if they can't do that, then they just don't want to perform. So at the end of the day, it just didn't happen."

FEBRUARY 26, 1992:
It's announced that Nirvana tops the prestigious New York weekly *Village Voice*'s annual Pazz & Jop Critic's Poll. *Nevermind* is named Best Album, and "Smells Like Teen Spirit" is named Best Single and Best Video. This marks the first time since 1983 that a group swept those three categories. The poll runs in the March 3, 1992 issue of the *Village Voice*.

MARCH–JUNE 1992:
There was talk of a spring US arena tour, but Kurt wanted to stay home with his pregnant new bride in their Los Angeles apartment. The band doesn't have a show scheduled until June 21.

During the down time, Kurt admitted to still doing a lot of drugs – and hiding it from Courtney by shooting up in a locked closet. "I just got up and got drugs and listened to music and painted and played guitar. That's about it." Kurt tells Michael Azerrad in *Come As You Are*. He also painted and wrote the bulk of *In Utero* ("I did all my best songs on heroin this year," he tells Azerrad.)

Craig Montgomery believes – if Kurt was clean, that is – the band should've capitalized on the momentum of *Nevermind* by touring the US at this time. "At that time, *Nevermind* was at its peak, and they should've been out delivering the goods. They didn't do it because Kurt was too fucked up."

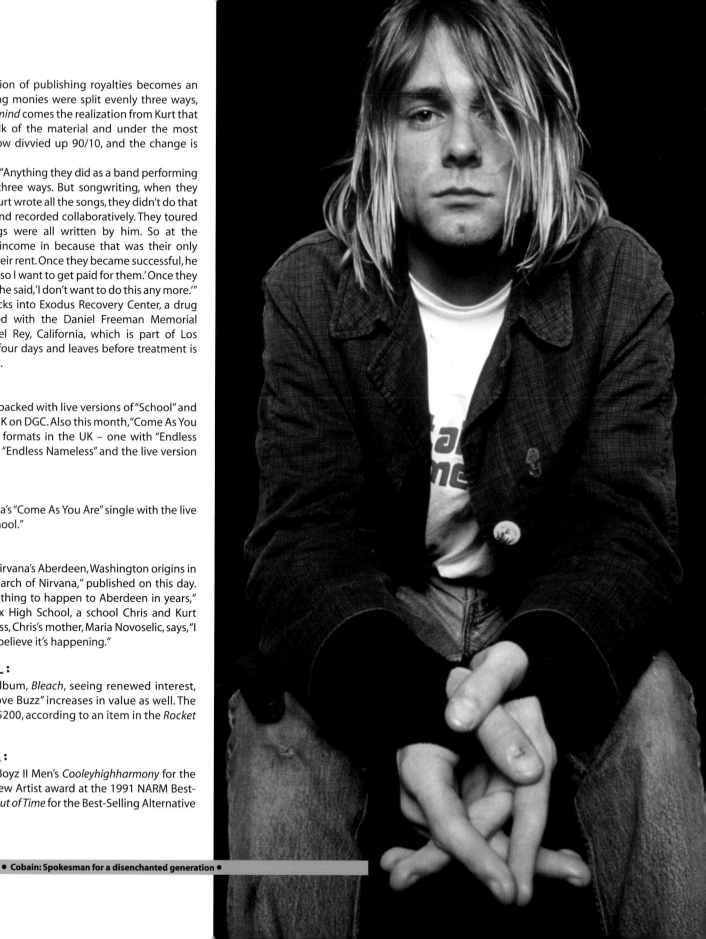

SPRING 1992:

Around springtime, the division of publishing royalties becomes an issue. Up until now, publishing monies were split evenly three ways, but with the success of *Nevermind* comes the realization from Kurt that he's the one writing the bulk of the material and under the most pressure. The royalties are now divvied up 90/10, and the change is made retroactively.

Danny Goldberg explains: "Anything they did as a band performing or artist royalties, they split three ways. But songwriting, when they were a little band, you know Kurt wrote all the songs, they didn't do that collaboratively. They played and recorded collaboratively. They toured collaboratively, but the songs were all written by him. So at the beginning, he threw all the income in because that was their only money, and they had to pay their rent. Once they became successful, he said, 'Look these are my songs so I want to get paid for them.' Once they had enough money to live on, he said, 'I don't want to do this any more.'"

Also this spring, Kurt checks into Exodus Recovery Center, a drug rehabilitation facility affiliated with the Daniel Freeman Memorial Hospital, based in Marina del Rey, California, which is part of Los Angeles County. He stays for four days and leaves before treatment is over to detox at home instead.

MARCH 1, 1992:

The "Come As You Are" single backed with live versions of "School" and "Drain You" is released in the UK on DGC. Also this month, "Come As You Are" is released in two other formats in the UK – one with "Endless Nameless" and the other with "Endless Nameless" and the live version of "School."

MARCH 3, 1992:

In the US, DGC releases Nirvana's "Come As You Are" single with the live version of "Drain You" and "School."

MARCH 8, 1992:

Patrick MacDonald digs into Nirvana's Aberdeen, Washington origins in the *Seattle Times* article "In Search of Nirvana," published on this day. "Nirvana's success is the best thing to happen to Aberdeen in years," says John Eko of Weatherwax High School, a school Chris and Kurt attended. On the band's success, Chris's mother, Maria Novoselic, says, "I still can't believe it. I still can't believe it's happening."

MARCH 15, 1992:

Not only is the band's first album, *Bleach*, seeing renewed interest, but the band's first single, "Love Buzz" increases in value as well. The single goes from $5 value to $200, according to an item in the *Rocket* on this day.

MARCH 16, 1992:

Nirvana's *Nevermind* loses to Boyz II Men's *Cooleyhighharmony* for the Best-Selling Recording by a New Artist award at the 1991 NARM Best-Seller Awards, and to R.E.M.'s *Out of Time* for the Best-Selling Alternative Music Recording.

Washington Governor Booth Gardner signs a bill, which was passed on February 25, making Washington the first state with a music censorship law. Under Washington State House Bill #2554, better known as the Erotic Music Bill, record store owners can be arrested for selling what the state deems offensive – or adult-only – music to minors. Members of Nirvana, Soundgarden, and Pearl Jam fight to get this bill thrown out, and later win.

MARCH 21, 1992:
"Come As You Are" debuts at No. 76 on *Billboard*'s Hot 100 Singles chart.

MARCH 22, 1992:
The 1992 Northwest Music Awards are held at the Paramount Theatre in Seattle. The band didn't show up, but they did win five awards for best group, song, alternative rock group, video, and alternative rock album of the year.

Meanwhile, news breaks in the *Los Angeles Times* that there is yet another band going by the name Nirvana that plans to sue the Seattle Nirvana over their name. This time it's a British group, who had some success in the '60s and '70s. The London-based musicians, Alex Spyropoulos and Patrick Campbell-Lyons, attempt to solve the problem through discussions with Geffen and Gold Mountain to no avail, so they take their story to the *Times* and will soon file suit against Kurt Cobain & Co.

MARCH 30, 1992:
As Nirvana's sales continue to soar, nearing 4 million at this point, A&R scouts at record labels scurry to find "the next Nirvana" and *Newsweek* published an article on this day titled "Searching for Nirvana II."

The feeding frenzy benefits a lot of "alternative" bands on indie labels, such as Afghan Whigs and Helmet, as well as newcomers and Nirvana sound-alikes like Bush and Silverchair. It benefits Mrs. Kurt Cobain's band as well. Hole ends up signing to DGC for more money than her husband's band. The *Rocket*'s Charles R. Cross tells *Newsweek*, "I had one A&R guy tell me, 'Sleeping with Kurt Cobain is worth half a million dollars.'" Close; Hole signed for a reported $1 million.

Helmet, on the indie label Amphetamine Reptile, also inked a major-label deal with Interscope Records in the midst of this alternative frenzy. "I had made a joke then when we got our record deal that we should send Nirvana a fruit basket," explains Helmet's Page Hamilton. "I didn't mean it in any sarcastic way, I meant that we were still Helmet, but if Nirvana hadn't exploded there wouldn't be this rush to sign quote unquote alternative bands, back when it was still called alternative. I'm forever thrilled to have been around at that time and really sad that this person is not with us. The whole thing just makes me sick thinking about it. I just hope people realize what a great contribution [Kurt] made. It affected all of our lives."

MARCH 31, 1992:
Nevermind: It's an Interview by Kurt St. Thomas and Troy Smith of WFNX in Boston is released. The disc features interviews with Kurt, Dave, and Chris conducted on January 11 and January 12, 1992, as well as live

Paramount in Seattle. It also includes the album versions of "Territoria Pissings" and "Smells Like Teen Spirit," and snippets of other songs.

MARCH 1992:
MTV starts playing the "Come As You Are" video.

APRIL 1, 1992:
The "Smells Like Teen Spirit" single is certified platinum for sales o 1 million by the RIAA. The band, label, and friends still can't get used to what's happening. Dave Grohl told *Spin* at the time, "Everything happened so quickly. I don't think anyone knows what's gonna happen next." "You ask yourself, 'How did this happen?' There's no answer, Geffen's VP of sales, Eddie Gilreath, tells *USA Today*. "We're fortunate to have this situation, but we can't explain it."

APRIL 4, 1992:
"Come As You Are" reaches its peak position on Mainstream Rock Tracks at No. 3.

APRIL 14, 1992:
Scotti Brothers Records releases Weird "Al" Yankovic's *Off the Deep End* which parodies the *Nevermind* album cover and includes the parody o "Smells Like Teen Spirit" titled "Smells Like Nirvana."

"The day that they did SNL the first time, I was friends with Victoria Jackson, who was part of the cast at that time, and I was trying to get a hold of Nirvana because I wanted to do a parody of 'Smells Like Teen Spirit' and I was having a hard time getting a hold of them or getting through to their management or something," recalls Al. "So I thought maybe I could talk to Kurt directly and bypass all the middlemen. So asked Victoria if she gets Kurt or anyone from the band alone to pu them on the phone for a minute, and that's what she did.

"She grabbed Kurt Cobain out of the hallway and said, 'Weird A wants to talk to you' and I got on the phone and he was really sweet and I said I'm a big fan and I just wanted to know if it was cool that I did a parody of 'Smells Like Teen Spirit.' And he said, 'Yeah, that would be great. I'm really honored.' And almost as an afterthought, he goes, 'So what, is it gonna be a song about food?' And I said, 'Well no, it's gonna be a song about how nobody can understand your lyrics.' And expected him to be offended, but he said, 'That's cool. It's a great idea.'" (Sample lyric: "Now I'm mumblin', and I'm screaming. And, I don't know what I'm singing.")

Al even used some of the same extras and cheerleaders from Nirvana's video for the song – and the same man who played the janito and the same soundstage – for his video of the parody. "We got the same art director and backdrops and everything," says Al. "Kurt late said that he didn't realize Nirvana had really made it until he saw the Weird Al video. That's one of my favorite quotes of all time."

APRIL 15, 1992:
Nirvana wins three awards at the Boston Phoenix/WFNX 4th Annua Music Poll at the Orpheum Theater in Boston. "Smells Like Teen Spirit" is named Best Song, and Nirvana is named Best New Artist and Bes

APRIL 16, 1992:

The *Rolling Stone* cover story runs on this date featuring Kurt wearing his now famous "Corporate Magazines Still Suck" homemade T-shirt. In the story, "Inside the Heart and Mind of Nirvana" by Michael Azerrad, he takes another shot at Pearl Jam, where he warns kids of fake bands that claim to be alternative like Pearl Jam, saying they're "jumping on the alternative bandwagon." Soon, Pearl Jam begins to outsell Nirvana.

"I had so much pressure from my management and the band members – they wanted to do it, and I just agreed," Kurt explains to the *Advocate* about doing the *Rolling Stone* cover story. "On my way there I just decided, I'm going to write something on my shirt that's offensive enough to stop getting our picture on the cover. This way I could say that I actually played along with it and wasn't necessarily challenging *Rolling Stone*, saying, 'You suck' and 'We don't want to have anything to do with you, but we'll still use you for exposure.'"

APRIL 17, 1992:

A taped Nirvana performance appears on the late-night syndicated TV music show, "In Concert."

APRIL 19, 1992:

Nirvana's television performance on "The Word" in London on November 8, 1991 appears on "The Best of The Word."

APRIL 24, 1992:

Kurt and Courtney attend a concert by Teenage Fanclub – a Scottish band also on DGC – at Fairfax High School in Hollywood. "I went backstage after the show and Kurt and Courtney were on the bus and I sat and talked with them a little bit," says ex-Geffen GM Bill Bennett. "I always liked her. I think I was afraid of her the first time I ever met her. She said, 'Take me to the Ivy!' [a high-priced LA restaurant favored by celebrities and Hollywood executives]. So I took her to the Ivy. And I consider her a friend. I've stayed in touch with her all these years and I went up for the funeral. Frances plays with my children. I like all these people."

APRIL 27, 1992:

The Wild Planet music store in Ventura, California gets complaints about the cover of *Nevermind*. City officials claim the baby's penis is offensive and want the poster for the album taken out of the store window.

"The issue was nudity, whether it was a one-year-old or an 88-year-old," Ventura City Council code enforcement officer Dan Emry said in the Ventura County edition of the *LA Times*. "I got a call from a fellow who was offended. He asked me if there was anything we could do about it."

Former Geffen art director Robert Fisher says that the label did have a back-up plan in case there were more complaints. "Later on, after the album was out and they wanted to get it into the big chains like Wal-Mart, we actually prepared a version where we cut off, or we airbrushed off the penis, but we never had to use that," he says. Kurt Cobain told *Hits* that the band is "proud of the penis. I hope it's OK to show a baby's genitals. We were prepared to put a sticker on the baby's penis, if it was a problem, that said, 'If you are offended by this, you must be a closet pedophile.'" It never actually became a problem.

● **No encore: Nirvana close the set** ●

APRIL 1992:

April also sees the reissue of *Bleach*, which was re-mastered, by DGC, the publication of the *Sassy* cover story, and recording sessions with Barrett Jones at Laundry Room Studios, which had moved from its Arlington, Virginia origins to West Seattle.

In the *Sassy* piece – "Kurt and Courtney Sitting In a Tree" – the couple seem genuinely happy and in love. Kurt declares, "I'm just so overwhelmed by the fact that I'm in love on this scale." The writer, Christina Kelley, also innocently observes that the two were looking "very Sid and Nancy."

The Nirvana session with Barrett lasted for two days, according to a *Goldmine* article. The band records "Oh the Guilt" for the Jesus Lizard split 7-inch, "Return of the Rat" for the Wipers 7-inch box set, *Eight Songs for Greg Sage and the Wipers*, and "Curmudgeon." "I don't think they'd ever really played them before," Barrett tells *Goldmine*. "But they figured them out pretty quick. They're all pretty easy. I think they were trying to be a little more punk rock about the whole thing; trying to get away from the *Nevermind* glossiness. I think that was the purpose."

● Kurt in his favorite coat ●

JUNE 3, 1992:

Nirvana, Geffen, Geffen's distributor MCA, and Sub Pop are sued by Patrick Campbell-Lyons and Alex Spyropoulos of the British '60s group Nirvana over their name. The suit is filed June 3, then slightly amended and re-filed on June 5 in Los Angeles Superior Court (case no. BC 056621) for violation of the Lanham Act, statutory unfair competition, common law unfair competition, violation of business and professions code S14300, and injunctive relief is requested.

The London-based Nirvana claims they had been using the name since 1967 and registered it in 1970. The group recorded at least nine albums under the name Nirvana and had a 1968 hit with "Rainbow Chaser." The group's Alex Spyropoulos told *LA Times'* Steve Hochman, "We want our name clean. We want to be fair. Nothing against [the other Nirvana]. They're great. But they're destroying over 25 years of work we've done, and for us that's something we can't take lying down."

JUNE 5, 1992:

Entertainment Weekly has some fun with Kurt's unintelligible lyrics in "Smells Like Teen Spirit" in an article by Melissa Rawlins titled "From Bad To Verse Sounds Like 'Teen Spirit,' But What Are They Really Singing?" Now, this is before the "Lithium" single is released with the lyrics to *Nevermind*, so all the country was still guessing as to just what Kurt was saying. Melissa's take on the first line was "Now all punk girls/Bring your friends." The real line, of course, is "Load up on guns, and bring your friends."

JUNE 10, 1992:

Geffen and MCA are officially served with the legal papers filed by the London-based Nirvana, according to court documents. A hearing is set for July 27, 1992.

JUNE 11, 1992:

Chris Novoselic attends a press conference held by the Washington Music Industry Coalition to announce that the American Civil Liberties Union (Danny Goldberg was chairman of ACLU's LA chapter) plans to file a lawsuit challenging the constitutionality of the Erotic Music Bill (HB2554), which went into effect this day. The organization wins their battle in November of this year when a Superior Court judge in Washington struck down the statute on the grounds that it violated free speech.

JUNE 12, 1992:

The RIAA certifies *Nevermind* for 4 million copies sold in the US.

MID-JUNE 1992:

Before heading off on the European tour, Kurt and Courtney put some of their personal belongings, including lyric sheets and notebooks, in the bathtub for safekeeping in case an intruder broke in. Ironically, upon their return from the tour, they discovered that a pipe had broken in the bathroom and ruined the contents of the tub. They soon moved out of the Spaulding Avenue apartment and into another apartment in the Hollywood Hills.

MAY 2, 1992:

"Come As You Are" reaches its peak position on the *Billboard* Hot 100 chart at No. 32.

MAY 16, 1992:

Chris Novoselic turns 27 years old.

MAY 17, 1992:

With a summer concert season packed with superstar acts like Bruce Springsteen, Guns N' Roses, Metallica, and U2, the media wonders why Nirvana isn't mounting a big tour as well. In a *Los Angeles Times* article titled "Why is Nirvana Missing From a Heavenly Tour Season?," Steve Hochman says the band's "low profile has renewed published speculation that singer/guitarist Kurt Cobain has a heroin problem." At the time, a spokesperson for the band, however, said the reason for not touring is due to Cobain's stomach problems.

MAY 30, 1992:

After an impressive 28 weeks in the top 10 of The Billboard 200 – 14 of those consecutive weeks were spent in the top 5 – Nirvana's *Nevermind* falls out of the top 10 down to No. 15.

June 20, 1992:

Nirvana's cover of the Wipers' "Return of the Rat" for the box set of 7-inches titled *Eight Songs for Greg Sage and the Wipers* is released on Tim/Kerr Records. The other Wipers covers (each on red or blue vinyl) are: Hole, "Over the Edge," Poison Idea, "Up Front," Whirlees, "Land of the Lost," M-99, "Astro Cloud," Napalm Beach, "Potential Suicide," Dharma Bums, "On the Run," and Crackerbash, "I Don't Know What I Am/Mystery."

Originally, Nirvana was going to contribute their cover of the Wipers' "D-7," but once it appeared on the *Hormoaning* EP earlier this year, licensing it from Geffen proved too difficult. So Kurt "got pissed off and said 'Fuck it. I'll record another track,'" T/K's Thor Lindsay told *Goldmine* in 1997.

June 21, 1992:

The band makes up the dates they canceled in Europe in December 1991. The first gig, with the Breeders opening, is at the Point Theater in Dublin, Ireland. Dave Grohl later tells Michael Azerrad that "there was a lot of crazy shit going on" during this tour. But for Nirvana sound man Craig Montgomery: "This tour was fun. It might be my favorite tour."

"Kurt Cobain's voice began ragged and rough as he screamed out the words of 'Drain You' and 'Stay Away,'" wrote Kevin Courtney in his review of the show for the *Irish Times*. "But by the time the band launched into 'Lounge Act,' he had harnessed the anger and venom that fuels his vocal power." "Smells Like Teen Spirit" and "Come As You Are" were left for the encores.

June 22, 1992:

Nirvana plays King's Hall in Belfast, Ireland. According to an article by Everett True, Kurt was "repeatedly punched by a bouncer after going to stop an altercation between security and a fan." A band spokesperson told *Melody Maker* at the time, "Kurt saw a bouncer beating up a kid so he went to intervene. A scuffle broke out and the bouncer came round behind him and punched him in the side of his stomach a couple of times. I think the guy has since been sacked. Kurt was complaining of a pain the next day."

June 23, 1992:

Kurt collapses in the morning and is taken to the hospital. The rumor is that he overdosed. At the time, his people say that he had a bleeding ulcer from eating too much junk food, while Kurt would later tell Michael Azerrad that he simply forgot to take his Methadone pills and woke up suffering from Methadone withdrawal.

"We had breakfast about nine in the morning in the hotel with a couple of the crew," explains a band spokesperson to *Melody Maker* shortly after the incident. "Kurt was complaining that he had a stomach ache. The next moment he was violently sick. Everyone thought he'd just had too much to drink. We spoke to the tour manager and he called in the doctor. She came and said 'Get him to hospital.' They called an ambulance. He was in hospital for about half an hour and they gave him some tablets. It's a weeping ulcer. I've known him for three years and he's always had it. It's because he eats a lot of junk food."

Also on this date, the Breeders' 1990 album, *Pod*, is re-released on 4AD/Elektra and Kurt Cobain tells *Spin* later this year that this is one of his favorite albums of the year.

June 24, 1992:

Nirvana performs in Paris at Le Zenith. The set list for this tour normally consists of "Aneurysm," "Drain You," "Stay Away," "Sliver," "School," "In Bloom," "Breed," "About a Girl," "Scoff," "Polly," "Lithium," "Blew," "Been a Son," "On a Plain," "Negative Creep," "Love Buzz," "Smells Like Teen Spirit," "Come As You Are," "Territorial Pissings," and "Endless, Nameless."

By the time Kurt and Courtney arrived in Paris, management had people keep an eye on the two for fear of what they might do. Kurt told Michael Azerrad that he was "being monitored by two goons." The couple then secretly switched hotels.

June 26, 1992:

The next stop is the Roskilde Festival in Roskilde, Denmark. Nirvana was the headliner on the larger of the two stages, the 60,000-seat stage, and Helmet were the closing band on the 8,000-seat stage.

"They were amazing," recalls Helmet's Page Hamilton. "These guys had it so together, they had 60,000 Danish people singing along. It was fucking awesome. Dave Grohl is a phenomenal drummer and a great back-up singer. He was the perfect guy for the band and just straightened everything out. He just tightened everything up. Even with Kurt, having the ability to be either really on or off as drastic as he was, Dave was still always on. That's the beauty of live music, some nights you have it and some nights you don't, and on this night in Denmark Kurt had it. It wasn't the nasally, whiney Cobain, it was the powerful, in-tune Cobain. And, as I've experienced later when we played a couple shows with them in a row, it can change from night to night."

After the show, Page says, "Chris shoved Kurt into our dressing room window in these trailers we had to get some beer; it was pretty funny."

JUNE 27, 1992:

"Lithium" debuts at No. 32 on *Billboard*'s Mainstream Rock Tracks chart. This night, Nirvana plays the Ruisrock Festival in Turku, Finland. Teenage Fanclub was on the bill.

"Pearl Jam were supposed to play, and this one fan had a big sign that on one side said 'Negative Creep' [a Nirvana song] and on the other side it said 'Even Flow' [a Pearl Jam song]," remembers Nirvana sound man Craig Montgomery. "And during 'Teen Spirit,' this fan is right in front of the stage and the 'Even Flow' side is facing toward the stage, so during 'Teen Spirit,' instead of going 'How low, how low, how low, how low,' Kurt goes, 'Even flow, even flow, even flow.'"

JUNE 28, 1992:

Most of the shows are going over pretty well, but the Isle of Calf Festival in Oslo, Norway is described as "slightly lackluster, contrary and full of unanswered questions as to Nirvana's role as a stadium rock band" in *Melody Maker*. "Kurt simply stands immobile as 20,000 kids go berserk." Tori Amos' cover of "Smells Like Teen Spirit" is used as the intro music before the show.

JUNE 29, 1992:

The day after the Oslo show, Everett True says in his *Melody Maker* article "In My Head I'm So Ugly" that he, the band, and a few others smoked a joint atop a hill and then found a deserted playground to let off some steam. "Both Dave and Chris picked up on this as one of the happiest incidents in the last year and a half of touring," he wrote.

JUNE 30, 1992:

Nirvana opens their show at Sjohistoriska, a naval museum, in Stockholm, Sweden with the Fang song, "The Money Will Roll Right In." The band brings 50 fans onstage with them for the encore of "Smells Like Teen Spirit" and "Territorial Pissings." The morning of the show, Chris Novoselic does yet another interview with Everett True, and in the afternoon the band does a brief spot on a Swedish TV station.

JUNE 1992:

Hard Rock Comics, a division of Revolutionary Comics, releases the unauthorized Nirvana comic book, *Nirvana: Smells Like Territorial Pissings*. It's issue No. 4 and boldly states on the front cover, "Unauthorized and proud of it." The 33-page book was written by Spike Steffenhagen, edited by Todd Loren, with art and lettering by Scott Pentzer. Kurt's fear of being a rock and roll caricature literally came true.

JULY 1, 1992:

After a major-label bidding war and lots of meetings, Hole officially signs to Geffen on this date for a reported $1 million. Courtney even asked Geffen to pull out Nirvana's contract so she could make sure her deal was sweeter. Everyone from Madonna's Maverick label to Def American, Arista, Virgin, and Charisma were after Hole. The deal calls for

two albums with an option for five more. However, the first of these albums isn't released until two years later, when *Live Through This* hits the stores on April 12, 1994. The second album, *Celebrity Skin*, takes even longer, coming out in 1998. On January 19, 2000, Geffen ends up filing a lawsuit against Hole for breach of written contract in Los Angeles Superior Court (case no. BC 223364) for failing to live up to this recording contract.

JULY 2, 1992:

Nirvana performs at the Plaza de Toros de Valencia in Valencia, Spain, with Teenage Fanclub opening. "The show was in a bull fighting ring at night outside – that was kind of fun," says Craig Montgomery. "But I don't think we were seeing that much of Kurt and Courtney at that time. By then, things were pretty tense, and pretty professional."

On this day, Keith Cameron interviews the band for *Sounds* magazine for an article titled "Love Will Tear Us Apart," which talks about Kurt's drug use and rock star shenanigans, saying the band has gone from "nobodies to superstars to fuck-ups in the space of six months."

JULY 3, 1992:

The band plays a second show in Spain, at Pabellon de Real Madrid. Courtney gets contractions before the show, and they cut the tour off early to head home. After the show, they took her to the hospital and with a clean bill of health sent the two home on the next flight.

JULY 4-5, 1992:

The two remaining shows – Pabellon de la Casilla de Bilboa in Bilboa, Spain and Velodromo de Anoeta in San Sebastian, Spain – are canceled.

JULY 4, 1992:

News breaks about Kurt's trip to the hospital in Belfast the week prior. In true British tabloid fashion, *Melody Maker*'s headline reads: "Kurt KO'd in Belfast. Nirvana Star Rushed to Hospital with 'Mystery Stomach Bug.'" This news, along with the canceled Spain shows and rumors about the band not getting along leads to speculation that the band is breaking up.

JULY 7, 1992:

MTV announces the nominations for the 1992 MTV Video Music Awards. Nirvana is up for Best New Artist, Best Alternative Video, and Video of the Year for "Smells Like Teen Spirit." And even Weird "Al" Yankovic's Nirvana parody, "Smells Like Nirvana," grabs a nomination for Best Male Video. MTV also announces that Nirvana will be among the performers on the awards show.

JULY 9, 1992:

The "Lithium" single backed with "Curmudgeon" is released commercially in the UK on DGC. Courtney Love turns 27 years old. It's on this day that she poses for the photos taken by Michel Comte for the infamous *Vanity Fair* piece, which show her eight months pregnant with a cigarette in her hand. *Vanity Fair* editor Tina Brown had the cigarette airbrushed out, but once tabloids heard of the photos a bidding war ensued. Courtney and Kurt ended up paying $50,000 to buy back all of the negatives.

While there was much ado about covering up these photos, there was little talk over the candid photos of a three-months' pregnant Courtney on her wedding day holding a cigarette that were published in Poppy Z. Brite's *Courtney Love: The Real Story*.

JULY 20, 1992:
The UK gets another version of the "Lithium" single, this time with a live version of "Been a Son" added.

JULY 21, 1992:
"Lithium" with the live version of "Been a Son" and "Curmudgeon" is released commercially in the US. The mystery of the lyrics is finally solved when DGC issues "Lithium" with full *Nevermind* lyrics in the liner notes.

"People who are secluded for too long go insane and as a last resort they often use religion to keep alive," explains Kurt Cobain in the press release about "Lithium.""In the song, a guy's lost his girl and his friends and he's brooding. He's decided to find God before he kills himself. It's hard for me to understand the need for a vice like that but I can appreciate it too. People need vices."

JULY 25, 1992:
"Lithium," which has been all over the radio since early this year, reaches its highest position on *Billboard*'s Mainstream Rock Tracks chart at No. 16.

JULY 27, 1992:
A hearing is set in the US District Court for the Central District of California in the British Nirvana vs. Seattle Nirvana name dispute. The two groups end up settling the matter out of court, with Kurt Cobain's Nirvana paying $100,000 this time in order to keep their band name.

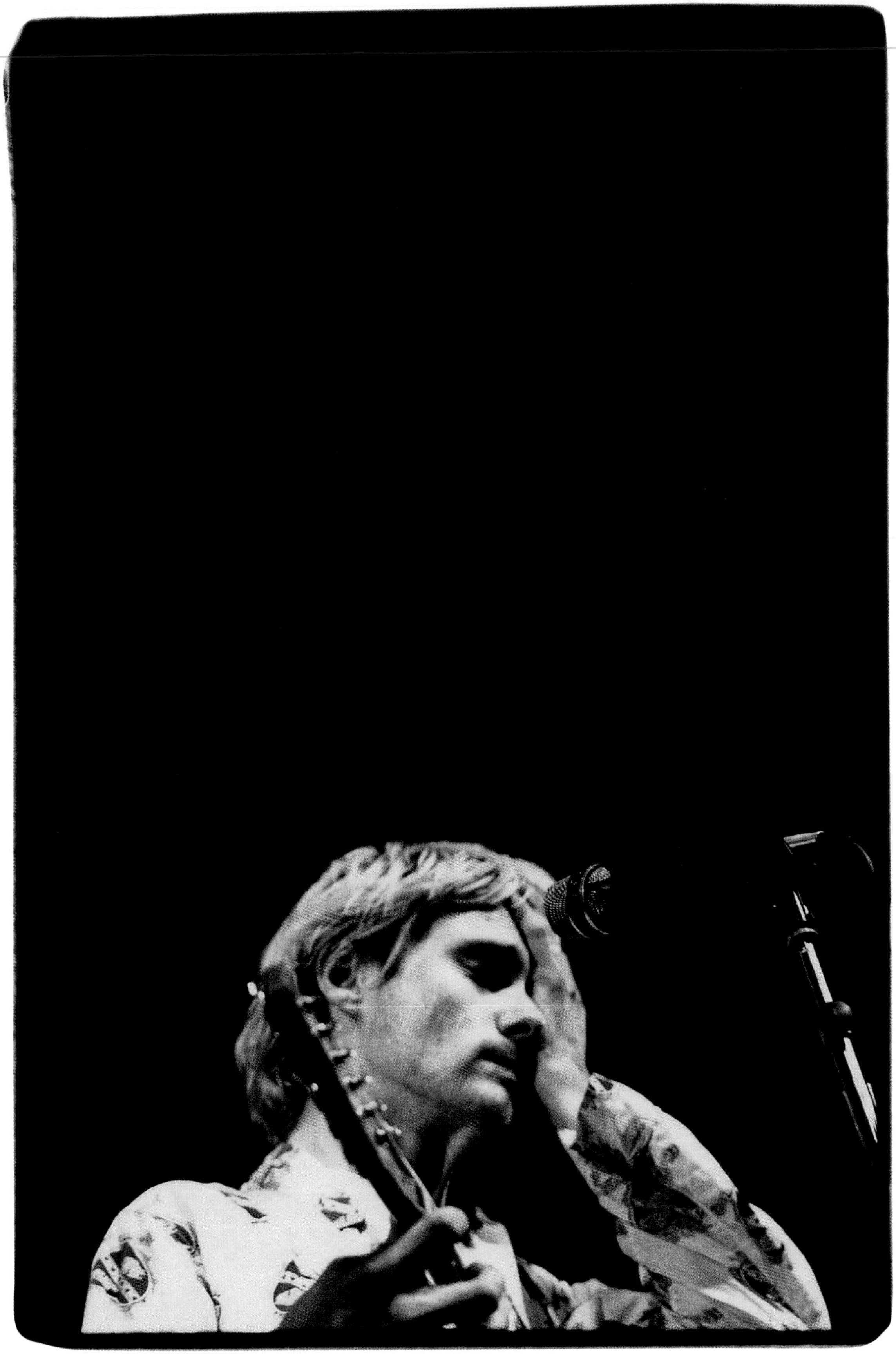

• The touring begins to take its toll. Onstage 1992 •

AUGUST/SEPTEMBER 1992:

Kurt works on the Melvins' *Houdini* record at Razor's Edge Studio in San Francisco and at Brilliant Studios. He produces seven songs and plays guitar on one song, "Sky Pup." Jack Endino, who recorded some of Nirvana's early work, including *Bleach*, tells *Goldmine* that Kurt called him for advice before producing *Houdini* because he'd never produced a band before.

AUGUST 4, 1992:

Kurt checks himself into Cedars-Sinai Medical Center in LA to detox from drugs once again, spending approximately 25 days there. This time he can't just take Methadone and sweat it out in his apartment; instead, he's more weak and very sick and hooked up to an IV. Eric Erlandson was there during this time for support.

Kurt had always maintained that he wasn't a junkie for very long. "I did heroin for three weeks," he would later tell the *Los Angeles Times*. "Then I went through a detox program, but my stomach started up again on tour. I was vomiting really bad... couldn't hold anything down."

AUGUST 7, 1992:

Courtney checks herself into Cedars-Sinai on this date, which is two weeks before the baby was due. The *Los Angeles Times'* Steve Hochman reported that Courtney had checked into the hospital under an assumed name, and that "a pregnant woman identified by a hospital source as the San Francisco-born singer was receiving daily doses of prenatal vitamins and Methadone, a heroin substitute used to treat narcotics addiction." The *Times* story goes on to describe further who this person is by saying that the woman's admission record states Kurt as her husband and Eric Erlandson as the second contact.

However, Courtney has said that she checked into the hospital early for fear of what she might do to herself after reading an advance copy of the *Vanity Fair* article that claimed she was using heroin while pregnant.

AUGUST 8, 1992:

Chris Novoselic was going to sit in with the Seattle band the Posies at the EndFest at the Kitsap County Fairgrounds in Bremerton, Washington, but it didn't happen.

"There was the rumor that he was going to sit in with us," says the Posies' drummer Mike Musburger. "Dave Fox, our new bass player, actually played his first big show with us that day and I think he wore a shirt that said 'Chris Novoselic' because it was in the newspaper that he was gonna play with us."

On the charts, "Lithium" debuts at No. 69 on the *Billboard* Hot 100 chart.

AUGUST 11–15, 1992:

The September issue of *Vanity Fair*, featuring the Lynn Hirschberg article "Strange Love," hits the newsstands nationwide. Courtney's comment – "We got high and went to SNL. After that, I did heroin for a couple of months." – made it look as though Courtney was admitting to doing heroin while pregnant, because she had previously been quoted saying she knew she was pregnant around the time of Nirvana's SNL appearance. It is believed that this article is what prompted the Los Angeles Department of Children's Services to investigate, and

eventually take Kurt and Courtney's baby away from them temporarily.

Courtney later explains to the *Advocate*: "When I first talked to her, I had just found out that I was pregnant, and I had done some drugs in the beginning of my pregnancy, that's what I told her." Kurt's response in the press was a bit more irrational. He says in *Come As You Are*, "First I'm going to take her dog and slit its guts out in front of her and then shit all over her and stab her to death."

"It drove Courtney crazy and she drove him crazy about it, and it literally caused the county to challenge custody [of Frances Bean]," says Danny Goldberg of the situation.

Kurt and Courtney issued a statement about the article through their management that claims the story "contains many inaccuracies and distortions, and generally gives a false picture of both of us." They "unequivocally deny" the allegations that she used heroin while pregnant.

"Because we were stupid enough to do drugs at one time, we realize that we opened ourselves up to gossip by people in the rock world who want desperately to pretend they have some inside information on famous people," they say in the statement. "We never dreamed that such gossip would be reported as if it were true without us even having the ability to comment on it, especially when the gossip reflects on such a personal and important event as the birth of our first child."

AUGUST 14, 1992:

Entertainment Weekly reports, "The opiate invasion can be observed in microcosm in Seattle, alternative rock's hot spot and the fastest-growing capital for heroin overdoses in America" and that there is a "225% increase in heroin-related emergency room visits."

AUGUST 15, 1992:

"Lithium" peaks at No. 64 on *Billboard*'s Hot 100 chart.

AUGUST 18, 1992:

"You get out of this bed and you come down now. You are not leaving me to do this by myself, fuck you," screamed Courtney at Kurt after wheeling her IV stand down the hall to the room where her husband was detoxing from drugs.

With Kurt – who passed out during the birth due to his fragile state – by her side, Courtney gave birth to a healthy baby girl, who weighed in at 7 pounds and 1 ounce at 7:48 a.m. at Cedars-Sinai Medical Center. Frances Bean is named after Frances McKee of the Vaselines, and not after the late actress Frances Farmer as most had thought. Her middle name was chosen because the couple thought she look like a bean in the sonogram.

"I'm just glad I had a girl, but I want to have a son with him too. Just so I can help him make up for the relationship he never had [with his father]," Courtney told the *Los Angeles Times* just prior to her husband's death.

The good news of a healthy baby was soon overshadowed by the visits from the social workers who had already begun taking steps to take Frances Bean away from Kurt and Courtney. Courtney later tells the *Rocket*, "This has hurt us incredibly. When I had Frances, tabloid reporters from the *Enquirer* and the *Globe* were being dragged off my floor at the hospital. People were going through my garbage and my faxes. My medical records were xeroxed and sent to the *Los Angeles Times.* Social workers were coming into my room with *Vanity Fair* under their arm – 'I've heard you did all these drugs during your pregnancy and we want to send your child to a foster home!' I had to hire a lawyer just to deal with that!"

AUGUST 19, 1992:

"[Kurt] brought a gun to the hospital the day after our daughter was born," Courtney told *Rolling Stone* in 1994. "I was like, 'I'll go first. I can't have you do it first. I'll go first.'" Wondering what Frances would think knowing that her parents killed themselves the day after she was born, they handed the gun over to Eric Erlandson.

• **New arrival: Kurt and Frances Bean Cobain** •

AUGUST 23, 1992:

The aforementioned *Los Angeles Times* article by Steve Hochman that alleges a woman fitting Courtney Love's description checked into Cedars and began Methadone treatment on August 7 is published on this day. This article is the subject of the lawsuit filed by Courtney against her former doctor Michael Horwitz and Cedars-Sinai Medical Center, where she gave birth to the healthy Frances Bean just five days earlier.

Steve Hochman explains how the story unfolded: "I got a call from a man, who called himself Sore Throat [Yes, like Watergate's Deep Throat], and he told me that Courtney had checked into the hospital under an assumed name. He said her behavior was atrocious and she was very cavalier about the drug thing, and just nasty. We arranged a meeting, but before that I went to the hospital to see if there was indeed someone under that name checked in, and I found that there was.

"So, I met with this person in a lab coat," Steve continues. "But I didn't even want to know his name – if it went to court I wanted to honestly say I didn't now who it was. He looked like a doctor, but it could've been an orderly dressed as a doctor, so I told him that I needed something more concrete before I would do the story. He pulls out a file from his coat pocket and it was her main records chart. It had the alias on it, but it listed Kurt as the husband and it had her birth date and listed Eric Erlandson as the second contact. And it very clearly stated that she was being treated with Methadone."

Meanwhile, Nirvana had a Seattle Center Coliseum show scheduled on this date, but it was postponed until September 11.

AUGUST 27, 1992:

The *Globe* article, "Rock Star's Baby is Born a Junkie," hits newsstands. The article, dated September 8, 1992, states: "They've got money and fame but no damn heart. Nirvana singer's pregnant wife boasted they took heroin – now tiny tot pays the shocking price." The article featured a grossly underdeveloped newborn that was *not* Frances, and quotes "sources" claiming that Courtney was "spaced out" during the birth and that Frances was suffering from "agonizing withdrawal."

Gold Mountain quickly issues a statement saying, "The vicious rumors that Frances was suffering any withdrawals at the time of birth are completely false, and in fact, she has not suffered any discomfort since delivery." Everybody who saw the blonde-haired, blue-eyed baby shortly after her birth – and even to this day – can vouch for the fact that Frances is a beautiful, healthy child.

AUGUST 28, 1992:

Amidst rumors of a Nirvana break-up, speculation on the health of Frances Bean, and concern over Kurt's physical state, Nirvana leave for London for their appearance at the Reading Festival in Reading, England.

"The biggest thing that affected me was all the insane rumors, the heroin rumors... All this speculation going on. I felt totally violated. I never realized that my private life would be such an issue," Kurt tells the *LA Times'* Robert Hilburn, citing the reason why he says he "must have quit the band about 10 different times" in the last year.

AUGUST 30, 1992:

Kurt Cobain is slowly pushed out on to the stage at the Reading Festival in a wheelchair and wearing a white hospital gown and a Courtney-looking wig. With a lot of faux effort, he lifts himself from the chair toward the microphone and pretends to collapse to the floor, and then jumps back up and starts singing "The Rose" by Bette Midler. Nirvana is back and seemingly debunking all of the pre-arrival rumors.

Chris Novoselic has said this show was the tour highlight of the year. "I have to say that hearing tens of thousands of people sing along with 'Lithium' was a very cool moment in the history of the band," he wrote in the *From the Muddy Banks of the Wishkah* liner notes.

The set also includes, ironically, Boston's "More Than a Feeling," which "Smells Like Teen Spirit" has drawn comparisons to, Fang's "The Money Will Roll Right In," and closes with the American National Anthem, "The Star Spangled Banner." Onstage, the band jokes around about whether this is their last show or not ("This is our last show... 'til the next one," remarked Kurt), and Kurt tells the crowd that Courtney thinks everyone hates her, so he asked the thousands gathered to yell, 'We love you, Courtney." Kurt dedicates "All Apologies" to his wife and newborn baby.

Also onstage is Tony, the dancer, wearing plaid trousers with God Is Gay painted on his chest, which is something Kurt spray-painted over Aberdeen, Washington in his teens. Someone in the band joked that, "Tony, the dancer, wrote every song we're playing tonight."

AUGUST 31, 1992:

The Courtney Love backlash continues with this poignant Letter to the Editor in the *LA Times* from Daniel J. Bulla of Van Nuys, California: "John chose Yoko. Kurt chose Courtney. How can geniuses be so stupid? Are the Gods just dorky humans after all? Oh well, Nevermind."

Late August/Early September 1992: About two weeks after the birth of the healthy Frances Bean, the Los Angeles County Children's Department takes Frances away from the Cobains and orders Kurt back to rehab for 30 days. The baby is put in the temporary care of Courtney's sister Jamie, and neither Kurt nor Courtney are allowed to be alone with their child for one month. After that, they were ordered by the court to submit to regular urine tests and visits from a social worker.

Living in the apartment next to Courtney's sister, the Cobains saw their child every day, but weren't free from the watchful eye of Children's Services for another six months. They estimated that they spent approximately $240,000 in 1992 in legal fees all because of the *Vanity Fair* article.

SEPTEMBER 2, 1992:

Axl Rose bashes Kurt and Courtney onstage at Guns N' Roses' Citrus Bowl show in Orlando, Florida. Taken from a Real Audio clip of his spiel, Axl starts out ranting about the word "alternative" and what it's supposed to mean.

Then he says, "I think that the problem starts when you start thinking that you're different from everybody else on the fucking planet. You may be a little different in what you're doing and how you go about doing it. But I've got a good feeling that you're probably a human. Right? You're probably a human being? And so right now, alternative, the only thing that means to me is someone like Kurt

● **The proud new parents** ●

Cobain in Nirvana, who basically is a fucking junkie with a junkie wife. And if the baby's born deformed, I think they both oughta go to prison. That's my feeling. He's too good and too cool to bring his rock and roll to you, because the majority of you he doesn't like or want to play to or even have you like his music… I don't know, you can tell me that you really like to be alienated, but I think underneath it all you're probably nothing but a double-talking jive mother fucker."

SEPTEMBER 8, 1992:
Nirvana messes around with "Rape Me" and a new song called "New Poopy" at their sound check for the MTV awards. MTV catches wind of it and asks the band to play one of their hits instead – either "Smells Like Teen Spirit" or "Lithium."

SEPTEMBER 9, 1992:
When Kurt started strumming the first few bars of "Rape Me" live on MTV, the network's executives collectively cringed, fearing the song's lyrics weren't quite right for mainstream America. The joke on MTV only lasted a few seconds, as the band quickly went into "Lithium" at the 1992 MTV Video Music Awards, held at UCLA's Pauley Pavilion in Los Angeles.

This is also the infamous night of the Axl Rose incident in which Kurt and Courtney jokingly ask Axl to be the godfather of Frances, and then his supermodel girlfriend Stephanie Seymour asked Courtney if she was a model. Courtney's response? "Are you a brain surgeon?" Kurt gets the best and last word when Axl tells him to shut his bitch up, and Kurt turns to Courtney and goes, "Shut up, bitch." Also backstage, Courtney and Eddie Vedder danced.

Onstage, Chris clocks himself in the head when he throws his bass in the air and fails to catch it, knocking himself to the ground. Irked by the media, the band isn't too keen on the idea of accepting their awards, so they send up a Michael Jackson impersonator to pick up their first award of the night for Best Alternative Video for "Smells Like Teen Spirit." Kurt finally goes up for the second award, Best New Artist, and looks straight into the camera and says, "You know, it's really hard to believe everything you read."

This is also the first date that Kurt and Courtney are required by the courts to submit urine samples for drug testing, in order to keep Frances Bean in their care.

SEPTEMBER 10, 1992:
Nirvana performs at a benefit concert at Portland Meadows Racetrack for the "No On 9" campaign to protest Oregon's Initiative 9, which would limit homosexuals' rights. Kurt talks about the Axl Rose incident at the MTV Awards onstage. Helmet, Poison Idea, and Calamity Jane are on the bill, and Dead Kennedys' Jello Biafra is the emcee. The benefit raises $25,000.

"It was one of his off nights – Kurt was out of tune and he sounded whiney," recalls Helmet's Page Hamilton. "Backstage, he's kind of slouched back and was a scrawny little guy and he just looked sickly. He didn't look healthy at all. It didn't have anything to do with heroin, that certainly didn't help him, but he just looked like he wasn't healthy anyway."

• Winding up and winding down on stage •

• Axl Rose and friend •

SEPTEMBER 11, 1992:

Nirvana plays a triumphant homecoming show at the Seattle Center Coliseum with Helmet and Fitz of Depression on the bill. The gig benefits the anti-censorship organization, the Washington Music Industry Coalition.

"This followed the MTV awards, and there were all these rumors that they couldn't do it. And ultimately I look at this show as sort of Kurt's 'Fuck you' to the critics," says Charles R. Cross. "And he really intended to do an awesome show, if for no other reason than to prove that he could. It was the American version of Reading. This was his hometown, and from the first moment it's completely rocking. It was Kurt's return to Seattle. The resurrection of Kurt Cobain in Seattle, really."

Kurt also goes into a long diatribe about how they were banned from Seattle, relating an incident at the venue a few years ago where he and Chris got into some trouble and they were put on a list of people "banned for life" from the venue. Thus this show is know as the "Banned for Life" show, according to Charles.

Gillian G. Gaar noted in the *Rocket* that the floor looked like the world's largest mosh pit. "The Coliseum held about 15,000 people," says Gillian. "I was in the stands, and I remember looking at the main floor and it just seemed like the entire floor was jumping up and down."

Kurt's father, Don Cobain, found his way backstage. He hadn't seen his son in several years, and had never met his daughter-in-law or granddaughter. Kurt later told Jon Savage in *Guitar World* that he was happy to see him because he wanted him to know that he didn't hate him anymore; however, "I didn't want to encourage our relationship because I just didn't have anything to say to him."

SEPTEMBER 12, 1992:

Many of the thousands of fans at Lollapalooza '92 at Irvine Meadows Amphitheater in Irvine, California, an hour's drive from Los Angeles, were fooled into thinking that Kurt Cobain joined Pearl Jam onstage to help sing Neil Young's "Rockin' in the Free World." Pearl Jam's Eddie Vedder introduced a guy wearing a wig that looked like Kurt's trademark unwashed blonde hair as Kurt, but it was actually drummer Jack Irons (a friend of Eddie's who later joined Pearl Jam).

SEPTEMBER 14, 1992:

The *Los Angeles Times* mistakenly runs a review of Lollapalooza that says Kurt performed at the show.

SEPTEMBER 21, 1992:

Kurt Cobain tries to set the record straight about his drug use in a *Los Angeles Times* article by Robert Hilburn. This is Kurt's first major interview in nearly a year.

"I don't want my daughter to grow up and someday be hassled by kids at school," he told the paper. "I don't want people telling her that her parents were junkies... I can't tell you how much my attitude has changed since we've got Frances. Holding my baby is the best drug in the world."

SEPTEMBER 22, 1992:

A letter written on this date by Courtney's new doctor, Robert P. Fremont, explains what the Cobains had to go through in order to keep their daughter. The letter, published in *Courtney Love: The Real Story* by Poppy Z. Brite, reads: "Starting September 9, 1992 [Courtney] has been given random urine tests which have all been entirely clean. She is seeing a drug counselor, a clinical psychologist, attending aftercare meetings at CPC Westwood and is examined in my office weekly. She seems determined to succeed and her prognosis is very good with the above safeguards in place."

SEPTEMBER 25, 1992:

William S. Burroughs records his part of "The 'Priest' They Called Him" at Red House Studios in Lawrence, Kansas. The 10-inch vinyl release featured vocals by Burroughs and guitar by Kurt Cobain, who recorded his parts at Laundry Room Studios in Seattle in November 1992.

SEPTEMBER 26, 1992:

Kurt joins Sonic Youth and Mudhoney onstage at their show at Castaic Lake Natural Amphitheater in Valencia, California. He performs "Where

Did You Sleep Last Night?" solo, and then joins Mudhoney on guitar for "The Money Will Roll Right In."

SEPTEMBER 28, 1992:

Now it's Courtney's turn to play a solo show. She performs a brief set at the cozy Largo on Robertson Boulevard in West Hollywood, California for a benefit for the Bohemian Women's Political Alliance. Kurt is in attendance. She performs two songs: "Doll Parts" and Nirvana's "Pennyroyal Tea," telling the crowd she co-wrote the song with Kurt; however, the album doesn't credit her as a co-writer.

"Love and Cobain have made more news offstage than on in the past several months, much of it centering on drug problems, but lately they've cut the Sid and Nancy act and have been busily clearing the

air," writes Richard Cromelin in his *LA Times* review of the show. "What tends to get lost in this sideshow is that Love has the makings of a striking artist."

OCTOBER 3, 1992:

Nirvana plays an unannounced show at Western Washington University's Carver Gymnasium in Bellingham, Washington, which is about two hours from Seattle. They're actually the opening band for Mudhoney.

At the end of the set, Mudhoney's Matt Lukin brings two kids – around 10 years old – onstage. Chris Novoselic hands one kid a bass, and Kurt and Matt hand the other kid a guitar, and the crowd starts chanting, "Smash it! Smash it!" The kid with the bass does.

● Dave Grohl gets angry ●

"It was a really fun show," says Nils Bernstein. "They were really upbeat, and they had those kids onstage, so it was just really fun. There were a ton of people from Seattle who road-tripped up for the show, and they had a huge backstage area. Dave and Chris put me in this kayak and rammed me through the wall."

OCTOBER 4, 1992:

The last of the secret, unannounced shows of the year is at the Crocodile Café in Seattle. Once again, they open for Mudhoney. Kurt addresses the crowd saying, "I want to thank you all for coming. We just wanted to know what it felt like to be an alternative band in a nightclub again." Then he paused, according to the *Seattle Times*, and quipped, "Do you know how much money we have?"

"Courtney was sitting out at the diner counter, and she was wearing Kurt's coat, the big brown one with the fleece, during Mudhoney's set," recalls Gillian, "and Kurt came out jokingly pulling on her arm, 'Come on, let's go watch inside.' And she goes, 'No I'd rather just sit here.' It was just kind of sweet to watch them like that. They seemed relaxed. During the show, Kurt asked if there were any requests, and Chris leans over and in this funny voice goes, 'Play "Teen Spirit"' Play "Teen Spirit." They didn't play "Teen Spirit." It was probably one of the few shows at that time where they didn't have to play it." During Mudhoney's set, Kurt got onstage to play guitar during one song, then dove into the crowd.

The day of the show, Courtney did an interview with Gillian for the *Rocket* to tell her side of the *Vanity Fair* story. "At the end of the day, people can make up their own mind about Courtney. We just wanted to give her a chance to say her side, which she did," says Gillian, who found Courtney to be a bit defensive, a bit self-deprecating, and very funny during the interview. "She and Kurt were planning to move back to Seattle at the time, and she kind of said that she wanted to let people know who they were, you know, clear the way a little. Because they actually didn't do many interviews right after the *Vanity Fair* article."

OCTOBER 6, 1992:

Chris Novoselic, Dave Grohl, Mudhoney's manager Bobby Whitiker, Posies' Mike Musburger and Ken Stringfellow, and the Fastbacks' Kim Warnick attend the Metallica/Guns N' Roses show at the Kingdome in Seattle. Backstage, Chris gets drunk and is almost thrown out.

"After that whole debacle about opening for Guns N' Roses, Chris and Dave went to the show that year, on the tour they were asked to be on," recalls Mike Musburger. "And I didn't see everything that went down, but Chris and Bobby were so damn drunk they were like mock fighting everywhere they went and getting security on them in the hospitality area. They would knock over a table, cause a huge scene."

Security was about to throw them out until one guard recognized Chris and let them stay. "A Metallica roadie came out and bitched at them about disrespecting their scene, or something like that. It was great," he says. Mike was standing next to Chris and Dave during GNR's

"set and everyone was "joking about how bad they were. I thought it was kind of funny that they were there, but it's Seattle and it's a huge rock show, so why not?"

OCTOBER 22, 1992:

Victoria Clarke and Britt Collins, two Seattle-based British writers who were working on an unauthorized biography of Nirvana, claimed that Kurt Cobain left a threatening message on their answering machine on this day.

The message says: "This is Kurt Cobain. [long pause] If anything comes out in this book that hurts my wife, I'll fucking hurt you. I don't care if this is a recorded threat. I'm at the end of my ropes. You'll understand when you see me in person. I've never been more fucking serious in my life... I suppose I could throw out a few thousand dollars and have you snuffed, but maybe I'll try it the legal way first."

After hearing the messages, Victoria moved out of her Seattle house and down to LA because she was afraid of the couple. "I knew they weren't joking. It was serious," Victoria says in *Kurt & Courtney*. Danny Goldberg's response at the time was, "Kurt absolutely denies the notion that he or any member of the band made such phone calls." It is soon learned that it was indeed Kurt's voice on the tape, which was circulated around the music industry at the time and later aired in the documentary *Kurt & Courtney*.

The book the two writers were working on was tentatively titled *Nirvana: Flower Sniffin', Kitty Pettin', Baby Kissin' Corporate Rock Whores* (an early T-shirt motto). The writers have claimed that the band initially authorized the book. However, when the writers interviewed one of the couple's many enemies, *Vanity Fair*'s Lynn Hirschberg, and started digging up more dirt on the couple, Kurt and Courtney got upset and tried to halt the publication of the book. Gold Mountain, which maintains that the band never agreed to participate in the book, soon called potential interviewees and warned them not to talk.

OCTOBER 23-31, 1992:

Between these days, more threatening messages were left on Victoria Clarke and Britt Collins' answering machine from Courtney over the book the two were writing.

"I will never fucking forgive you," says Courtney in one of the answering machine messages. "As a matter of fact, I will haunt you two fucking cunts for the rest of your God damn lives... You're gonna pay and pay and pay and pay out your ass and that's a fact... Your fucking list of enemies is gonna be longer than you can wrap your fucking finger around and you're gonna be so fucking humiliated this time next week you're gonna wish you never were born."

Courtney at first denied the she left the messages, telling the *Seattle Times*, "We were in Argentina like that whole week." But then she later told *Entertainment Weekly*, "Imagine if you were being harassed [by writers] and you called them up and you go, 'Fuck you, stop it, leave me

"...YOU'RE GONNA PAY AND PAY AND PAY AND PAY OUT YOUR ASS AND THAT'S A FACT..."

> **"...THEY WERE JUST OOHING AND AAHING AND BEING TYPICAL DISGUSTING PARENTS. BUT AROUND THE BAND, HE WAS TENSE."**

alone'... I don't think it's that bad. I mean, I know we're right. I mean, we might have been mean to them, but they violated us and raped us, and it's just scary. I remember saying, like, 'I'll fucking haunt you 'til you fucking die,' and I meant it, because this kind of shit cannot go on."

OCTOBER 24-25, 1992:

Nirvana work with producer Jack Endino to lay down some demos for *In Utero* at Word of Mouth Studios, the studio formerly known as Reciprocal. They record "Dumb," "Heart-Shaped Box," "Pennyroyal Tea," "Rape Me," "tourette's," and "Scentless Apprentice." The only track that was recorded with vocals was "Rape Me."

"Kurt acted like he could hardly be bothered to be there," says Jack. "He did vocals on one song and then left, not even taking a cassette rough mix. No one ever called to ask for one either, either band or label. The songs were left unfinished. Partly this was because of Frances Bean who was only a few weeks old at the time, so can you blame him? Courtney brought Frances down to the studio on the second night and I remember thinking what a perfect little family they appeared to be right at that second. They were just oohing and aahing and being typical disgusting parents. But around the band, he was tense."

The band chose to record on the same 8-track machine that was used for *Bleach*.

OCTOBER 25, 1992:

Nirvana hangs out with Joshua Hardy, a 17-year-old with a brain tumor, as part of a Make-A-Wish Foundation dream come true promotion. Make-A-Wish is a non-profit organization that fulfils the dreams of terminally ill children. Joshua's wish was to hang out with his favorite Seattle bands, including Nirvana and some other bands.

"They met at [Sub Pop] for pizza; it was pretty low key," says Susan McConnell, the marketing director for Make-A-Wish Foundation at the time. "Kurt wasn't there at first, he was late, and the other guys were very nice to this young man. He had come all the way from New Hampshire to meet them and he passed away about four to five months after that."

OCTOBER 26, 1992:

Victoria Clarke files a police report with the Seattle Police claiming that Kurt Cobain left threatening messages on her answering machine about the unauthorized biography she was writing on the band.

The police report reads, "The victim reported that the suspect had called and left a long, hostile, threatening message on her answering machine. The victim said that she and a colleague are writing a book about the rock band. The suspect is upset about some of the book's material. The victim is afraid the suspect will take action on those threats."

OCTOBER 30, 1992:

Nirvana performs at Velez Sarsfield Stadium in Buenos Aires, Argentina in front of approximately 50,000 people. Calamity Jane opened, but much to Kurt's dismay, the crowd heckled them. And instead of the audience chanting "Nirvana! Nirvana!," this time they yelled "Cobain! Cobain!"

OCTOBER 1992:

Sometime this month, Nirvana shoots the "In Bloom" video with director Kevin Kerslake. Courtney and Frances accompanied the band on shoot, which was held at Sunset Stage Studios in Hollywood and shot on the old-fashioned Kinescopes parodying "The Ed Sullivan Show." Three versions were shot: one with the band in dresses, one with the band in suits and dresses, and another with the band in suits. Some of the footage was shot in black and white.

Geffen's Art Director at the time, Robert Fisher, was there for part of the shoot. "They looked like they were having fun," he says, "but by that time there were a lot of hangers-on. I was only there for a few hours to talk about the artwork." Initially, the three versions were going to be rolled out to MTV one by one, but that didn't happen as planned. The second version, the hybrid of the band in suits and in dresses, was released to MTV first and it's this clip that wins the 1993 MTV Video Music Award.

Also in October, Julian Cope, who Courtney was friends with while she lived in London, places an ad in the British press that indirectly attacks Courtney. "Free us (the rock and roll fans) from Nancy Spungen-fixated heroin a-holes who cling to our greatest rock groups and suck out their brains." Courtney told *Q*, "It hurt me so much. Yeah, I'm insane and crazy, but I didn't do anything inappropriate, weird or bad."

NOVEMBER 1, 1992:

Danny Goldberg tells the *New York Times* that the threatening messages alleged to have been left on Victoria Clarke's answering machine are either a "prank that someone has played on these women or this is something they are fabricating to publicize an unauthorized biography. The band is not very happy about the book, based on what they know about it."

NOVEMBER 2, 1992:

A Washington state Superior Court judge in King County strikes down the five-month-old Erotic Music Bill, which Governor Booth Gardner signed in March and Nirvana opposed. The bill, #2554, banned the sale of offensive music to minors and was the subject of a lawsuit filed in June by the Washington Music Industry Coalition.

NOVEMBER 10, 1992:

Pansy Division covers "Smells Like Teen Spirit" with an alternate title of "Smells Like Queer Spirit." The song is released as the B-side to their single on Lookout! Records, "Fem in a Black Leather Jacket."

"In the spring of '92, we were driving down to LA to play our first out-of-town show," says Jon Ginoli, lead singer/guitarist of the San Francisco-based, all-gay rock band Pansy Division. "And 'Teen Spirit' came on the radio; it had been months after the song was out and we still couldn't figure out the words. So we thought, well, here are some

● **Sunglasses... to hide behind?** ●

really well concealed lyrics, what if they're gay? What if the reason we can't understand these lyrics is because they're really gay and they're trying to sneak something on the radio. So then we thought, if they were gay lyrics, what would they say? So we basically wrote a whole set of gay lyrics to 'Smells Like Teen Spirit.' It wasn't a slap at Nirvana, we weren't making fun of them, we were making fun of the fact that we had no idea what the song was about."

Here's a sample of the "Smells Like Gay Spirit" lyrics:

Against all odds, we appear
Grew up brainwashed, but turned out queer
Bunsplitters, rugmunchers too
We screw just how we want to screw
Hello hello hello homo...

Impressed with Nirvana's pro-gay stance, Pansy Division also included this on the sleeve to the single: "With kisses to Nirvana. No superstar American rock band has ever before had the guts to take on such an overtly pro-gay stance. Right on." Kurt Cobain told British writer Jon Savage that the note was "a real flattering thing."

NOVEMBER 11, 1992:

DGC sends advance cassettes of *Incesticide*, the compilation of demos, B-sides, and outtakes, to the press, which welcomed it with great reviews. The album's sarcastic working titles were *Filler* and *Throw-Aways*.

"It was like, we're selling so many records, let's put something together for the Christmas season," explains Lisa Gladfelter Bell of the impetus to release new Nirvana product at this time. Chris Novoselic told *Rolling Stone* that they decided to release the collection because, "We thought it would be something nice for the fans just to see where we're coming from. Some of the stuff's kind of wild."

NOVEMBER 15, 1992:

With the meteoric rise of Nirvana came more stories on the Seattle scene, grunge, and grunge-wear. But the most ridiculous came when the author of the *New York Times* article on "Grunge: A Success Story" was tricked into thinking there was a lexicon of grunge. Irked by the media coverage of all things Seattle, Megan Jasper, who was with Caroline Records at the time, decided to toy with the *Times* by giving fictitious words and their equally fictitious grunge meanings. Such as Wack Slacks = old ripped jeans; Lamestain = uncool person.

"This total goofball called up and he said, 'Hi. I was referred to you by Jonathan Pon-Man,' which is not how his name is pronounced. I said, uh-huh. 'He told me you have the lexicon of grunge words.' And I just thought, 'Oh, my God.' It was crazy. I was just making up words that rhyme with each other. You take words like riddle and biddle and cat and shat and mix and match them like mixing up Garanimal tags. And all I could hear was this typing in the background. He didn't even take a

moment to think about what I was saying. At the time, you have to understand, there were so many magazines and newspapers and A&R people up here, it had really become an invasion. The city was completely torn open. There were lots of ways that people could say 'Fuck you,' and this was just one of them."

NOVEMBER 30, 1992:

The third single from *Nevermind*, "In Bloom," is released backed with "Sliver" and a live version of "Polly." On "In Bloom," Courtney Love tells the *Los Angeles Times*: "I felt his voice… that sadness. You know the idea that every abused child in America bought Nirvana's album? It's so right. I felt a comfort and soul in his voice… a solace that I needed."

NOVEMBER 1992:

Kurt records his vocal parts for the 10-inch he did with William S. Burroughs, "The 'Priest' They Called Him." Kurt told *Spin's* Darcy Steinke that the project "probably pleases me more than it pleases anybody else." Thor Lindsay of T/K once gave Kurt a signed first edition of Burroughs' *Naked Lunch* for which he is thanked in the liner notes to *Incesticide*. Meanwhile, Kurt and Courtney move back to Seattle.

• **Going gold gold gold** •

DECEMBER 4, 1992:

Kurt and Courtney attend Mudhoney's show at the Palace in Los Angeles.

DECEMBER 15, 1992:

The 15-song *Incesticide* is released. The lengthy liner notes, written by "Kurdt (the blond one)", serves as a letter to all those who have scorned him and his wife. In it he states that none of the musical experiences he's had over the years "were half as rewarding as having a baby with a person who is the supreme example of dignity, ethics and honesty." He also gives a "big fuck you to those of you who have the audacity to claim that I'm so naïve and stupid that I would allow myself to be taken advantage of and manipulated." More importantly, Kurt airs his anger toward the "two wastes of sperm and eggs" who raped a girl in 1991 while they sang the lyrics to "Polly."

DECEMBER 18, 1992:

As early as 15 months after the release of their major-label debut, and amidst the drug rumors, break-up rumors, and rock and roll shenanigans, the press starts wondering how long the chaos can last. The *Buffalo News* writes "Will Nirvana Survive the Hype?"

DECEMBER 23, 1992:

Courtney Love's attorneys at the LA-based law firm Novian, Novian & Younesi draw up papers to sue Cedars-Sinai Medical Center and Courtney's former doctor, Dr. Michael Horwitz, over allegedly leaking Love's medical records to the *LA Times*, which ran in their August 23, 1992 article. The lawsuit is filed six days later.

DECEMBER 25, 1992:

More absurd press spurred by Nirvana's success is published. The "Grunge-A-Go-Go" article runs in the *LA Times*. Also on newsstands this month is *Vogue* magazine's 10-page fashion spread on grunge-wear. Teenage fans flock to stores to get the "Nirvana look" of flannels, Converse sneakers, long johns, and lots of layers. Layering for Kurt was merely a way to look bigger than his frail 5'7", 125-pound frame.

"Things just got so crazy. It irritates me now," says Gillian. "People said it was Seattle's turn to have a big scene; it was Atlanta before and Minneapolis. But there was something different about the way the media just started getting really out of control. There wasn't anything about what the people in Minneapolis wore, or what the people in Atlanta drank. Pretty soon it wasn't just the bands, it was pretty much everything about the Northwest. For us, it was grunge-wear, flannel, micro brews, coffee, and heroin. The most ridiculous was the silk flannel shirts meant to look like flannel for $500."

Mike Musburger of the Posies says when grunge fashions hit J.C. Penny, that's when he had to laugh. "A lot of people laughed at it, but they didn't realize what the long-term perceptions of it would be. We were all just wondering, 'How long is this going to go on? What's gonna happen next?'" Today, he's still annoyed that Seattle is known for grunge, coffee, heroin. "We're just a normal American city. We still have a pretty vibrant music scene, people do drink coffee, but they drink coffee everywhere in the world, and people do heroin everywhere in the world too."

DECEMBER 26, 1992:

"In Bloom" debuts at No. 31 on *Billboard*'s Mainstream Rock Tracks chart. In *Billboard*'s 1992 Year-End charts issue, Nirvana ranks No. 2 on Top Billboard 200 Album Artists, Duo or Group; No. 13 of all Top Pop Artists of the year; and No. 2 among Top New Pop Artists, among other accolades.

DECEMBER 29, 1992:

Courtney files a lawsuit (case no. BC 071675) in the Superior Court of the State of California, County of Los Angeles, against Cedars-Sinai Medical Center and her former doctor Michael Horwitz for allegedly revealing her medical records to the press.

Courtney Cobain (whose aliases are listed on the suit as Courtney Love, Courtney Love-Cobain, Courtney Menely, Lorrie Glass, and Michelle Rodriquez) is suing for medical fraud, medical negligence, wrongful disclosure of medical information, invasion of privacy – public disclosure of private facts, invasion of privacy – publicity placing person in false light in public eye, intentional infliction of emotional distress, and negligent infliction of emotional distress. She is seeking more than $250,000 in damages. The suit is settled out of court in April 1993, and the details of the settlement are in a sealed document, which means they are not for public record.

DECEMBER 1992:

Courtney allegedly hits Victoria Clarke in the face with a glass at an LA club. Victoria tells her side of the story in *Kurt & Courtney*: "She sort of grabbed me and attacked me with something. I think it was a glass or something. And I ended up covered in beer on the ground and she pulled me along the floor by my hair and tried to get me outside. It was quite a scary thing." The day after the incident, Victoria filed a complaint with the Los Angeles Police Department. Courtney then filed a counter complaint, saying she was acting in self-defense.

Also this month, trying to show that they're just a normal American family, the Cobains are the subject of a *Spin* story by Jonathan Poneman, co-founder of Nirvana's former label Sub Pop, titled "Family Values," in which Courtney declares, "I just want to have kids by the same person and stay with the same person." In the same issue, Nirvana is named Artist of the Year.

"I JUST WANT TO HAVE KIDS BY THE SAME PERSON AND STAY WITH THE SAME PERSON."

MOMENTS OF BRILLIANCE

JANUARY 1, 1993:

Long-time friend and band photographer Charles Peterson photographs Kurt Cobain at the Four Seasons Olympic Hotel in Seattle for the cover of the *Advocate*, a prominent gay magazine.

"It was nice," Charles told Gillian G. Gaar in the 1997 *Goldmine* story "Verse Chorus Verse: The Recording History of Nirvana." "There were no publicity people. I didn't have an assistant. There was no hair and make-up [person]. It was just in his bedroom at his hotel." The resulting February 9, 1993 *Advocate* sports Kurt on the cover in his pajamas, his favorite form of clothing around this time.

JANUARY 2, 1993:

Incesticide debuts at No. 51 on The Billboard 200. Sub Pop had reportedly wanted to issue a Nirvana collection of rarities called *Cash Cow*, but DGC beat them to the punch. Geffen's head of marketing Robert Smith has said the album was issued to help educate fans on where Nirvana came from. "Nirvana is not just a punk band that got really big," Robert told *Billboard*'s Craig Rosen. "There's a real route of progression to follow."

JANUARY 7, 1993:

The National Academy of Recording Arts and Sciences announces the nominees for the 35th annual Grammy Awards at the Hard Rock Café in NY. Nirvana is nominated for "Smells Like Teen Spirit" in the Best Hard Rock Performance with Vocal category. The song is up against Red Hot Chili Peppers' "Give It Away," Guns N' Roses' "Live and Let Die," Alice in Chains' *Dirt*, Pearl Jam's "Jeremy" and Faith No More's *Angel Dust*.

JANUARY 9, 1993:

Like everything Nirvana released, *Incesticide* garners great reviews in every major and not-so-major publication. *Billboard* wrote: "Although material spans different producers and phases of the young trio, it plays like a deliberately consistent recording – a testament to the band's acute writing and impassioned delivery in any setting. While not the much-anticipated Nirvana studio album, this one will whet fans' appetites until that one is unleashed in the spring."

JANUARY 11, 1993:

In London, the nominations for England's most prestigious awards show, the Brit Awards, are announced. Nirvana grabs one nomination for Best International Newcomer.

JANUARY 13, 1993:

The nominations for the National Association of Recording Merchandisers (NARM)'s Best Seller Awards are announced. Nirvana's *Nevermind* is nominated for Best Selling Alternative Recording, up against R.E.M.'s *Automatic For the People*, Red Hot Chili Peppers' *Blood Sugar Sex Magik*, and Pearl Jam's *Ten*. The album is also up for Best Selling Recording by a Group, against U2's *Achtung Baby*, RHCPs, Pearl Jam, and Metallica's *Metallica*.

JANUARY 14, 1993:

Dave Grohl turns 24 years old.

JANUARY 16, 1993:

Nirvana, L7, Alice in Chains, and the Red Hot Chili Peppers perform at the Hollywood Rocks Festival at the 80,000-seat soccer stadium, Morumbi Stadium, in Sao Paulo, Brazil. The show, one of their biggest, was sponsored by Hollywood cigarettes.

"We had a mental breakdown on the stage and played 'Seasons in the Sun' and ['Rio'] from Duran Duran," recalls Chris Novoselic in an MTV News interview in October 1993. Dave described the show to MTV as "a mess," but Kurt countered, "That was great!" Kurt also revealed to MTV News that "Seasons in the Sun," a No. 1 hit in 1974 for Terry Jacks, was one of his favorite singles from his childhood, and a song he used to cry to.

● Kurt with the acoustic that was to feature increasingly in Nirvana's live act ●

• Early rehearsal sessions for *In Utero* •

Meanwhile, at home, *Incesticide* barely becomes a top 40 album as it reaches its peak position of No. 39 on The Billboard 200.

JANUARY 17, 1993:
The band and their entourage – which included Courtney, Hole's Patty Schemel, sound man Craig Montgomery, and others – fly to Rio de Janeiro where they remain at the Intercontinental Hotel on the beach until January 23. "Brazil was a peak," says Craig. "Definitely. We were doing these big soccer stadiums, and it was fun."

JANUARY 18, 1993:
Before entering the BMG Ariola Studios to record demos for Nirvana's *In Utero* (which had the working titles of *I Hate Myself And I Want To Die*, *Radio Friendly Unit Shifter*, and *Verse Chorus Verse* before *In Utero* was decided

upon in May) and Hole's *Live Through This*, some of the band and crew – including Kurt and Courtney, Patty, Dave, Craig, and others – went hang-gliding over the mountains and on to the beaches of the Atlantic Ocean.

"We had a day off before we went into the studio," recalls Craig. "We were staying a little bit up from the main beaches like Copacabana, down this road a mile or two, where there's some hills and another section of beach. Just behind the hotel, there were these mountains. These guys who were sort of our security guards knew a guy who had a hang-gliding business, so they offered to take us. We were having fun. We were all pretty jazzed to be in Rio; it was really sunny and hot and the hotel had a nice pool. The water at the beach was sort of grungy so we didn't go in there. We had to drive out into woods for a while to get to the top of this hill to hang-glide. We'd cruise around and end up on the beach right in front of the hotel."

JANUARY 19-22, 1993:

Demo recording sessions for *In Utero* and *Live Through This* took about three or four days, according to Craig, though he couldn't recall the exact dates. Among the songs recorded were "Heart-Shaped Box," "Milk It," "Very Ape," (which had the working title of "Perky New Wave Number"), "Gallons of Rubbing Alcohol Flow Through the Strip," (which appears on the European version of *In Utero*), "Closing Time (a.k.a. Drunk in Rio)," and Hole's "Miss World," among others. Some have reported that these sessions were for a Kurt Cobain solo album, but Craig says that is absolutely not true.

"I have a version of 'Heart-Shaped Box' that I think is really cool. It's a warmer sounding [version], more direct, less roomy and diffused. He didn't have all the lyrics together yet, though, at that time," says Craig, who recorded these sessions. "They were just in there doing more demos for *In Utero*, to get more stuff on tape. Five or six songs were done, some songs didn't make *In Utero*. We did everything live in one take with a vocal added if he had the lyrics written. He didn't have many lyrics written, so usually it was just what we call a scratch vocal, which is him singing as we're tracking it live. ['Gallons of Rubbing Alcohol...'] was totally improvisational. It was a jam, but Kurt did this kind of monologue over it with a scream at the end.

"Since we had the studio time and Nirvana didn't have anything else to record, we did some Hole stuff too, including 'Miss World.' Kurt played bass, Courtney sang and played guitar, and Patty's on drums. It wasn't meant to be released, Courtney just wanted to use the time to get some ideas down," continues Craig. "The most fleshed-out song was 'Miss World.' It was a really nice studio with a great board and tape machine and tons of really nice microphones, so we got some neat-sounding stuff."

JANUARY 23, 1993:

The second show in Brazil for the Hollywood Rocks Festival is at Apotoese Stadium in Rio de Janeiro, which seats about 70,000. "I don't think it was quite as good as the first show, just because we were tired," says Craig.

Highlights of the show include Flea from the Red Hot Chili Peppers joining the band onstage to play trumpet during the guitar solo in "Smells Like Teen Spirit." "It's not that they didn't like 'Teen Spirit,' but at the time, they were sort of sick of playing it," says Craig. "So anything they could do to make it different or interesting, they tried to do." This is also the show where Kurt is wearing a black, lacey slip dress, Dave is in a bra, and a 17-minute version of "Scentless Apprentice" is played.

JANUARY 24, 1993:

Nirvana and the gang fly home to Seattle.

JANUARY 30, 1993:

"In Bloom" moves from No. 8 to No. 5 – the highest position it will reach – on *Billboard*'s Mainstream Rock Tracks chart. And the *Ottawa Citizen* declares: "Grunge is history."

EARLY FEBRUARY 1993:

Before heading to Minnesota, Kurt, who had a hard time finding decent left-handed guitars, designed a Fender custom guitar that was a hybrid of a Jaguar and a Mustang. "We were contacted and told that Kurt had an idea for a guitar," Fender's Mark Wittenberg told *Guitar World*. "His favorite guitar was a Mustang, but there were things about the lines of the Jaguar that he really liked too." Mark and Fender's Larry Brooks soon met Kurt in his apartment in the Hollywood Hills to plan what would become the "Jag-Stang."

FEBRUARY 1, 1993:

Courtney Love and writer Victoria Clarke are in a Los Angeles courthouse giving evidence about the alleged incident in which Courtney, angry over the book Victoria was writing on Nirvana, reportedly hit the British scribe in the face with a cocktail glass at a nightclub in Los Angeles in December 1992. This was a preliminary hearing, in which Courtney also admitted that it was indeed her voice on Clarke's answering machine that left the threatening messages in October 1992. The case was adjourned until the end of the month, and ultimately dropped.

FEBRUARY 9, 1993:

The *Advocate* cover story, "The Dark Side of Nirvana's Kurt Cobain," is published. The article, which Kurt set up himself instead of his publicist, is most remembered for his openness about bisexuality ("If I wouldn't have found Courtney, I probably would have carried on a bisexual lifestyle. But I just find her totally attractive in all ways."), and for his biting words about Guns N' Roses ("They're really talent-less people, and they write crap music...")

"He did that himself. Ughhh," groans Lisa Gladfelter Bell, who was at the tail end of her role as Nirvana's publicist at this point. "I just thought he was a loose cannon. I just couldn't believe it. It never does you any good [to talk badly about other bands]. The best thing he could do, if he felt that way about Guns N' Roses, was not say anything instead of going off about it, and being so hurtful. I thought it was wrong, but he called them up and wanted to do an interview. It was again, more damage control, and everyone at the label knew that. When I got a copy [of the article], I was like 'Oh, Jesus Christ.'"

FEBRUARY 14-24, 1993:

Nirvana, checked in as the Simon Ritchie Group (Simon Ritchie is Sid Vicious's real name and the Cobains' alias for checking into hotels while on tour), head to Pachyderm Studios in St. Cloud, Minnesota, outside of Minneapolis, to record *In Utero* with Steve Albini. Steve's hard-core indie rock ethics are just what Nirvana was looking for to make a credible follow-up to the commercial smash of *Nevermind*.

The band records their basic tracks in just six days, costing $24,000 for the studio and $100,000 for Steve Albini's fee. Steve, whose work on the Breeders' *Pod*, the Pixies' *Surfer Rosa*, and his own band Big Black is what impressed the band, didn't take points on the record like most "producers" and prefers to be credited as "recorded by" instead of "produced by."

"We intentionally made an aggressive record," Kurt told *Chicago Sun Times*' Jim DeRogatis about *In Utero*. "I'm proud of the fact that we introduced a different recording style, a different sound, and we're in a position where we're almost guaranteed a chance of it being played on radio." Meanwhile, Steve Albini tells *Billboard*, "The band and I were both

> "If I wouldn't have found Courtney, I probably would have carried on a bisexual lifestyle. But I just find her totally attractive in all ways."

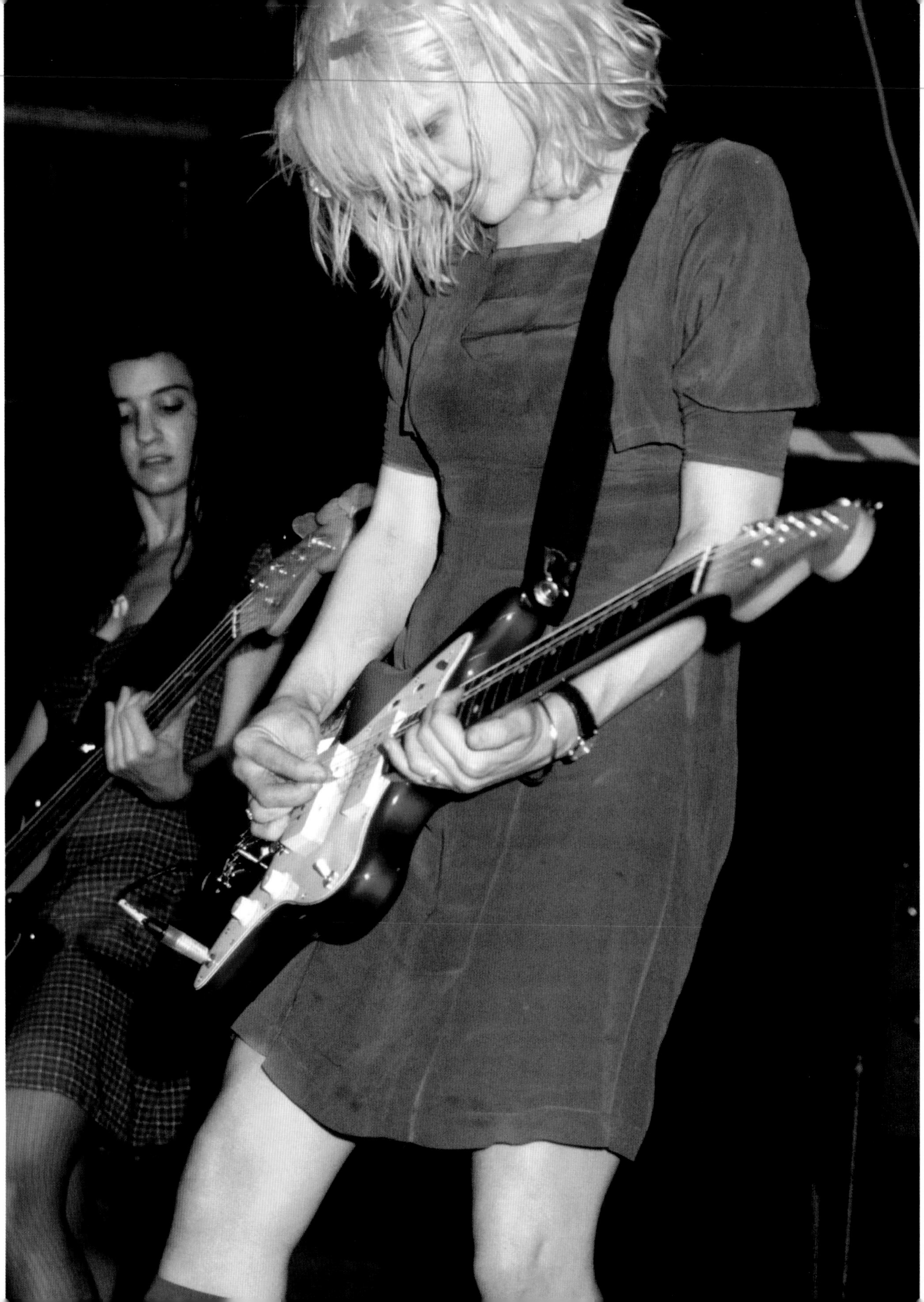

• Coutney live with Hole •

trying to make a record that was very straightforward, very accurate, powerful, hi-fi recording of the band, without doing the contemporary studio tricks. The band recorded essentially live in the studio."

About a week after the band's arrival, Courtney flies in, but her presence isn't exactly welcomed. She ends up in an argument with Dave Grohl, and Steve would later describe her as a "psycho hose-beast." During their down time in the studio, the band and entourage would make prank phone calls, including calls to John Silva, Madonna, and Evan Dando. On the last day of recording, Steve handed out cigars to celebrate.

FEBRUARY 16, 1993:
Nirvana wins the Best International Newcomer award at the 1993 Brit Awards, held in London. Still at work on *In Utero*, they don't attend the ceremony.

FEBRUARY 19, 1993:
Incesticide is certified gold by the RIAA for 500,000 copies sold in the US. The label and band chose not to heavily promote the album, therefore no interviews were set up to publicize it and only one video was made, for the song "Sliver."

FEBRUARY 20, 1993:
Kurt Cobain turns 26 years old.

FEBRUARY 22, 1993:
Chicago-based independent label Touch and Go releases the Nirvana/Jesus Lizard split 7-inch single featuring Nirvana's "Oh, the Guilt" and Jesus Lizard's "Puss." The single was actually in the works for a few years, but it didn't come to fruition until full into Nirvana-mania, which left Jesus Lizard's David Yow feeling a bit uncomfortable.

"Nirvana became like the Beatles of the '90s, but they still wanted to do it," David says in *The Rocket*. "And we had to figure out, well, do we want to do this and look like we're riding on Nirvana's coattails, or we could just do it and not worry about it, which is what we ended up doing."

FEBRUARY 24, 1993:
Nirvana's "Smells Like Teen Spirit" loses to the Red Hot Chili Peppers' "Give It Away" for the Best Hard Rock Performance with Vocal award at the 35th annual Grammy Awards. This is also Kurt and Courtney's one-year wedding anniversary.

FEBRUARY 1993:
Also this month, Sonic Youth's EP *Whores Moaning* (the title is a play on Nirvana's previously-released *Hormoaning* EP) is released in Australia featuring artwork by Kurt Cobain. A collage of Kurt's dolls is on the front cover and one of his drawings is on the back.

EARLY MARCH 1993:
After recording *In Utero*, Kurt, Courtney, and Frances Bean move into a rented house at 11301 Lakeside Ave. N.E. in the Sand Point area of Seattle, overlooking Lake Washington. They also buy a two-story house on 10-plus acres in Carnation, reportedly costing $400,000. They left the

Lakeside house a year later to purchase a much larger home in a more exclusive neighborhood. They weren't known as the best housekeepers or decorators, often using sheets for curtains and sparse furnishings. One thing in common at all of their residences was usually a room they referred to as the "mess room," cluttered with guitars, notebooks, art supplies, and Courtney's neglected Buddhist shrine.

Also around this time, indie rock's reigning couple – Kim Gordon and Thurston Moore of Sonic Youth – stay at Chris and Shelli's house at 2253 North 54th St. in the U-District (University District) of Seattle while they're in town on tour.

MARCH 6–9, 1993:
The NARM Best Seller Awards are given out during the 35th annual National Association of Recording Merchandisers Convention at the Marriott Orlando World Center in Orlando, Florida. Nirvana loses to Pearl Jam for the awards for Best Selling Alternative Recording and Best Selling Recording By a Group.

MARCH 15, 1993:
Eight Songs for Greg Sage and the Wipers, originally released as a box of four double-sided 7-inch singles on colored vinyl, is re-issued by Tim/Kerr Records on CD with six additional tracks, forcing a title change to *Fourteen Songs for Greg Sage and the Wipers*. It features Nirvana's cover of "Return of the Rat."

MARCH 19, 1993:
Kurt attends a secret show by Hole, featuring their new bassist Kristen Pfaff (who dies from a heroin overdose on June 16, 1994), at the Crocodile Café in Seattle.

"Kurt was standing way, way back out of sight," recalls Seattle journalist Tom Phalen. "They were playing new songs for *Live Through This*. [Courtney] played really well, the band sounded really good, and the songs sounded really good. They were way different from the first album and I remember thinking somebody has been giving her a hand. It was just so obvious. Some of the chord changes she was doing were way more sophisticated than anything she had written before. They were just too melodic, but it was a nice show. A lot of people walked away from the show very impressed."

MARCH 23, 1993:
Kurt and Courtney finally win their battle with the LA Department of Children's Services over Frances Bean. A Family Court judge rules on this day that the couple is no longer required to submit to drug testing or supervision from social workers.

LATE MARCH 1993:
Courtney is in England with Hole to appear on "The Word" on March 26 and record a John Peel session on March 27. She also plays a 20-minute set at Rough Trade Records to promote the group's new single, "Beautiful Son." While Courtney was away, Kurt, Frances, and a nanny are at home at their Lakeside Avenue house in Seattle.

During this time, Kevin Kerslake spends some time at the house to help Kurt go through footage the band has collected over the years for their long-form home video, *Live! Tonight! Sold Out!!*, which was conceived by Kurt and directed by Kevin. They also shot footage for the video of "Sliver," the only single released from *Incesticide*, on a Super 8 camera in the Cobain's garage. Frances Bean appears in the video.

Around this time, Kurt talked to Kevin about directing the band's next video, for "Heart-Shaped Box," according to the lawsuit filed in the United States District Court, Central District of California in 1994 over this video. The court papers state, "For some time, Plaintiff [Kevin Kerslake] had been developing a concept which he thought would work well for the 'Heart-Shaped Box' video. This involved complex and interplaying images of a young girl born into a Ku Klux Klan family; a flower-filled room; fields of poppies; a forest of gnarled trees; a 'scarecrow-like' character; and an old man on a cross."

Kevin, who directed four other Nirvana videos ("Come As You Are," "In Bloom," "Lithium," and "Sliver"), ends up not getting the job to direct the video and he files a lawsuit in 1994 after seeing some of his ideas for the video used in the final clip that was directed by Anton Corbijn later this year.

APRIL 3, 1993:

The *Guardian* newspaper in England runs a Q&A with Courtney asking her "How would you like to die?" She answers, "At the same time as my husband and be reborn as twins." Almost a year to this date, Kurt commits suicide.

APRIL 4, 1993:

Of the upcoming Bosnian rape benefit concert, Chris Novoselic, who organized the event, tells the *San Francisco Chronicle*'s Michael Snyder, "An epic tragedy is happening in Europe and nobody's doing anything about it. Mass executions, ethnic cleansing, the rapes. I don't have the ability to launch an invasion or an air strike. A benefit to raise money and awareness is the most I can do... That region of the world is where my family comes from." Around this time, Chris goes back to the birth spelling of his name, Krist.

APRIL 5, 1993:

Hole's "Beautiful Son" single released on City Slang Records featuring a cover photo of Kurt as a child – a fact they didn't want known at the time. The lyric "You look good in my dress/My beautiful son" is about how Kurt looks cute in Courtney's dresses. The song was released as a 7-inch, CD single, and 12-inch. The B-side is, ironically, an ode to Yoko Ono titled "Twenty Years in the Dakota."

APRIL 9, 1993:

Nirvana plays a benefit for Bosnian rape victims at the Cow Palace in San Francisco with the Breeders, L7, and Disposable Heroes of Hiphoprisy opening. It's their first US show in six months, and their first show in the Bay Area since 1991, so a lot is riding on this performance. Pearl Jam's Eddie Vedder and Dale Crover of the Melvins are there. The show raises $50,000 for the Tresnjevka Women's Group, a Zagreb-based organization that established shelters for women raped during the Bosnia-Herzegovina war.

The morning of the show, Geffen/DGC's San Francisco promotion rep Cheryl Kovalchik takes Krist and Michael Franti of Disposable Heroes of Hiphoprisy to three morning radio shows (modern rock station Live 105's Alex Bennett show, hip-hop station KMEL, and news/talk station KGO) to talk about the issue at hand. "They wanted to get an important message out, and they did," says Cheryl.

"It was a monstrous set," recalls Charles R. Cross. "Most fans consider this one of their best performances ever." Kurt switched the side of the stage he was on, and dedicated "Frances Farmer Will Have Her Revenge On Seattle" to Courtney and Frances – or "the Bean" as Kurt would call her.

Backstage, people were giving Courtney gifts for the baby. After the show and into the next morning, Krist, Shelli, Dave, guitar tech Ernie Bailey, tour manager Alex MacLeod, Mark Kates, and others are partying at the Phoenix hotel, according to Michael Azerrad's book *Come As You Are*.

APRIL 10, 1993:

During the day, *Come As You Are* reports that Krist goes to City Lights bookstore in San Francisco and outside is a cash machine where a homeless person calls out to him for a $20 bill in the spirit of the Easter holiday. Krist gives him one.

APRIL 13, 1993:

Dave Markey's concert documentary, *1991: The Year Punk Broke*, which chronicles Sonic Youth's summer 1991 European festival tour featuring Nirvana, is released. Also featured in the documentary are Dinosaur Jr., Gumball, Babes in Toyland, and the Ramones.

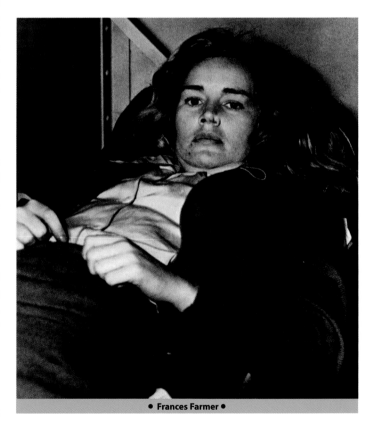

● **Frances Farmer** ●

Greg Kot starts the ball rolling on the controversy over *In Utero* when he opens the *Chicago Tribune* story "Record Label Finds Little Bliss In Nirvana's Latest." In it, Steve Albini says, "Geffen and the band's management hate the record. They considered it an indulgence when Nirvana asked to record with me. I have no faith this record will be released." To confirm Steve's comments, Greg quoted unnamed sources that also called the album "unreleaseable."

Bill Bennett, Geffen's GM at the time, now says, "That's a fact, there were people who said that. There were people who did not like it and they were vocal and that was forgotten once the record took off. He brought us the record his way, and he won. I remember the day we got in *In Utero*. People didn't really think it was the proper follow-up and yet it was a magnificent record. DGC was happy with the record, that's not to say there weren't people inside that didn't 'get it,' so to speak."

Greg, who tried unsuccessfully to interview the band for the article, explains how the story unfolded: "Albini sort of got nailed as the bad guy outlaw who revealed the story, when in fact Albini was the only guy who would go on record and actually say what was happening. I didn't go to Albini until I had gotten the story from three or four other people within the label's infrastructure. However, no one at the label would go on record. To get the story, I had to have someone 'in the know' go on the record to confirm those anonymous sources. And Albini, of course, I've always found him to be very blunt and he was perfectly willing to be quoted. And that's when I knew I had a story. At the end of the day, the story was proven to be correct. What more vindication do you need?"

Soon nearly every major media outlet picks up on the story, including *Newsweek*, *Rolling Stone*, and *Billboard*. And two of the album's songs are sent back to the studio for more work.

APRIL 21, 1993:
In Utero is mastered at Gateway Studios in Portland, Maine by Bob Ludwig.

APRIL 24, 1993:
Melody Maker publishes the article titled "Cobain't That Peculiar" by Everett True. Not taking the interview seriously, Kurt asks, in true punk rock fashion, "Look, when you type this up, can you fix it so the words end in mid-letter, at the end of each line. That looks far more punk rock." Maybe this explains why the credits on the "Love Buzz" single show Jack Endino's last name split on two lines, with "En" at the end of one line, and then "Dino" on the next line.

APRIL 1993:
Courtney and Cedars-Sinai Medical Center settle her medical negligence lawsuit filed December 29, 1992 out of court.

MAY 2, 1993:
Kurt overdoses on heroin at his rented Seattle home at 11301 Lakeside Ave. N.E. after coming home shaking, flushed, and incoherent after doing heroin at a friend's house. Scared, Courtney called 911 at 9:10 p.m.

According to the Incident Report filed with the Seattle Police

of a narcotic according to medical personnel on the scene. Cobain was conscious and able to answer questions, but was obviously impaired to some degree. Cobain was transported to Harborview Medical Center by Seattle Fire Department."

The report recounts the incident, which says that Kurt was at a "friend's house two hours earlier where he injected himself with $30-$40 worth of heroin. He then drove home to the address of the incident and stayed in his room." Three people there, including his wife, spoke to the responding officers and told them that Kurt's "physical condition gradually deteriorated to the point that he was shaking, became flushed, and delirious and talked incoherently." The report also said, "This type of incident had happened before to Cobain."

The incident happened shortly after Kurt returned home for a family dinner with his wife, mother and sister. After he started shaking, Love injected him with Buprenorphine, which she had done before, and which is known to revive an overdose victim. To make him vomit the substances out of his body, she gave him Valium, three Benadryl tablets, and four codeine tablets, while waiting for the ambulance to arrive, according to a *Rolling Stone* story on the incident. Even though he was clearly on drugs, Kurt was not – then or at any time – arrested for drugs.

MAY 11, 1993:
DGC issues a press release ("Nirvana's Kurt Cobain Debunks Rumors of Geffen Interference with New Album") to refute the *Chicago Tribune* story that DGC was going to reject *In Utero*.

"There has been no pressure from our record label to change the tracks we did with Albini. We have 100% control of our music... We – the band – felt the vocals were not loud enough on a few of the tracks. We want to change that," said Kurt in the release, in an attempt to prove that Nirvana is not a band to cave in to corporate pressures. "The simple truth is," added Geffen president Ed Rosenblatt in the press release, "as I have assured the members of Nirvana and their management all along, we will release whatever record the band delivers to us."

MAY 12, 1993:
The *Chicago Tribune* follows up the story with an item quoting Steve Albini saying, "The band has asked me not to comment any more on this situation, and I'm very glad they finally said something about it."

MAY 16, 1993:
Krist Novoselic turns 28 years old.

MAY 17, 1993:
Newsweek publishes a follow-up story on the *Chicago Tribune* piece about *In Utero*. The article, by Jeff Giles, runs with the headline "You Call This Nirvana? An abrasive album cools a romance with Geffen Records. There's got to be a morning after." The story reports that its sources confirmed that the *Chicago Tribune* story is true.

Nirvana takes a shot at Jeff in an ad in *Billboard*: "Although Giles did speak with representatives at Geffen Records and Gold Mountain Entertainment (our management), their quotes were rendered invalid in his piece by other quotes from unnamed sources... Most damaging to us is that Giles ridiculed our relationship with our label based on totally

[AUK] SJ... PHYSICAL CONDITION GRADUALLY DETERIORATED TO THE POINT THAT HE WAS SHAKING, BECAME FLUSHED AND DELIRIOUS AND TALKED INCOHERENTLY."

1 Serve The Servants 2 Scentless Apprentice 3 Heart-Shaped Box 4 Rape Me 5 Frances Farmer Will Have Her Revenge On Seattle 6 Dumb 7 Very Ape 8 Milk It 9 Pennyroyal Tea 10 Radio Friendly Unit Shifter 11 tourette's 12 All Apologies 13 Gallons Of Rubbing Alcohol Flow Through The Strip

GED24536 - F: BM650 Recorded by Steve Albini A&R: Gary Gersh Management: Gold Mountain Entertainment
℗ & © 1993 Geffen Records, Inc., an MCA Company. Distributed by BMG. A Bertelsmann Music Group Company.
All trademarks and logos are protected. Printed in Germany. Produced by special Arrangement with Sub Pop Records.

7 20642 45362 9

*Devalued American Dollar Purchase Incentive Track

● *In Utero*, from behind ●

MAY 18, 1993:

Nirvana's "Smells Like Teen Spirit" receives the award for the most-performed song on US college radio at the 41st annual BMI Pop Awards. Kurt's fears of losing the college audience were officially put to rest. "When the album first started getting heavy play [on alternative radio]," Kurt once told the *New York Times'* Jon Pareles, "I think we were mostly concerned with losing those college kids. For some reason, that didn't happen to us."

"It's hard to hear that song now in the same way," comments Nils Bernstein about how radio overplayed "Smells Like Teen Spirit." "Like 'Stairway to Heaven' is an amazing song and it's a shame that you can't hear that song the same way. It really is just this incredible song and it sucks that it's been ruined for so many people."

MAY 22, 1993:

In this issue of *Billboard*, a letter to Newsweek (dated 11 May) from Nirvana is published as a full-page advertisement. Also in this issue, an item on the controversy quotes Jeff Giles saying that he "made repeated requests for interviews with the band members. I stand by my sources and my story."

MID-MAY 1993:

"Sliver" debuts on MTV. Kurt was criticized for putting the young Frances Bean in the video.

MAY 1993:

While denying that DGC wasn't happy with *In Utero* and would accept anything the band delivered, the band has two songs reworked in early May. The "*In Utero* Clean-Up" is done by Scott Litt at Bad Animals Studios

in Seattle. The band first approached Albini, then even considered Andy Wallace, who Kurt had just two years ago criticized for making *Nevermind* too slick. Scott Litt, best known for his work on R.E.M.'s *Automatic For the People*, remixes "Heart-Shaped Box" and "All Apologies," and adds an extra guitar part and backing vocals on "Heart-Shaped Box."

Ex-Geffen GM Bill Bennett confirms what most already know: the two songs were re-done to sound more commercial. However, Janet Billig's explanation in the *Los Angeles Times* was that "after living with the recordings for a bit, they decided to do some more." Krist Novoselic's perspective was a little more direct: "We've got a single like 'Heart-Shaped Box' and 'All Apologies,' these really kind of nice songs, and the record's really aggressive," he told the *Chicago Sun Times'* Jim DeRogatis. "I wanted to make songs like 'Heart-Shaped Box' a gateway for people to buy the record, and then they'd put it on and have this aggressive wild sound. A true alternative record."

Geffen has a history of rejecting records over creative issues – they sued Neil Young for making an album "unrepresentative" of his work and rejected the first stab at Aerosmith's *Get a Grip*.

SUMMER 1993:

There is a lot of down time between finishing up *In Utero* and embarking on their massive tour to support the album in the fall. Sometime this summer, photographer Charles Peterson gets a call from Kurt to come to his Lakeside Ave. house to photograph the collage he made of pictures of fetuses, orchids, lilies, intestines, and umbilical chords that will serve as the controversial back cover of the album.

When asked what Kurt would do in between tours and recording, Danny Goldberg, who remained close to Kurt and Courtney after leaving Gold Mountain, says, "Kurt went through different periods. I mean once he was with Courtney, he was certainly with her. That was pretty early on. But he was very creative. He was always doing paintings and writing songs and working on that home video [*Live! Tonight! Sold Out!!*], so there was always something creative going on with him."

JUNE 4, 1993:

Kurt Cobain is taken into the Seattle Police Department for investigation of domestic assault for allegedly assaulting Courtney. He posted $950 bail and was released from King County jail three hours later. Formal charges were not filed, but the case is referred to the Seattle Police Department's Criminal Division for further examination.

The police report says the incident was over an argument the couple had about Kurt's guns. Courtney relayed her side of the story to the *Seattle Times* on July 1, 1993: "Kurt is not violent, he is not a wife beater. We are the most compatible people on Earth. It started because we were playing loud music in our garage and we live in a quiet neighborhood. All of a sudden there were sirens and like, three cop cars, six cops in the house."

She further explains that she had thrown juice in Kurt's face and he pushed her. She pushed him back, and according to the police report, he pushed her to the floor and choked her, leaving a scratch on her forearm and neck from the incident, though Love says the mark is from her guitar string. "Kurt spent three hours in jail. It was hell. I was crying the whole time," Courtney says in the *Seattle Times*.

Kurt later tells *Spin* magazine that he was surprised that the police report was so detailed, but "completely wrong." He tells his side of the story to *Spin*'s Darcy Steinke: "What really happened was that Courtney and I were running around the house screaming and wrestling – it was a bit Sid and Nancy-esque, I have to admit, but we were having a good time. And then we get this knock on the door and there are five cop cars outside and the cops all have their guns drawn." He then said the two argued over who was to go to jail so Kurt went. "I kind of regret that now because the idea of Courtney as a husband beater is kind of amusing. She did throw juice at me and I did push her but it was about who was going to jail."

June 26, 1993:

Kurt wasn't spotted around town much, especially in his later years, but Seattle writer Gillian G. Gaar caught a rare glimpse at him on this night at a cash machine at US Bank on Broadway in Seattle. This area is a well-known drug area.

"It was early evening, about 7 p.m., and I went up to my cash machine and there's this guy in front of me using the machine who's in really beat-up, scruffy clothes – he looked like this total derelict and I thought this guy is probably getting out his last 20 bucks, and it was Kurt, wearing his deer cap," recalls Gillian. "I recognized him because of those eyes, those piercing blue eyes, when you see them up close, it's quite stunning."

June 30, 1993:

"The Scream thing right now is the most important thing happening to me. Nirvana's not really happening at all, with the new record not coming out until September 14," Dave Grohl tells the *Washington Post* about the reunion tour with his former band, Washington, DC-based hardcore outfit Scream. The band features Grohl on drums; guitarist Franz Stahl, who later went on to replace Pat Smear in Dave's post-Nirvana success, the Foo Fighters, but quit in 1999; singer Peter Stahl; and bassist Skeeter Thompson.

"I'm so glad we're doing this. I think this will throw everything back into perspective for me," he tells the *Post*. "We'll play these clubs, and maybe sleep on people's floors like we always did, then in the fall I go out with Nirvana and fly into cities, and play in front of 10 or 15,000 people, go to the nice hotel and watch TV till I fall asleep. It's not the same as playing on a small stage with guys who are basically my brothers."

June 1993:

According to the Courtney Love biography by Melissa Rossi, *Courtney Love: Queen of Noise*, Courtney "instigated an in-home rehab session [for Kurt] this June. Kurt protested, but she proceeded with her plan, even calling in a psychic." Prior to this, the bio says Courtney started going to Narcotics Anonymous meetings and made a concerted effort to clean up her act. Also this month, Nirvana poses for a photo shoot with Anton Corbijn in Seattle.

July 1, 1993:

Tim/Kerr Records releases "The 'Priest' They Called Him" 10-inch featuring Kurt Cobain's guitar to William S. Burroughs' spoken word. While his name is spelled properly as Kurt Cobain on the back cover, etched on the black vinyl itself of the first 20,000 copies is yet another spelling of Kurt's name: Kurtis Donald Cohbaine, with a dot over the "o" in Cohbaine.

This night, Courtney plays a gig at the Off Ramp in Seattle. "She was playing some songs that would be on *Live Through This*," recalls Gillian, "because I remember the last thing she did was 'Doll Parts,' her on

● **Smiles for the camera from the boys in the band** ●

acoustic guitar. I remember being really struck at how powerful the lyrics were. This was the same day that news broke about Kurt's arrest for beating Courtney up and she was making a lot of references to that. She goes, 'Yeah, my husband is this total wife beater... NOT!'"

Kurt and Krist, who had been at a Leonard Cohen show, showed up backstage after the show. Even later, *New Musical Express* writer Brian Willis is invited to the Cobains' house to listen to *In Utero*. It became a cover story in *NME*, much to management's dismay. The exclusive cover story, "Domicile on Cobain St.," runs in the July 24, 1993 issue of *NME*.

And on this day, the news breaks in the *Seattle Times* about Kurt's June arrest.

July 4, 1993:

Dave Grohl plays his first reunion show with Scream at the annual Smoke Out Bash on the Mall in Washington, DC. The idea for the tour came from Peter Stahl after learning that Dischord Records was planning to reissue the Scream back catalogue on CD this month, as well release the album *Fumble/Banging the Drum* on July 21.

"When Pete said all this was going to come out on CD, first he just asked me some questions about remixing the stuff," Dave told the *Washington Post*. "Then it turned into, 'Why not do a show at the 9:30?' Then it turned into a whole tour."

July 5-6, 1993:

Scream plays two shows at the 9:30 Club in Washington, DC on July 5 and 6, with shows to follow in New York, Boston, Detroit, Minneapolis, Seattle, San Francisco, and Los Angeles.

July 7, 1993:

The Seattle music scene is shaken by the horrid death of the Gits' lead singer Mia Zapata who was raped, strangled and killed on a street in Seattle. Bands quickly come together to organize a tribute concert for her to help pay for the investigation. Her murder remained unsolved until January 2003.

July 8, 1993:

The first review of the Scream reunion (from the 9:30 Club show on July 5) runs in the *Washington Post*, saying that the band "played with passion and precision; the music's chest-rattling impact came only partially from the extreme over-amplification" and that Dave "was solid throughout."

July 9, 1993:

Kurt attends a PJ Harvey concert at Under the Rail in Seattle. "He was just standing on his own watching," says Gillian. "He was kind of hunched over, just out with the rest of us, not in the VIP area. Kurt's appearance made such a big impression on us, because he didn't go out a lot. He was really a slight guy, when you saw him up close, it looked like you could beat him up easily." It's also Courtney's 28th birthday.

July 14, 1993:

"At the urging and insistence of Cobain, Plaintiff further developed his ideas along with corresponding images and directorial cues" for the "Heart-Shaped Box" video, according to the lawsuit filed by Kevin Kerslake over "Heart-Shaped Box." On this date, Kevin writes his first of five video treatments, which are registered with the U.S. Copyright Office, for "Heart-Shaped Box." A treatment is a written description of the ideas, images, and directorial cues to be used for a video and the script of the video.

The court documents include details of Kevin's treatments for this clip. Part of it reads: "Flowers/red slippers/radio under water, underwater portrait of the girl; Flowers/slippers pulled from water and portrait of girl at water's edge; Girl skips across hills with flowers and slippers, the witch shuffles across the crest of the hill." It also claims that the following ideas were Kevin's: The entire concept of the flower room; girl in front of the closet of Klan robes and chasing the Klan's hat in the wind; William S. Burroughs as a scarecrow and on the cross [Burroughs never did appear in the video]; fetuses hanging from trees; and many other images.

July 17, 1993:

After 92 weeks on The Billboard 200, *Nevermind* finally falls off the chart.

July 18, 1993:

Adding fuel to the still blazing Nirvana/Pearl Jam fire is a *Los Angeles Times* article that poses the question of "If Pearl Jam's *Vs.* and Nirvana's *In Utero* come out on the same date, whose album will fans buy?" Of the dozen radio programmers the *Times* polled, only one picked Nirvana. Retailers who were polled said the same, estimating that demand for the Pearl Jam release would be at least 33% higher than for Nirvana.

Kurt apparently sensed the potential problem and said he didn't want the albums released on the same date, telling MTV that he feels "sorry for the kids who have to decide on what they should buy." The albums don't end up released on the same date, and both albums debut at No. 1 in their respective weeks. However, Pearl Jam's first-week sales are 950,000 and Nirvana's are 180,000. *Vs.* set a new record for opening week sales in the SoundScan era, which began May 15, 1991.

On this night, Grohl's Scream reunion tour wraps up in LA at the Whisky. the *Los Angeles Times* review says, "drummer Dave Grohl supercharged the usual punk-rock polka stuff with an extraordinary array of back-beat flams and paradiddles."

July 22, 1993:

Guitar World's Jon Savage interviews Kurt Cobain for an article that is not published until after his death. The interview is conducted after a Melvins show; he was only one of a handful of interviews scheduled in NY for UK press. As usual Kurt didn't really want to do the interview and asked Jon, "Do I have to do this now?" He did.

"The idea on the press campaign – and I didn't really design the press campaign – was for them to do interviews where you can get more bang for the bucks and [only] if you could really trust the writer," explains Jim Merlis, the band's publicist for *In Utero*. "It was really difficult. You were really on a fine line. And it was never like they'd come out and say 'No, we won't do it.' It was always a maybe. They wanted to play their shows and that was about it. They wanted to do the least promotion that they possibly could. They didn't like interviews. And they thought they really had gotten burned by the press too. It was just very tension filled."

"YEAH, MY HUSBAND IS THIS TOTAL WIFE BEATER ... NOT!"

"I BELIEVE IF YOU DIE YOU'RE COMPLETELY HAPPY AND YOUR SOUL SOMEWHERE LIVES ON AND THERE'S THIS POSITIVE ENERGY. I'M NOT IN ANY WAY AFRAID OF DEATH."

JULY 23, 1993:

"On the morning of July 23, Love heard something fall in the bathroom of the New York hotel where the couple was staying. She opened the door and found Cobain on the floor unconscious. He had overdosed again," *Rolling Stone* reported in a posthumous Cobain article. Later Krist told Seattle writer Tom Phalen that towards the end Kurt was "always fucked up. He just kept putting himself to sleep and one day he didn't wake up. He was always ODing. He just wanted to be unconscious all the time, even when he was conscious he was only semi-conscious."

Courtney once again revived Kurt from the overdose and he went through with the band's unannounced, last-minute show at Roseland Ballroom during the annual music convention New Music Seminar. This is the first time they performed with the acoustic section featuring a cellist, which they would do for the entire *In Utero* tour to come. The cello player was Lori Goldston of Seattle's Black Cat Orchestra. Big John Duncan was on board as second guitarist, but only played this one show with the band. The Jesus Lizard opens the show.

"It wasn't a very good show," recalls Jim Merlis. "It was kind of a mess. It just seemed sloppy. It was early on. I knew he was experimenting with [the acoustic section]. The audience seemed to like it though, and the reviews were positive. We had a conversation at the show about left-handed guitars, and he talked about how he wanted to buy Leadbelly's guitar, but someone in Japan was buying it for like $100,000 and he couldn't afford that."

JULY 24-26, 1993:

Nirvana stay in NY for a few days, and Kurt does some interviews, including one with *The Face* where he says, "I believe if you die you're completely happy and your soul somewhere lives on and there's this positive energy. I'm not in any way afraid of death." Also in the interview, he notes, "I've been suicidal all my life. I just don't want to die now. Having a child and being in love is the only thing I feel I've been blessed with."

July 30, 1993:

After discussing Kevin Kerslake's first treatment for the "Heart-Shaped Box" video, Kurt asked for a second treatment to be prepared based on his suggestions for the clip. The second treatment is submitted to Kurt on this day, according to the court document. The document also states that the last treatment of the video "did not include any substantive additions by Cobain."

July 1993:

Also this month, Dave Thompson, who wrote the Nirvana biography *Never Fade Away: The Kurt Cobain Story*, interviews the band at the Broadway Bar & Grill on Broadway in Seattle for a story in *Alternative Press*'s October 1993 issue. He can't remember the date of the interview, but he clearly remembers what happened:

"I met the three of them at a hotel. We get in the car and drive up to Broadway and Kurt was really edgy even in the car," says Dave, who also wrote about this incident in the *Alternative Press* piece. "Krist was telling this long-involved story about this guy having sex with a chicken and Kurt was just like really quiet and really edgy and we got to the bar and Kurt just announced, 'I've got to go out.' And just disappeared. So there was Dave and Krist and the publicist [Luke Wood, who was dismissed of his duties as their publicist after only three months] sitting there. After about 20 minutes Krist is like, 'This is fucking ridiculous. We're supposed to be doing an interview, he walked off, I'm going home.' Krist walked out, so now there's Dave and me and Luke.

"So Dave and I are talking about antique clocks (he's a collector) and all of a sudden Kurt just bounces in, smiling, and goes, 'I'm sorry I had to go see my chiropractor.' It was about 40 minutes," continues Dave. "There was a big change in his attitude. Broadway is not renowned for chiropractors. His mood had completely changed, he was so bouncy and Luke was sitting there looking completely horrified. So Kurt asks where Krist is, and we tell him he's gone. Kurt just launches into this rant about how much he hates Krist. Every time he sees him when he's out, Krist backs away like, 'Oh God, here comes the junkie' and it's like he can't stand him and he's always walking off. And Luke's sitting there looking more and more horrified and Kurt looked over at him, saw the effect it had and then gave him this huge wink and a grin. It was like, wind up the babysitter. Purely for effect, but it was really funny."

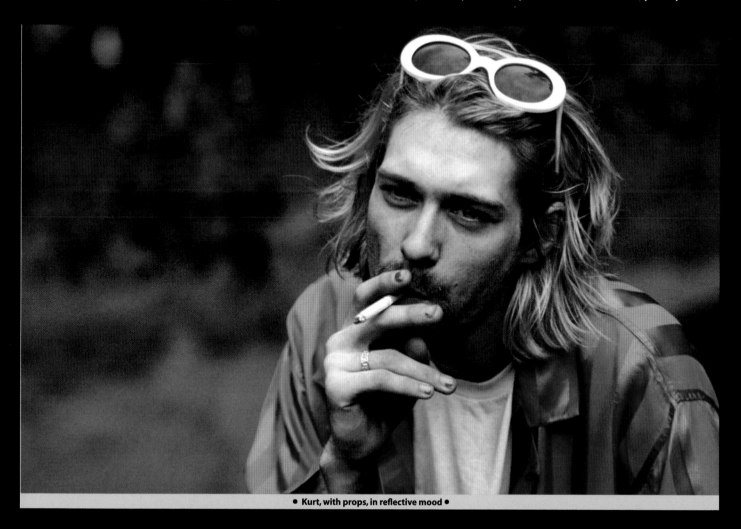

• **Kurt, with props, in reflective mood** •

AUGUST 2, 1993:

The third treatment for "Heart-Shaped Box" by director Kevin Kerslake is submitted to Kurt Cobain for approval. According to the lawsuit filed in 1994, "Cobain later commented that the Third Treatment was 'Perfect – the best treatment that he had ever read.' Cobain approved the Third Treatment for shooting, as did Nirvana's record company. "The normal procedure with making videos would be once a treatment is approved, the director and his production company would start the process of hiring the people who would work on the video.

AUGUST 6, 1993:

Nirvana performs at a benefit for the Mia Zapata Investigation Fund at the King Theater (a movie theater) in Seattle. Hell Smells, Kill Sybil, Voodoo Gearshift, and Tad are also on the bill. This is Nirvana's last show as a trio.

"Nirvana was the last-minute headliner. On the ticket, it's printed that Tad is the headliner," says Gillian G. Gaar. "After Tad played, there was this feeling like, 'Well is it really going to happen?' because it had

been so last-minute, but Nirvana did go on, and we all breathed a sigh of release. They started doing 'Seasons in the Sun,' kind of a slow dirge-like version, and you know how Kurt could scream and his voice would sound all raw and scraped? Well he began doing that on the chorus: 'We had joy we had fun!' It was so funny. Did the whole song. And again they didn't do 'Teen Spirit.'

Members of Pearl Jam, Mudhoney, 7 Year Bitch, Imij, Stymime, Helmet, and Hole were also in attendance, as was Tad Doyle's then bride-to-be Barbara Beymer, who got into a fight with Courtney backstage. "She was kind of a big girl, someone Courtney shouldn't have been fucking with," says Page Hamilton of Helmet. "She could've ripped her limb from limb. I came backstage after all hell broke loose, and it was just a weird scene. One thing I remember from the show was they did a condensed version of Led Zeppelin's 'No Quarter' and it sounded really cool."

The event raised $3,500, which went toward hiring a private investigator to solve the case.

AUGUST 10 - 12, 1993:

Kevin modifies his third treatment for the "Heart-Shaped Box" video by creating two other versions of the clip (treatments four and five). The suit claims, "These additional treatments were modifications of the third treatment that retained all of Plaintiff's original imagery, but contained modifications to reduce the proposed budget for the video."

Around this time, Kevin has moved ahead with his plans for the video by hiring a crew, production designer/art director, and cameraman, developing a shooting script, and completing film tests, according to the lawsuit papers. All of this was done with Kurt's knowledge, according to court papers. However, the papers state, "[Kevin Kerslake] placed several calls to Cobain to finalize the shooting schedule. These calls were not returned."

AUGUST 27, 1993:

The *Chicago Tribune* reports that DGC had delayed the release of *In Utero* by one week. Originally due September 14, it's now slated for September 21.

AUGUST 28, 1993:

Kevin finds out through Robin Sloane, who handled videos and creative services at Geffen, that he is no longer directing the "Heart-Shaped Box" video. Noted photographer Anton Corbijn gets the gig instead.

When Kevin found out, he sent Anton a letter to make sure that his video treatments would not be used by the Anton-directed clip. This letter is Exhibit B in the lawsuit. In his letter to Anton, he writes, "I'm not sure if you are aware of the circumstances that predicated Nirvana choosing you to direct the 'Heart-Shaped Box' video, and you certainly should not be burdened with a list of events; suffice to say, we had been awarded the job and Kurt became discontent with something (What? We still don't know). Out of concern that some of the images we were set to shoot would end up in a video shot by someone else, a breakdown was made..."

Also upon learning that another director got the gig, Kevin's attorneys sent a letter around this time to Robin Sloane that delineates the responsibility of images appearing in the five treatments by Kevin for "Heart-Shaped Box" as a proactive move to ensure that none of Kevin's ideas are used by another director. In the end, the video does indeed contain many of the images that the lawsuit states were Kevin's ideas.

AUGUST 31, 1993:

An accounting for Giant Merchandise on this date is part of the subject of a lawsuit filed on August 30, 1996 for breach of contract. The suit, filed by Nirvana in Superior Court of the State of California, Los Angeles County (case no. C156615) against Giant Merchandising Corp and Kenneth Lemunyon for breach of contract and accounting, reads, in part:

"Nirvana is informed and believes and thereupon alleges that the accountings performed by Giant are incomplete and inaccurate. Among other things, an accounting dated August 31, 1993, which is predicated in part upon earlier accountings performed by Giant, calculates royalties payable to Nirvana on the foreign sales of Nirvana merchandise at a lesser rate than is required under the merchandising agreement." In brief, Nirvana claimed that Giant underpaid their royalties for the retail merchandising agreement. They were looking for damages in excess of $25,000.

AUGUST 1993:

"Heart-Shaped Box," the first single from *In Utero*, is issued in the UK on Geffen, backed with "Marigold," which was written and sung by Dave Grohl. While singles were released commercially in the UK, the band and their label chose not to release every radio song as a single in the US because they felt it cannibalized album sales. The initial copies of the single in the UK were issued on red vinyl. The 12-inch and CD single version also included "Milk It."

Sometime in late August or early September, Anton Corbijn directs Nirvana's "Heart-Shaped Box" video at Raleigh Studios in Los Angeles.

SEPTEMBER 1, 1993:

Kurt calls up Kevin Kerslake and invites him to the MTV Video Music Awards because the "In Bloom" video that he directed is up for an award. Kevin accepts the invitation. At this time the sets for the "Heart-Shaped Box" video had been built.

Also at this time, "Plaintiff and Cobain began talking about the Nirvana long-form home video which Plaintiff was developing, and the 'Heart-Shaped Box' project, and who created which image," states the lawsuit. "Cobain admitted to Plaintiff that Plaintiff had come up with the images set forth in Plaintiff's video treatments, and assured Plaintiff that he would not use the images developed by Plaintiff in the 'Heart-Shaped Box' video."

SEPTEMBER 2, 1993:

Nirvana and Kevin take home the Best Alternative Video for "In Bloom" at the 1993 MTV Video Music Awards at Universal Amphitheater in Universal City, California.

"We knew they were going to win the first award for the night – MTV tells you to make sure you show up," says Jim Merlis. "And I don't know how this happened, but we were really, really late and Krist ended up driving the van there and we get up to Universal and Krist almost runs over Jeff Ament from Pearl Jam in his rush to get in. Courtney immediately pushes over to the media and starts waving, and I'm trying to push everyone along because we're the first ones up. Then in the press tent afterwards, I think Kurt was really fucked up at the time, one guy in the media tent, and I don't know if he was trying to insult Kurt or what, but he kept asking, 'Do you even know what award you just won?'"

Also backstage in the press tent, journalists were asking artists about the current celebrity scandal – Michael Jackson's molestation charges. Kurt's comment was, "There are way too many gold diggers out there... I wish they'd leave the poor guy alone." Krist added, "I think he's getting a bad rap." When asked backstage if there was pressure to follow up the hugely successful *Nevermind*, Dave Grohl said, "There was no pressure," with Krist adding, "We just did a record. The pressure is on the label to sell it."

● A family night out: The MTV Video Music Awards in California ●

"Do you even know what award you just won?"

● Kurt, Courtney, and the Bean at the MTV Video Awards ●

After the awards this night, Kevin finds out from a friend who worked as a crew member for the "Heart-Shaped Box" video that the video had been completed "and that all of the images that Cobain had promised Plaintiff would not be shot were included," according to the suit.

EARLY SEPTEMBER 1993:

Kevin writes Kurt a letter (Exhibit C in the forthcoming lawsuit) about the video situation. The letter, which Kevin addressed to "kurdt," thanks Kurt for acknowledging his work on the "In Bloom" video by asking the director to accept the award onstage with them and then goes into how he found out about the "Heart-Shaped Box" video.

Kevin writes, "A crew member I use frequently... had worked on the Anton crew and he told me about the shoot. As he was telling me my heart sunk deeper and deeper. It was as though you and I had never spoke about the dilemma of using those images of the cross or the flower room. Then he told me that you shot images of the Klan hat and robe transformations. It was like a train ran right through me." Kevin didn't receive a response from the letter, but a meeting between attorneys and the record label was soon set up to view and discuss the video.

SEPTEMBER 7, 1993:

The "Heart-Shaped Box" single, backed with "Milk It" and "Marigold," ships to radio.

SEPTEMBER 8, 1993:

Kurt and Courtney perform together – for the first and last time – at Club Lingerie in Hollywood. Courtney was booked as a solo, acoustic act, along with Johnette Napolitano, 7 Year Bitch, Exene Cervenka, and Pinching Judy. The show benefited Rock Against Rape, which was trying to raise money for the First Strike Rape Prevention program.

"It was one of those things where she wasn't sure if she could make it," recalls Lynda Stenge, one of the promoters for the show. "And then she just showed up with Kurt, and we didn't even know at that moment that they were going to perform together. She did a few songs then called him up onstage… It was just incredible to see them onstage together."

Courtney played "Doll Parts" (she would later cast a young Kurt Cobain look-alike for her 1994 video of the song) and "Miss World" before Kurt joined her onstage for "Pennyroyal Tea" and "Where Did You Sleep Last Night?" Poking fun at the couple's John Lennon/Yoko Ono comparisons, she introduced Kurt as her "husband, Yoko."

SEPTEMBER 9, 1993:

According to published reports, in a memo filed on this day by the Seattle Police Criminal Division's director, the authorities decided to drop any domestic violence abuse charges against Kurt stemming from the June 4, 1993 incident.

The memo reads: "The victim [Courtney] will testify that nothing happened, contrary to the police report. Additionally the [emergency] tape is probably not admissible because it neither describes an assault, nor do her hearsay statements fall under an exception to the hearsay rule. Most notably, her statements do not fall under the excited utterance exception because her speech gives no indication that she was under the stress of a startling event such as an assault... Since we

● **Kurt and Courtney together on stage – for one time only – at Hollywood's Club Lingerie** ●

are unable to prove that an attack causing bodily injury occurred and there was an absence of self-defense, the City declines to file."

SEPTEMBER 13, 1993:

In Utero is released in the UK on vinyl and cassette. The European version of the album featured the additional song "Gallons of Rubbing Alcohol Flow Through the Strip," which was recorded by Craig Montgomery during the Brazil sessions in January of this year.

SEPTEMBER 14, 1993:

A limited run of 25,000 copies of *In Utero* on clear vinyl is released in the US, and the CD version of the album is released in the UK.

Robert Smith, head of marketing at Geffen, has said that they decided to release the vinyl version of the album first because the label wanted to re-establish their roots as a punk band. Kurt, while an avid collector of vinyl records (he's said that vinyl is "sacred" to him), also admitted to MTV News that the label wanted to postpone the release of the album, which was originally due on this date. As a compromise, the label got to push back the CD release one week if they would release the vinyl on the original date.

SEPTEMBER 18, 1993:

"Heart-Shaped Box" debuts at No. 7 on *Billboard*'s Modern Rock Tracks chart, at No. 23 on *Billboard*'s Mainstream Rock Tracks, and at No. 5 on the UK singles chart. Meanwhile, after two months off *Billboard*'s album chart, *Nevermind* re-enters The Billboard 200 at No. 188. The surge in sales is partially due to exposure from the MTV Video Music Awards a few weeks earlier.

SEPTEMBER 21, 1993:

In Utero is released in the US on CD, and word quickly gets out that Wal-Mart, a mass merchant store known as a "rack," isn't carrying the record because of the fetuses on the back cover and because of the song title "Rape Me."

"The grown-ups don't like it," Kurt told Nirvana biographer Michael Azerrad in 1993 right before the album came out. "I should just re-record this record and do the same thing we did last year because we sold out last year."

Also on this day, the Melvins' *Houdini* is released on Atlantic. Kurt Cobain produced seven songs and played guitar on "Sky Pup."

SEPTEMBER 23, 1993:

Nirvana has rehearsals at NBC's studios in New York for their second and last appearance on "Saturday Night Live." Meanwhile, Wal-Mart confirms that its near 2,000 stores in the US will not carry *In Utero*. They claimed that their "customers are different from those at other stores. The decision is based on customers' desires. They are more interested in country music." In actuality, the chain was afraid that mainstream America would be offended by the fetus collage and the song "Rape Me."

SEPTEMBER 24, 1993:

News breaks that Kmart, another 2,000-store mass merchant chain, is following in Wal-Mart's footsteps, refusing to carry *In Utero*. In order to have their music available to all of their fans, the band later decides to alter the artwork to make it suitable to these chains. The decision seems to coincide with Kurt's goals; he once told the *New York Times*, "One of the main reasons I signed to a major label was so people could buy our records at Kmart. In some small towns, Kmart is the only place that kids can buy records."

SEPTEMBER 25, 1993:

Nirvana – with second guitarist Pat Smear in tow – perform "Heart-Shaped Box" and "Rape Me" on "Saturday Night Live." Charles Barkley hosted. This performance of "Rape Me" is now included on the CD *Saturday Night Live: The Musical Performances, Vol. 2* (released September 21, 1999 on DreamWorks Records). The sticker on the back cover of the CD, however, lists Nirvana, but doesn't list the song title, "Rape Me."

"This was a very tense day," says Jim Merlis, who was at SNL with the group. "Everyone was incredibly high strung, because it's live and 10 minutes before the performance no one knew where Kurt was. It turned out that he and Courtney were in RuPaul's dressing room. It was just very nerve-wracking – everyone was there, the head of Geffen, everyone's wives, journalists. During rehearsals, Adam Sandler did his Eddie Vedder impersonation, but it didn't end up on the show. Courtney was really offended by it because she didn't want [Pearl Jam] to think they were responsible for it. It didn't air on the show because of time, but everyone thought Nirvana had it killed, but they didn't."

● New talent? RuPaul lines up with Nirvana ●

SEPTEMBER 27, 1993:
"Heart-Shaped Box" is released in the UK in a version backed with "Milk It" and "Marigold."

SEPTEMBER 28, 1993:
Rolling Stone names Nirvana's "Smells Like Teen Spirit" video the second best music video ever in their list of 100. Peter Gabriel's "Sledgehammer" ranked No. 1.

SEPTEMBER 29, 1993:
Kevin, his attorney Lee Phillips, and Nirvana's attorney Rosemary Carroll view the "Heart-Shaped Box" video. According to the suit, "A short time later, Nirvana re-cuts the 'Heart-Shaped Box' video. The Second Cut of the 'Heart-Shaped Box' video incorporated even more elements of [Kevin's] video treatment than did the First Cut."

LATE SEPTEMBER/ EARLY OCTOBER 1993:
Nirvana gets their tour manager, Alex MacLeod, to fire their sound man Craig Montgomery, who has worked with the band since 1989. Craig says he was fired because the band wasn't happy with their sound on "Saturday Night Live."

"I mean on SNL, I don't really do the sound," explains Craig. "I just go there and I help the show's mixer do the sound, but I didn't think there was anything wrong with it. I went down to the rehearsal space in Seattle after that, on First Avenue South above Jukebox City. I got there and I could tell there was something negative about the vibe, and people were angry with me. And Kurt, this is totally not like him at all to care about the sound, he said, 'What happened at "Saturday Night Live"? I'm not saying that you did bad sound, but people are telling me that it didn't sound good on TV.'

"And then at this time we were getting ready to go out on the *In Utero* tour," he continues. "I had hired the sound company, a bunch of us on the crew are down at the sound company putting the gear together, painting names and numbers on the road cases and stuff, and then Alex calls me into the office and tells me I'm not doing the tour. The band didn't really want to talk about it at all. At the time, it was pretty devastating for me, but it ended up working out for the best because that was not a very fun tour to be on."

SEPTEMBER/ OCTOBER 1993:
Recording sessions for Hole's *Live Through This* take place at Triclops Studios in Atlanta, Georgia. Kurt sings backing vocals on "Asking For It." Around this time, Kurt is said to have met with Michael Stipe about working together; Kurt apparently put some demos together for Michael but they never had a chance to actually record anything. Courtney would later say that toward the end of his life, all he wanted to do was work with Michael. And Kurt talked to Michael Azerrad about how Courtney was one of the few people he could easily collaborate with, though nothing was officially recorded, and about starting his own label called Exploitation Records.

"I'm extremely proud of what we've accomplished together," Kurt explains to Chuck Crisafulli in the *Fender Frontline* interview. "Having said that, however, I don't know how long we can continue as Nirvana without a radical shift in direction. I have lots of ideas and ambitions

• Pearl Jam's Eddie Vedder •

that have nothing to do with the mass conception of 'grunge' that has been force fed to the record buying public for the last few years. Whether I will be able to do everything I want to do as part of Nirvana remains to be seen. To be fair, I also know that both Krist and Dave have musical ideas that may not work in the context of Nirvana. We're all tired of being labeled. You can't imagine how stifling it is."

OCTOBER 9, 1993:
Even with the album banned at a collective 4,000 Wal-Mart and Kmart stores, *In Utero* debuts at No. 1 on The Billboard 200 with first-week sales of 180,000 units, according to SoundScan.

"We're certain that we won't sell a quarter as much [as *Nevermind*], and we're totally comfortable with that because we like this record so much," Kurt projected in the *Chicago Sun Times* a month earlier. "I wasn't half as proud of *Nevermind* as I am of this record."

OCTOBER 15, 1993:
The *Seattle Times* prints an item saying that the Pearl Jam/Nirvana feud is over and a planned story on the so-called war in *Time* magazine has been squashed. When asked about the feud, Jim Merlis says, "Honestly, it's Courtney. Kurt doesn't like Pearl Jam. It's clear. I don't know how deep it was and quite why it was. He would do these interviews, he would be like 'I have no problem with Pearl Jam' and five minutes later he starts slagging them. And it was almost like he couldn't help himself." Kurt's apparent issue with the group was that they were supposedly "grunge," but he deemed them mainstream, safe rock. "I'm pretty sure they didn't go out of their way to challenge their audience as much as we did with [*In Utero*]," Kurt once told *Rolling Stone*.

OCTOBER 16, 1993:
"Heart-Shaped Box" hits No. 1 and remains there the next week on *Billboard*'s Modern Rock Tracks chart. It is No. 1 for a total of four weeks (October 16, October 23, November 6, and November 13). The song spends the next eight weeks in the top 5 of the chart.

OCTOBER 18, 1993:

Nirvana kicks off their tour for *In Utero* – their first US tour in two years – at Veterans Memorial Coliseum at the Arizona State Fairgrounds in Phoenix, Arizona. Pat Smear, formerly of the Germs, is on board as the second guitarist, Lori Goldston is on cello, and the stage is adorned by two replicas of the see-through bodies with angel wings on the cover of *In Utero* and a few creepy-looking fake trees. Frances Bean and her nanny accompany Kurt for most the dates, while Courtney is recording her new album, *Live Through This*. The band hand-picks their favorite bands to open, including Mudhoney, Meat Puppets, the Boredoms, Half Japanese, Breeders and others.

Krist described the opening night to MTV News: "With all the lighters out there, it felt like we were doing Aerosmith 'Dream On' or something. I felt like Tom Hamilton, the bass player from Aerosmith." In the same interview, Kurt's frustration with larger crowds is evident as he describes the moment in the show where he's standing on the ledge about to jump into the crowd: "I stood for a long time and I know they couldn't read my mind but I was trying to with my eyes tell them, 'Don't hurt me.'... They immediately just started grabbing for me, trying to rip my flesh off for souvenirs... It used to be so much fun in the clubs... It was like a celebration... but these kids, some of 'em don't understand that, they're not used to that. All they know how to do is tear people apart."

Also on this day, Michael Azerrad's biography on the band, *Come As You Are: The Story of Nirvana*, is released. On the release form for the book, Kurt lists his address as "Hell on Earth."

OCTOBER 19, 1993:

Nirvana plays the Albuquerque Convention Center in Albuquerque, New Mexico. The set list stays pretty constant throughout this tour, usually consisting of 21 songs for about 95 minutes, and including "Breed," "Serve the Servants," "In Bloom," "Come As You Are," "Lithium," "Radio Friendly Unit Shifter," "Heart-Shaped Box," "All Apologies" and "Dumb" (both with Goldston on cello), "Polly," "Jesus Wants Me For A Sunbeam," "Pennyroyal Tea," "Rape Me," and "Smells Like Teen Spirit," though the band didn't always play that song.

"The one thing that was amazing to me is that I heard all those songs every night for months and I never got sick of them," Lori Goldston told Gillian G. Gaar in *Goldmine*. During this tour, she also heard the band kick around ideas for what could have been the next album. "I got the sense it would maybe be noticeably different in some way. But the idea of using oboes was the only concrete recurring theme on that subject."

Meanwhile, the "Heart-Shaped Box" video debuts on MTV. Around this time, Kurt tells MTV News that the band's falling out with Kevin Kerslake was over the concept and the budget for the video and that he swears on a stack of Bibles that the whole video was his idea.

OCTOBER 20, 1993:

Reviews start rolling in of the kick-off show in Phoenix. The *Los Angeles Times*' Robert Hilburn wrote that the "pacing was sluggish, and the playing at times reflected the tentativeness of learning to work together onstage." *USA Today*'s Edna Gunderson wrote, "Creative anarchy deteriorated into bad performance art as the band overindulged a tendency toward willful chaos."

"Everyone was down," says Jim Merlis about the *USA Today* review. "And the person that saved everything was Pat Smear. He said, 'I thought the review was the funniest thing I've read in my life.' Him saying that took the whole edge off it." Krist too has said that Pat had a good effect on the band: "He's got a lot of spirit and spunk, and that rubs off on the band," he told *Billboard*.

Jim says that after reading the reviews, Kurt, who is known for being supersensitive about criticism, "actually gets drunk which he rarely, rarely, rarely does, and he meets a guy that's a cross-dresser or something like that. At the [Kansas City show the next night], Kurt asks him to come onstage, but he's not at the show. I can't remember his name but he keeps calling his name out."

OCTOBER 21, 1993:

Nirvana plays Memorial Hall in Kansas City, Kansas. "Backstage was a groupie or a woman trying to be a groupie," says Jim, "and she came up and was like 'Why isn't anything going on backstage?' Nothing ever happened backstage at a Nirvana show, at least not at this point. The band's drinking sodas and eating pretzels." As for the show itself, Jim says that it was just "OK." "They were just sort of getting their legs for touring and they hadn't really got them yet. The next night they really hit it."

OCTOBER 22, 1993:

Nirvana plays Palmer Alumni Auditorium in Davenport, Iowa. "This was a show where you knew it was going to be great even before they went on because the crowd was slam dancing before there was any music playing," says Jim. "There was a great vibe to it. The show was just great. Same set I believe as the night before. So much more powerful, so much more energetic."

After the show Kurt wants to stop at Taco Bell for a bite. Jim was there: "He says, 'You know taco day at school was my favorite day.' I'm not sure if it was Taco Bell, or some knock off, maybe Del Taco? Anyway, we walk in – it's two blocks away from the venue – and everyone that's there has been to the show. The looks on their faces were incredible, but no one would approach him. Finally, someone came up to him with a napkin and asked for an autograph, and he signed it."

OCTOBER 23, 1993:

The first show at the Aragon Ballroom in Chicago goes over well, but the second night, by most accounts, is a disaster. Not all of the dates were sold out on this tour either, but this one was. Kurt jumps off an equipment rack and takes down one of the dummies on the stage. One of the highlights of the show is an unknown song that doesn't appear on any album.

"That's the best show I ever saw the band play," says Jim. "This is the night they did other songs that I hadn't heard them do before. Including a song I have no idea what the name of it is that they never did again." Some Internet reports say the song is either called "On the Mountain" or "You've Got No Right." The song was never titled at the time, but Courtney later performed it with Hole on "MTV Unplugged" under the name "You've Got No Right."

Reviews of the Aragon Ballroom show are phenomenal, with Greg Kot of the *Chicago Tribune* writing, "Nirvana threads rock's

● Life's a blur for Dave Grohl ●

disparate tradition: folk confessionalism, Beatlesque pop, metal roar, and underground skronk [sic]."

After the show, Gary Graff of *Detroit Free Press* does a phone interview with who he thinks is Dave Grohl. It's actually comedian Bobcat Goldthwait as part of a prank pulled by the band's tour manager Alex MacLeod. "We were really trying to make this interview happen," recalls Gary. "But at one point, the guys were just being so difficult, so Jim Merlis kind of threw his hands up and gave me all of their numbers. So, I started pestering the road manager and a couple of times were set up but then fell through. Finally, he got Dave for me. We did a nice interview, he said nothing outlandish. I was totally convinced that I had interviewed Dave Grohl. Jim called me up after in a panic telling me not to run the story because it wasn't Dave Grohl. It was Bobcat Goldthwait. Needless to say, there was a little retribution in their hotel room after that."

OCTOBER 24, 1993:

A rumor circulates that Nirvana is going to play the Lounge Ax club in Chicago on their day off. A few hundred fans even wait outside the club, but the band didn't play, nor were they planning to play. Instead, they lounged around their hotel and watched an advance copy of *Wayne's World 2*.

OCTOBER 25, 1993:

At their second show at the Aragon Ballroom in Chicago, the band is booed by the audience. Kurt complained of sound problems with the monitors, and ended the show prematurely without playing the expected "Smells Like Teen Spirit."

"It was a mess," says Jim Merlis. "Probably the worst show of the tour. I think that part of it was because Kurt was really nervous about the *Rolling Stone* interview that he was doing after the show. But, when we went backstage, the mood was so light and happy. Kurt was playing with Frances. I drive Kurt and David back to the hotel, where I have a suite. I have a tape recorder because we're supposed to tape every interview. I put the tape recorder on Kurt. And I think he did this to show his feathers in front of David Fricke, but he's like, 'This is David Fricke. I totally trust him. You don't need to record this.'" The interview, like many with Kurt, lasted from about midnight until 3:30 in the morning; it was the last major magazine interview Kurt Cobain ever did.

Backstage, it was hard to tell by looking at Kurt that the band just had a bad show. "He was happy because Frances was there," says Jim. "I don't remember seeing Kurt happier. The whole thing about him being so depressed all the time really wasn't the case. He was playing with Frances and beaming. I remember Danny Goldberg saying to Rosemary Carroll that he's never seen him so happy either. [Fatherhood] just seemed very natural for him. Part of him was really like a kid, and even though she was just an infant, he could relate to her. He was just really good with her."

OCTOBER 26, 1993:

Nirvana plays the Mecca Auditorium in Milwaukee, Wisconsin. Second guitarist Pat Smear is going over well. Kurt later told Chuck Crisafulli for the *Fender Frontline* interview that Pat worked out great from day one. "In addition to being one of my closest friends, Pat has found a niche in our music that compliments what was already there without forcing any major changes. I don't see myself ever becoming Mick Jagger, but having Pat onstage has freed me to spend more time connecting with my audience. I've become more of a showman. Let's just say that having Pat to hold down the rhythm allows me to concentrate on the performance as a whole. I think it's improved our live show 100%."

OCTOBER 27, 1993:

Nirvana plays the K-Wings Stadium in Kalamazoo, Michigan. The Meat Puppets and Boredoms take over the opening slot from Mudhoney. The morning of the show, the band does a photo shoot with Mark Seliger for the cover of *Rolling Stone* dressed in suits.

"The Kalamazoo show was amazing because it was the Boredoms and Meat Puppets' first show," says Jim. "Now, there's a change in the opening line-up. I remember Kurt and I watching from the stage just to see the reaction and remembering that is was really cool."

Derrick Bostrom, drummer of the Meat Puppets, was given a little "welcome to the tour" token gift from Dave Grohl and his fiancée at the time, Jennifer. "They gave me one of those lollipops that are on a little

● **In Utero on stage: Lost in music** ●

motor that rotate around. That was his welcome to the tour gift," says Derrick. "Kurt pretty much stayed to himself as much as I did, and I pretty much stayed out of the way."

OCTOBER 29, 1993:

Nirvana plays Michigan State Fairgrounds Coliseum in Detroit, Michigan. "The biggest problem the show had was the venue, it's a horrible concert facility and it just swallows up all the sound," says Gary Graff. "It was packed, hot and sweaty. It was the best recreation of a sweaty rock club on a larger level as you can hope for. The one thing that I remember about it was how almost surprisingly straightforward of a show it was. It wasn't like the show at the Blind Pig in '89 or '90, which was like, 'Oh my God!' They played well, but something was missing. I tend to blame it on the venue, because it kind of sucks the energy out of shows there."

OCTOBER 30, 1993:

Nirvana plays the Hara Arena in Dayton, Ohio. For some reason, Kurt and Krist think that their former drummer Chad Channing is in the audience and they call out to him from the stage to join them for "School," one of their earliest songs that appears on *Bleach*.

"I wasn't there," says Chad Channing. "I heard a tape of that show for the first time [in 1998] and I thought, 'Wow, they stopped the show' and Kurt said, 'OK, we're not gonna play another note, Chad. So you better just get up here.' And they waited quite a while; Kurt was serious about it. There was a good 10-minute gap on the tape where they're yanking around waiting for me to show up and they're yelling for me every now and then. I was never there. It was pretty funny. Had I been there, I would have shown up."

OCTOBER 31, 1993:

The band dresses up for Halloween at their University of Akron show in Akron, Ohio. Kurt is dressed as the purple dinosaur Barney. Pat is dressed as Slash from Guns N' Roses. Dave is a mummy. And Krist is a black-faced Ted Danson (in response to Ted's stunt with his then girlfriend Whoopie Goldberg.)

"They had a fight between Barney and Slash. It was a 'Guitar Battle TO THE DEATH!' as they said. Barney died of course," says the Meat Puppets' Derrick. "And, I can't remember if I saw this, read about it, or someone told me, but I recall someone hitting [Kurt] in the head with a shoe and I think it was this night and he took out his wang and pissed in the shoe and then threw it out back into the crowd." When asked if the band goofed around onstage much during these shows, Derrick countered, "They were a hard-working unit. Both members of the rhythm section were no nonsense and Cobain was more than willing to do his thing. He wasn't a showman, but he wasn't unprofessional either. He just sort of went up and did an unassuming thing."

"Smells Like Teen Spirit" was once again omitted from the set list, but the show was a success nonetheless. *Cleveland Plain Dealer*'s Michael Norman wrote, "The band proved that it has taken the artistic innovation and power of *Nevermind* to an exciting new level."

NOVEMBER 1, 1993:

Travel Day. It was around these shows that Kurt wanted to fire the catering company hired to feed the band, according to Derrick, because the food wasn't what he needed for his sensitive stomach. "I remember, there was a situation where Kurt wanted to fire the caterers. And I was thought that this is the best food we ever had, what's wrong with this guy?" says Derrick. "And of course, it came out later that he was having stomach problems and he couldn't get the bland food that I was eating my whole life and was glad to be away from. So, it made more sense then."

NOVEMBER 2, 1993:

The band delivers yet another amazing show to another sold-out crowd at Verdun Auditorium in Montreal, Quebec, Canada. "Drain You," "Serve the Servants," and "Dumb" were the standouts. "To hear Cobain's voice crack singing 'My heart is broke' in 'Dumb' was to understand it," wrote Mark LePage in the *Montreal Gazette*.

NOVEMBER 4, 1993:

Nirvana sells out one of the biggest venues of tour, the 8,500 capacity Maple Leaf Gardens in Toronto, Ontario, Canada. However, Kurt was crabbier than usual, according to the review in the *Toronto Star*. "Teen Spirit" didn't rear its head, either. "They got a little tired of *Nevermind*, after they played those songs a bunch of times, so long," explains Danny Goldberg. "So the newer songs had a different quality to them."

Krist later joined the Meat Puppets' Derrick Bostrom and Cris and Curt Kirkwood at a party. "We jammed with Krist at an after hours party at some friends of ours in Toronto," says Derrick. "It was after the show sometime after midnight – me and Cris were there, and then their Krist was there. My friends had some gear so we ended up doing a jam. I think Krist played guitar and my Cris and I played our own instrument, no one sang. It was just a jam – some noodling, noise. It was just kind of

● The Meat Puppets – one of Nirvana's favorite bands ●

vamping on chord changes, just kind of like rock noise jam; kind of a typical Meat Puppets kind of a jam."

NOVEMBER 5, 1993:

Amidst the promotion for *In Utero*, sales of *Nevermind* remain steady. The album is certified by the Recording Industry Association of America for 5 million copies. Danny Goldberg told *Newsweek* that MTV is to thank for pushing album sales to the 5 million mark.

The band plays the University of Buffalo's North Campus Alumni Arena in Amherst, NY and is joined by the Meat Puppets and Boredoms for a jam on "Smells Like Teen Spirit." Earlier in the set, Kurt yells at the security guards, who are keeping fans at bay – "You guys in the yellow shirts, get the fuck out of here, you're spoiling the fun. They're not hurting anybody, so let them stay." Kurt then jumps into the crowd, speaks to security, then returns asking fans not to get on top of anyone else because if they don't stop they'll get thrown out. He added, "And if you don't like it, go home, we got your money." Now, that's the spirit. Spotted in the audience were City Council members Greg Olma and Dave Czajka.

"Courtney and Frances were there," recalls Derrick, "and I remember at some point Kurt was asking my Curt, 'So, Curt, you're a father. Courtney and I were arguing this issue about if the baby is crying at night should we bring her into our bed or just let her cry?' I don't remember the answer, but I do remember him asking what he had learned as a father."

By the last night of their stint on the tour, the Meat Puppets knew they were going to join Nirvana at their "MTV Unplugged" taping the following month. According to Derrick, this is how it came about: "There had been talk of my guys teaching their guys how to do the songs that they wanted to do, because apparently it's not really obvious song structures. And I remember joking with my guys, 'Hell, you should just put off teaching them as long as you can, maybe they'll end up having to invite you on the show.' It was a half-serious notion, and that's what ended up happening. They never got around to learning the songs so it was like just come along, 'This is gonna be a stressful enough thing anyway, we'll just have some friends along.' It wasn't like we were best buds from day one, we just happened to be there."

NOVEMBER 6, 1993:

"Heart-Shaped Box" peaks at No. 4 on *Billboard*'s Mainstream Rock Tracks chart and is the most played video on MTV. An article in *Billboard* magazine quotes Geffen's head of marketing Robert Smith as saying that the "trend of grunge is probably dead and almost buried."

NOVEMBER 7, 1993:

Nirvana performs at William and Mary Hall in Williamsburg, Virginia. Strangely, in all of their years of touring, the band never played one of the largest cities in the Mid-Atlantic region: Baltimore. Back in LA, Mrs. Kurt Cobain and her band play the Palace in Hollywood supporting the Lemonheads. Rumors start to circulate that Courtney and lead Lemonhead Evan Dando are having a fling. Right around this time, there is also talk that Courtney is rekindling her affair with Billy Corgan, and she told the press around this time that he was great in bed.

NOVEMBER 8, 1993:

The Armory in Philadelphia is next. "Krist went up to the mike and said something like, 'Was anyone here when we played J.C. Dobbs that one time?' Then he ran back to the mike [embarrassed] and said, 'I mean *three* times,'" according to Tom Sheehy, publicist for the Philly club J.C. Dobbs. "It was an amazing show," recalls writer Marci Cohen. "The band seemed like they were having fun."

NOVEMBER 9, 1993:

"All Apologies" is sent to radio in the US and released commercially in the UK backed with "Rape Me." The band plays the Stabler Arena at LeHigh University in Bethlehem, Pennsylvania. And the *No Alternative* compilation is released on Arista Records, featuring Nirvana's "Verse Chorus Verse" as the unlisted secret track.

NOVEMBER 10, 1993:

Nirvana's performance of "Sliver" from the Springfield Civic Center in Springfield, Massachusetts on this date is later used for the *From the Muddy Banks of the Wishkah* live album.

Kurt messed up in the middle of "Dumb" because he was distracted by a disturbance in the crowd. "Kurt was, what can I say, he seemed pretty wasted, but it was a great show," recalls John R. Wallace, a long-time fan and collector. "He went off on certain things, played longer on some songs, extra on the leads, such as on 'Territorial Pissings,' 'Teen Spirit,' and 'Rape Me.' It seemed like he was going to walk off halfway through the set warning the crowd, 'If you throw one more shoe or coin, I'm gonna to leave for an hour.'"

Regardless of the flashes of happiness some might have seen from Kurt on this tour, *Boston Globe*'s Jim Sullivan observed quite the opposite, saying that Cobain's outpouring of emotions on this night "didn't seem the confessions of an overpaid rock star, but the cries of an over-stressed human being."

NOVEMBER 11, 1993:

On their day off, the band check out a Buzzcocks show in Boston and meet them after the show.

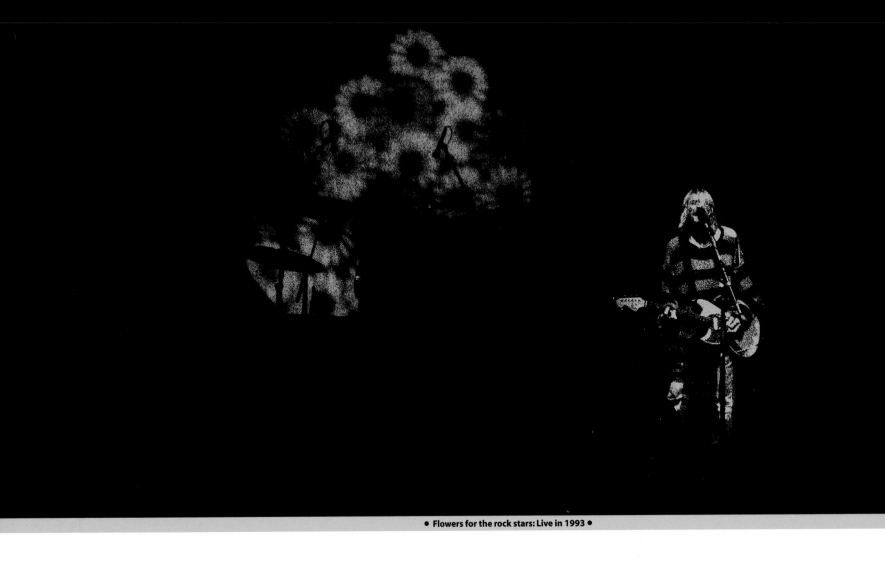

● **Flowers for the rock stars: Live in 1993** ●

NOVEMBER 12, 1993:

Nirvana plays the George Wallace Civic Center, a hockey rink, in Fitchburg, Massachusetts. Backstage after the show, Kurt was gracious with some friends and fans who asked for autographs. John R. Wallace brought three collectibles, including the 7-inch single of "Love Buzz" for Kurt to sign. He signed his name three different ways for John: Kurtis, Kurt, and Kurdt.

Also backstage, Alex Coletti of MTV brought Kurt some sketches of the stage he had planned for the "MTV Unplugged" show a week away. After Kurt described that he wanted lots of candles and lilies on the stage, Alex Coletti asked, "You mean like a funeral?" Kurt replied, "Yeah."

NOVEMBER 13, 1993:

Nirvana plays Bender Arena at American University in Washington, DC. The band jams on "Donuts" by the Legend, which is Everett True of *Melody Maker*'s band. Everett sang vocals with Kurt.

NOVEMBER 14, 1993:

Everett True once again screams into the mike with the band at their New York Coliseum show. "Kurt wasn't even singing. It was Everett by himself. It was so terrible. Kurt brought him onstage, and he just screamed into the microphone," says Jim Merlis. The show's 7,000 seats sold out immediately; however, the sound was terrible. "I remember during 'Rape Me' seeing little girls singing it, and thinking it was a little twisted," adds Jim. "The band played really well."

NOVEMBER 15, 1993:

The band's second night in New York is at the Roseland Ballroom, where just four months earlier they test-drove the acoustic part of the set. This time around, the kinks are worked out and the band hits their mark. The show includes a jam on the Stooges' "I Wanna Be Your Dog."

● **Nirvana's MTV Unplugged session, November 18** ●

NOVEMBER 16, 1993:

A review of the November 14 show runs in the *New York Times*, with the keen observation by writer Peter Watrous: "Mr. Cobain has presented himself as the reluctant pop performer (though a stage seems like an odd place to hide) and in performance he tries his best to come off as an anti-star, standing still for the most part and drawling his words unemotionally. But there's no escape from the pop mechanism, and it seems as if Mr. Cobain hasn't quite come to terms with it."

NOVEMBER 18, 1993:

In the morning, Nirvana rehearses for their pivotal "MTV Unplugged" performance, and isn't 100% clear on what they're going to play. "I just remember after rehearsals, John Silva was around and he was saying, not just to me, that they have not a clue what they're going to do," says Jim Merlis. "The Stone Temple Pilots had done their 'Unplugged' show recently and it took about six hours or four hours and everyone was saying how they did songs over and over again. And I was just like, 'Oh God, this is going to be miserable,' because in the back of my mind is Silva saying they have no idea what they're even going to play."

The band performs an eclectic mix of songs on the show: "About a Girl," "Come As You Are," the Vaselines' "Jesus Doesn't Want Me For a Sunbeam," David Bowie's "The Man Who Sold the World," "Pennyroyal Tea," "Dumb," "Polly," "On a Plain," "Something in the Way," the Meat Puppets' "Plateau," "Oh Me," and "Lake of Fire," featuring Cris and Curt Kirkwood of the Meat Puppets, "All Apologies," and Leadbelly's "Where Did You Sleep Last Night?" The performance was captured in one take; there were no encores.

While this is arguably one of the best musical moments on TV, MTV execs didn't initially see it that way. Alex Coletti, the show's producer, told

Guitar World, "I said to MTV, 'They're going to bring some guests on.' And at first everybody's eyes lit up, like, 'Who's it gonna be?' They wanted to hear the 'right' names – Eddie Vedder or Tori Amos or God knows who. But when I said, 'The Meat Puppets,' it was kind of like, 'Oh great. They're not doing any hits, and they're inviting guests who don't have any hits to come play. Great.'" It was great.

The "Unplugged" performance was very important to Kurt and, at the time, to the future of Nirvana. "He loved doing 'Unplugged,'" says Danny Goldberg. "He called me afterward and he was very proud of it and said it was the best thing they'd ever done and it was gonna broaden the band's appeal." Jim remembers Kurt calling his mother afterwards to tell her about the show: "He was really proud, I mean really proud. It was very special."

"After the show, there were all these kids there and he started hugging the kids. They were calling 'Kurt! Kurt!' And, he's hugging them. It was really cool," says Kurt St. Thomas of WFNX.

NOVEMBER 23, 1993:

The Beavis and Butt-Head Experience soundtrack album is released on Geffen featuring Nirvana's previously unreleased, "I Hate Myself and I Want to Die." Kurt was a fan of the animated MTV show. When *People* magazine came to interview Courtney in June 1993, he told the magazine, "I know Beavis and Butt-Head. I grew up with people like that. I recognize them."

NOVEMBER 26, 1993:

For whatever strange reason, fans threw a lot of shoes at the band on this tour. But at the Jacksonville, Florida show at the Moroccan Temple Shrine Auditorium, it was opening act the Breeders who got the footwear thrown at them. When Nirvana took the stage, Kurt asked fans to "keep your shoes to yourselves."

NOVEMBER 27, 1993:

Nirvana performs at Bayfront Amphitheater in Miami, Florida. An Internet report says that Kurt's guitar solo features a snippet of Led Zeppelin's "Heartbreaker."

"The one thing that was completely striking about the show was they had the angels onstage and every time Kurt moved in front them he looked like an angel himself. It was completely creepy later on thinking of that image," recalls Jessicka, lead singer of the Florida-bred band Jack Off Jill, who was at the show with Twiggy Ramirez from Marilyn Manson.

NOVEMBER 28, 1993:

Nirvana performs at Lakeland Civic Center in Lakeland, Florida. Speaking in general about the larger arenas that Nirvana played, Danny Goldberg says, "Kurt liked to be close to the fans. I didn't think he liked when there was a large physical distance from the fans. And he loved breaking guitars, it was just one of his favorite things."

NOVEMBER 29, 1993:

Kurt yells at a guy from the stage to stop grabbing a woman's breasts at their gig in Atlanta at the Omni.

• Angelic: Kurt on stage •

NOVEMBER 30, 1993:

Last month, *Nevermind* was certified for 5 million units; now, on this day, *In Utero* is certified for 1 million copies, making it a platinum record.

Commercial success like this – and the fame it brought – was tough for Kurt to handle. Kurt's Aunt Mari Earl explains it to *Goldmine*'s Gillian G. Gaar: "Music was for Kurt, as it was for me at one time, an escape, a way to express what was inside himself. It was an understanding friend, predictable and comforting. When he became famous, music was no longer an escape for him, it was a nightmare of scheduled 'creativity' and harried performances. It was almost as if he became a caricature of himself and the whole grunge movement. Kurt's success only reinforced my suspicions of how the music business operates. By that, I mean the artist becomes a commodity, a can of beans, if you will, merely a saleable product. Can anything drain the human spirit more?"

DECEMBER 1, 1993:

Nirvana plays Boutwell Auditorium in Birmingham, Alabama.

DECEMBER 2, 1993:

Tall-Leon City Civic Center in Tallahassee, Florida is the next tour stop.

DECEMBER 3, 1993:

Nirvana plays UNO Lakefront Arena in New Orleans. The *Times-Picayune*'s Scott Aiges described the show as "businesslike, crisp, confident, and clear-eyed." The tour clearly differs from the band's early performances filled with more emotion and fun. The reviewer notices, "The musicians interacted neither with the crowd nor with one another. At the most, Cobain would give a quick glance at his band mates to see if they were ready before he plunged from one tune into the next."

DECEMBER 4, 1993:

"All Apologies" debuts at No. 27 on *Billboard*'s Modern Rock Tracks chart. The line in the song that says, "Married, Buried" had led some to believe it was Cobain's statement on his own marriage to Courtney.

DECEMBER 5, 1993:

Nirvana plays Fairpark Coliseum in Dallas.

DECEMBER 6, 1993:

"Lap by lap, song by song, in a most orderly fashion" is how the *Houston Chronicle*'s Marty Racine described the group's AstroArena show in Houston, Texas. Near the end of the show, Kurt asked fans how they like their new Pearl Jam album, in reaction to their rivals outselling them.

When asked if he liked playing larger arenas, Krist Novoselic joked with Gillian G. Gaar in the *Rocket* that they were upset they didn't play the even larger venue in town, the Astrodome. "We want to play huge enormo-domes," he kids, "but the reality dictates that we play the small halls; so much for our egos. We wanted to play the Astrodome, and what we played was the AstroArena. It's right next to the Astrodome. We drove up to it and we saw the Astrodome and we saw the AstroArena, which held like 8 or 9,000 and maybe 6,000 showed up. Maybe we're not so big in Houston. Everything's big in Texas except Nirvana."

DECEMBER 8, 1993:
Nirvana plays the TNT Building in Oklahoma City, Oklahoma.

DECEMBER 9, 1993:
Nirvana plays the Ak-Sar-Ben Coliseum in Omaha, Nebraska.

DECEMBER 10, 1993:
Their Roy Wilkins Auditorium show in St. Paul, Minnesota is an instant sell-out, but garners more attacks from the media. "Kurt Cobain hardly lived up to his over the edge image," wrote the *Star Tribune*'s Jon Bream. "He was in control… never flirting with the kind of danger that has helped make Nirvana an appealing champion with its sound of anger, cynicism, escapism and affirmation that it's OK to be sad, it's OK to be a slacker, it's OK to be misunderstood. During the final feedback-drenched encore, he did carry on like a punk rock star, eventually simulating a suicide by electrocution." Also at the show, Kim Deal of the Breeders walked onstage during "Scentless Apprentice" and stage dove.

After the show, there was an alleged incident involving a trashed hotel room, which Krist later spoke to Gillian G. Gaar about: "There's wine all over the walls. Ask Kurt Loder [of MTV News]. He'll tell you about it. He was there. He did it. And since I was so drunk, he did it, not me." Of course, Krist is joking, but he did say that the hotel was going to charge the band $3,000 for damages.

DECEMBER 12, 1993:
The "All Apologies" video, from their "MTV Unplugged" performance, debuts on MTV. And rehearsals for MTV's "Live and Loud" New Year's Eve special take place at Pier 48 in Seattle. The show featured Nirvana, the Breeders, and Cypress Hill. Pearl Jam was supposed to perform, but bailed at the last minute because Eddie Vedder was sick. Nirvana hangs out on the set on this day, but they don't actually rehearse until the day of the show.

"Everyone was there all day, there was a big cafeteria where all the bands ate and hung out," says Tom Phalen, who was covering the event for the *Seattle Times* and *Rolling Stone*. "The vibe was good, except for Pearl Jam because Eddie didn't show for rehearsals and then we found out that they weren't going to play. So Nirvana immediately decided they wanted Mudhoney to play, so Dave and Krist start going, 'We want the Honeys! We want the Honeys!' And they're jumping up on the table, going 'Honeys! Honeys! Honeys!' They went off to find someone to see if they could get the band on the bill, but it didn't happen."

DECEMBER 13, 1993:
MTV's "Live and Loud" is taped at Pier 48 in Seattle. The band's performance of "Scentless Apprentice" is later included on *From the Muddy Banks of the Wishkah*. The band did their rehearsal for the show on this morning.

Tom Phalen recalls seeing Courtney, Frances, and the nanny (they went through a lot of nannies) backstage: "He was onstage and I think it was during sound check before the actual show and I went by the tech truck for MTV, it had monitors in it, and Courtney was sitting there with Frances in her lap, and Kurt was on the screen and the kid was reaching up to the screen going 'Daddy.' I was like, wow, family man.

With Frances around, Kurt just seemed lighter. He wasn't dragging his ass around. He was walking with a spring in his step; he looked good. He just had more energy and it came across when they played too."

At the end of the show, Charles R. Cross, Editor of the *Rocket*, says, "They not only destroyed their instruments, they destroyed the set, the speakers, bits of the stage. It was out of control. He was just smashing everything."

During a brief interview with Gillian G. Gaar in a hallway at the show, she asked Krist how he felt about doing all the corporate promotional things like this show with MTV. Krist answered, "We're dancing with the devil. There's no denying it. We always have been, from the day we signed that contract. Not the contract with Geffen, but the contract at the crossroads. There's just no denying it."

DECEMBER 14, 1993:
The *In Utero* tour rolls on, stopping at the Armory in Salem, Oregon on this night.

DECEMBER 15, 1993:
Nirvana plays Boise State University Pavilion in Boise, Idaho.

DECEMBER 16, 1993:
MTV airs Nirvana's "MTV Unplugged" show on the network for the first time. Meanwhile, the band plays the Golden Spike Arena in Ogden, Utah.

DECEMBER 18, 1993:
Nirvana plays the Denver Coliseum in Denver, Colorado.

DECEMBER 19, 1993:
The fallout from the *Chicago Tribune* article that said DGC might reject *In Utero* not only cost the label the price of a full-page ad in *Billboard* to refute the rumor, it also apparently cost the producer at the center of the controversy – Steve Albini – some work as well.

"I've gotten exactly one phone call out of a No. 1 record. It shows how pack-like these major label people are," Albini tells Chuck Crisafulli in a *Los Angeles Times* article on this day. "They all think the same thing: that Albini guy is trouble. Stay away." Since his work with Nirvana, Steve recorded Bush, PJ Harvey, Cheap Trick, and many others.

DECEMBER 23, 1993:
Nirvana plays the Arco Arena in Sacramento, California.

DECEMBER 24-28, 1993:
The band has some time off to spend with their families for the holidays. Around this time, Kurt and Courtney take a mini-vacation at Canyon Ranch Spa in Tucson, Arizona.

"...IT WAS OUT OF CONTROL. HE WAS JUST SMASHING EVERYTHING."

DECEMBER 25, 1993:

In Utero ranks at No. 74 on *Billboard*'s Top Pop Albums year-end chart and "Heart-Shaped Box" ranks No. 35 on the Top Album Rock Tracks year-end charts in *Billboard*'s 1993 Year in Review issue.

DECEMBER 29, 1993:

The San Diego Sports Arena in San Diego, California is the next stop on the tour.

DECEMBER 30, 1993:

Nirvana's performance of "Heart-Shaped Box" from the Great Western Forum in Inglewood, California, near Los Angeles, on this date is later used for *From the Muddy Banks of the Wishkah*.

Dave Navarro was among the many celebrities at the show this evening. "It was just phenomenal," remembers Dave. "And the one thing that I always thought was really an asset to them is they could never go wrong live. If they didn't care and looked like they didn't care, and looked like they were over it or weren't into it. The crowd kind of wanted them to look that way. So, if they had a show where it was showmanship and spectacular and throwing around guitars and jumping into drums, that was as exciting as seeing them be totally disenchanted with their success, which is part of the mystery that made that band exciting. So to watch Kurt be disinterested was interesting."

Backstage, Eddie Van Halen was spotted drunk and calling out to Krist, recalls Jim Merlis, who was also at the show. "I was talking to Krist and all of a sudden this person, who I thought was a kid, kept on saying, 'You should play basketball. You're so tall.' And I turn around and it's Eddie Van Halen. They were like, 'What the fuck's Eddie Van Halen doing down here?' And I missed part of this, but the lore of it goes that Eddie approached Kurt about jamming with him onstage, which you know they're not the kind of band to jam onstage. They're just not. It really didn't happen. Kurt was trying to be nice and he's like, 'What guitar are you going to use?' Eddie goes, 'I'll take the Mexican's,' meaning Pat Smear. Kurt got pissed and said to him, 'Why don't you go onstage after we finish playing, before our encore, by yourself. Courtney supposedly ran into the other room and told John Silva or someone that Kurt was about to be mean to Eddie Van Halen. Whoever it was, was like, 'OK, whatever.'"

DECEMBER 31, 1993:

Bobcat Goldthwait emcees the New Year's Eve show at the Oakland Coliseum Arena in Oakland, California. Meanwhile, MTV airs their "Live and Loud" special featuring Nirvana.

Cheryl Kovalchik recalls a funny comment Bobcat made about Krist, saying he wanted to make a movie of Curious George and cast Krist as the man in the big yellow hat. The morning of the show, Cheryl took Krist and Bobcat to KITS (Live 105, the alternative station in town) to promote the show. "It was not one of their better shows, in my opinion," says Cheryl. "Kurt wasn't in a bad mood, no, I don't think it was that. There were just moments of brilliance and there were moments of not so brilliance."

• **Post "Live and Loud"** •

PEACE, LOVE, EMPATHY

JANUARY 1, 1994:

The *Los Angeles Times* prints a not-so-flattering review of the band's December 30, 1993 Great Western Forum concert in LA, criticizing the smashing of the guitars as a "ritual" that has "become tedious" and suggests, "As Nirvana moves confidently into the New Year, this is one part of its repertoire that is best left behind." On this night, the tour stops at Jackson County Expo Hall in Medford, Oregon.

JANUARY 3-4, 1994:

Nirvana plays two nights at the Pacific National Exhibition Forum in Vancouver, Canada. The Butthole Surfers and Tad open and comedian Bobcat Goldthwait was the emcee.

JANUARY 5, 1994:

Mistakes happen. Geffen made one on the live album, *From the Muddy Banks of the Wishkah*, when they listed "Milk It" was from a January 5, 1994 show at Seattle Center Arena. In fact, there was no show on this

date. The song is actually from the January 7, 1994 show. According to Robert Fisher, *From the Muddy Banks of the Wishkah*, once had a working title of *Donkey Show*. Robert explains: "A donkey show is a sex show where women fuck donkeys. No one at the record label cared until they found out what it meant. And it was gonna be a double album – like the 'MTV Unplugged' performance with a live record, but then they broke it up into two instead."

JANUARY 6, 1994:

Nirvana plays the Spokane Coliseum in Spokane, Washington with the Butthole Surfers and Chokebore opening up. And the 36th annual Grammy Awards, nominations are announced. Nirvana is nominated for Best Alternative Album for *In Utero*. Their competition is Belly's *Star*, R.E.M.'s *Automatic For the People*, Smashing Pumpkins' *Siamese Dream*, and U2's *Zooropa*.

January 7-8, 1994:

Nirvana performs a two-night stand at the Seattle Center Arena. Chokebore and Butthole Surfers open. On the first night of the show, they dedicate "Smells Like Teen Spirit" to Seattle. Kurt told the crowd, "This song made Seattle the most livable city in America."

Grant Alden, then Managing Editor of Seattle's the *Rocket*, remembers the first night well: "They had always been much better on record for me up until this show. Kurt was obviously a wounded creature by this point. It was one of those nights where your back just sort of tingles. His voice was amazing. It was the first time I saw him do onstage what he can do on record. And it was the first time I became painfully aware of the price he paid for making the hair on my back stand up."

Mike Musburger was impressed by how the band embraced the big production of a rock show with such integrity. "It was like, 'Wow production.' I never thought Nirvana would step up to the challenge of having rock and roll production," he says. "But I thought they did it really, really well. It looked cool. It fit them. It sounded really great. The second guitar and the cello, just was great. It really worked. They seemed totally at ease with it. Kurt even talked to the crowd more."

Backstage, the band wasn't letting many people in their dressing room with the exception of Jim Rose of the Circus Sideshow and his wife Bebe. "The band was holding court in the dressing room, and they weren't letting anyone in at this point, and Jim Rose comes down the hallway with Bebe. So they let him into the dressing room, a few minutes later all the other people got kicked out," recalls Mike.

These were their last ever U.S. shows.

January 10, 1994:

The 1994 Brit Awards nominations are announced at the Hard Rock Café in London and Nirvana is nominated for Best International Group up against Crowded House, Pearl Jam, the Spin Doctors, and U2.

January 14, 1994:

Dave Grohl turns 25 years old. Courtney Love has made claims that, toward the end, Kurt "hated" Dave. On Howard Stern's nationally syndicated radio show on December 9, 1999, Courtney said, "He hated his guts! For five years I've been quiet about this. [Kurt] loved him at first, because he was sweet, funny and lovely. And then he turned into such a dick. This whirlwind of success was happening for Dave, and he really turned his back on Kurt. His singer had a drug problem, and he wouldn't talk to him, he wouldn't take his phone calls. He wasn't his friend anymore."

Dave took the high road and didn't react in the press to Courtney's comments, though most believe that "Stacked Actors" from the Foo Fighters' third album, 2000's *There Is Nothing Left to Lose*, is about Ms. Love. Dave also described the band's relationship in a 1999 interview on www.allstarnews.com as, "It's like the greatest love affair but with three people. And no sex."

January 19, 1994:

Kurt and Courtney purchase a $1.13 million 1901 gray, shake-covered house on 171 Lake Washington Blvd. East in the upscale Madrona neighborhood of Seattle along the west shore of Lake Washington.

The purchase is a far cry from Kurt's earliest aspirations to earn enough money to buy a piece of land that both he and his best friend at the time, Krist, could live on with their girlfriends. Sub Pop's Megan Jasper recalls an early conversation: "I remember one time they were in my office waiting for Jonathan and Bruce and they were making jokes about why they were making records, they were half-joking, because they never thought it would be possible, but they wanted to buy a chunk of land in the middle of nowhere that was all farm land. And they wanted it to be big enough so Krist and Shelli could have a house built on that land, and Kurt and Tracy [Marander, Kurt's first girlfriend] wanted a house on the same chunk of property, so they could be neighbors and have these great farmhouses. And they were laughing because they never thought they'd be able to have it. Those two [Kurt and Krist] were inseparable at the time. They were so tight."

January 22, 1994:

"All Apologies" shoots to No. 1 from No. 9 on *Billboard*'s Modern Rock Tracks chart. This is the band's third No. 1 single in the US.

January 24, 1994:

The *Advocate* prints a Letter to the Editor from Kurt that reads: "Of all the gut spilling, and, uh, whining I did in 1993, I never felt more relaxed than with the *Advocate*. What can I say? Thank you to the editors. I'll always be an advocate for fagdom."

January 25, 1994:

The Meat Puppets' breakthrough album, *Too High to Die*, is released featuring a sticker on the cover with this quote from Kurt Cobain: "The Meat Puppets gave me a completely different attitude toward music. I owe so much to them." The Meat Puppets owed a bit to Nirvana too, as interest in the band grew after Cris and Curt Kirkwood performed with Nirvana on "MTV Unplugged" just two months earlier.

● **The new family home at 171 Lake Washington Blvd East, Seattle** ●

• Dave Grohl with new haircut •

JANUARY 27, 1994:

Nirvana's last *Rolling Stone* cover story – and Kurt Cobain's last major interview – is published. The cover line reads "Success Doesn't Suck." In it, Kurt tells David Fricke, "I still see stuff, descriptions of rock stars in some magazine – 'Sting the environmental guy' and 'Kurt Cobain, the whiny, complaining, neurotic, bitchy guy who hates everything, hates rock stardom, hates his life.' And I've never been happier in my life."

JANUARY 28-29, 1994:

Krist and Dave track bass and drum parts at Robert Lang Studios in North Seattle for what would've been their next album. Pat Smear was at home in Los Angeles.

"The first two days Krist and Dave did tracking on a couple songs," Robert Lang told Gillian G. Gaar in *Goldmine*. "And then they did some other tunes. One song was totally completed with Kurt's vocals on it; Kurt came in Sunday in the afternoon and did some vocals. Then they did some guitar tracks and then we went and had dinner. They were so happy; the way the tracks sounded, how quick it went down; the whole vibe was really good."

JANUARY 30, 1994:

With basic tracks laid down, Kurt records his vocal parts at Robert Lang Studios. Songs from these sessions were expected to be included on the Nirvana box set that Geffen was planning in early 2000 when the first edition of this book was being finished.

JANUARY 1994:

Sometime this month, word gets out that Nirvana might headline the touring rock festival Lollapalooza in the summer. They would have reportedly been paid $9 million. Courtney is said to have been displeased when Kurt turned down the tour.

FEBRUARY 2, 1994:

Nirvana departs for the European leg of their *In Utero* tour. Joining them for the first time on cello is Melora Creager, from the New York-based gothic cello trio Rasputina, who are known for their costumes of Victorian corsets and bloomers.

The classically-trained Melora was hired a few months earlier when her friend, photographer Michael Lavine, told her the band was looking for a replacement for Lori Goldston, who appeared on the US leg of the tour. "He said that Kurt wanted a new cellist and to send my stuff to their management," recalls Melora. "I never heard anything for a long time, and then Michael called me and told me they were going to hire me and that the shit's gonna hit the fan, so get ready for the phone call. Kurt called me himself. Michael had told Kurt what Rasputina was like and I think that's part of why Kurt was interested. I wore the corset [on the tour] sometimes because it freaked Pat out. He was so funny about it."

FEBRUARY 3, 1994:

The band arrives in Europe. While Krist and Dave's wives are with them, Courtney was off doing her own thing and Kurt reportedly missed her immensely. "She was constantly *about* to come. Her arrival was always impending, but she never came [until a month later]," says Melora.

FEBRUARY 4, 1994:

Nirvana's first performance on this tour was actually a television appearance in Javel, France at Canal + Nulle Part Ailleurs. They perform "Rape Me," "Pennyroyal Tea," and "Drain You."

"We all went to the taping of a TV show because they'd never know what song they were going to do, so I never knew if I was going to play or not," says Melora, who only played on the handful of songs that featured the cello. "Later, in Rome, the tour manager told Kurt to have me play because I'm always hanging around anyway, so I got to play on that TV show."

Melora says the band headed out to the shopping district while in France and bought "suits like the Knack. They were really into that. I got sent off with the wives and girlfriends, because being a girl, and being in the band, but not really being in the band, I would be put with the girlfriends."

FEBRUARY 5, 1994:

The band flies to Lisbon, Portugal for their first show. During the day, they go to an American pizza parlor next to the hotel. "Everyone recognized Kurt and he seemed surprised at this even though he was on the TV at the time," says Melora. "All I can remember from this day is that everyone had to fill out landing forms in Portugal, and it seemed really hard for them. It was like they didn't know their addresses and stuff like that."

● Coutney looks pensive in early 1994 ●

FEBRUARY 6, 1994:

The band plays their first show of the six-week trek at Pavilhao Dramatico in Cascais, Portugal. The Buzzcocks are the opening act through February 18.

Surprisingly, the band never rehearsed with the new cellist prior to the tour, who admits to being pretty scared when she first arrived in Europe. "We just started straight into these huge shows," she says. "I had never done anything on that scale at all. Kurt's funny because through the whole thing, he kind of pretends like he's a bad musician, like 'Oh make up whatever you want because the songs are really easy.' And I got really excited – or overexcited – so all my parts were all cadenzas and crazy cello everywhere and I'm playing and playing and Krist Novoselic kind of had a problem with that. So Krist would ask me, 'You're playing like the record, right?' And I was probably closest to Pat Smear so I would tell him, 'Uh, Krist is asking if I'm playing like the record and Kurt told me to play whatever I wanted.' Those guys didn't really talk much, you know how that happens with bands? And in my mind, Kurt's the leader and he told me to play whatever I wanted, but Krist didn't like it like that. It was really nerve-wracking."

To work it out, Kurt sat Melora down in a room with Krist – "like a teacher," she says – and listened to what she was playing. "We ended up mixing it up a bit. Some things, I made up. Some things were from the record."

FEBRUARY 7, 1994: TRAVEL DAY.

The band members were traveling in separate buses by this time. It could easily be argued that this was due to the sheer fact that some people smoked and others didn't, but it also seemed obvious that there was a lot of tension in the air that divided the camp. "Krist and Shelli and Dave and Jennifer were on one bus," explains Melora. "And Pat and Kurt and Alex MacLeod, the tour manager, were on the other and that was a smoking bus, so I went to the smoking bus. I remember Jennifer going 'Don't go there. Come with us. It's evil, don't go.' It was like there was the normal, happy bus and then the weird, tense smoking bus."

After the first gig, the band viewed a tape of the show to work out some other kinks with the cello parts. "There's a lot of technical problems with the cello and I couldn't hear myself. The cello would go out of tune with temperature changes where it would be freezing in the locker rooms and then really hot onstage. I had blisters on my hands from trying to tune it constantly, so it was very difficult. It took a while to work it out, but they were really nice about it," explains Melora.

FEBRUARY 8, 1994:

Nirvana plays their second European show at Pabellon de Deportes del Real in Madrid, Spain. Courtney later told *Rolling Stone* that Kurt called her from Spain on this tour very upset. "He hated everything, everybody. Hated, hated, hated. He called me from Spain crying. I was gone 40 days [the longest the two have been apart]. I was doing my thing with my band for the first time since forever," Courtney told the magazine. "He was in Madrid, and he'd walked through the audience. The kids were smoking heroin off tinfoil, and the kids were going, 'Kurt! Smack!' and giving him the thumbs up. He called me, crying… He did not want to become a junkie icon."

FEBRUARY 9, 1994:

In Barcelona, Spain, the entourage became a little more comfortable with each other. "It started to get a little bit more fun," says Melora. "We got to hang out in Barcelona, maybe that's why it was more fun. After the show [at Palalio Desportes], there were a lot of fans around the hotel. The band had to squeeze by, like the Beatles, and I got stuck accidentally outside with the fans. That would happen a lot. It was like, 'Please let me in.' I'm kind of shy, basically, so I was like should I tell them? Or do they give a shit? I wasn't aggressive enough to get through these fans, I guess.

"People would ask later about the groupies and this and that," she continues. "But it wasn't like that at all. The fans were nice – people you would want as friends in this weird situation of super rock stars. Some fans would be in such painful ecstasy [over the music]. Some people would give Kurt drawings and drugs and I know that would make him feel weird, drawings like him as Christ. It was really sick. And whenever he could, I think it happened in Barcelona or Madrid, he would start stuff from the dressing room. They [fans] never know if you're in there, but if he can see the line outside the window he'd like throw beers down there and they would see that he's up there and everyone would go crazy."

FEBRUARY 10, 1994:

The band plays Palais des Sports in Toulouse, France. While Melora was asked to learn the entire *MTV Unplugged in New York* album, the band usually only performed about five songs that required cello. "We did different songs each night," she says. "[David Bowie's] 'The Man Who Sold the World' I especially liked playing, but they didn't do that very often. The Leadbelly song, 'Where Did You Sleep Last Night?,' they never actually did, but I learned that anyway. I don't think we ever played it. 'Polly' was always played, 'Something in the Way' I learned, but we never played. 'All Apologies' was always played, and 'Dumb.'"

FEBRUARY 11, 1994:

Travel day. On the band's days off, they were usually just traveling and had little time to partake in much sightseeing. "There would just be a few minutes of holes and Kurt always wanted to see things in the different cities, and he always seemed to feel cheated that he couldn't see something," says Melora. "He wanted to see the Guillotine place, but we just drove by it, and he's like [in a sad voice] 'Oh, thanks a lot.' I worked out a system where I'd read the book on the city in the morning, go try to see something in the day, so I'd try to force myself to see things, mostly with Pat Smear. Pat was definitely my friend of them."

FEBRUARY 12, 1994:

The band plays in Toulon, France at Zenith Omega. "This was on the Riviera," says Melora. "All I remember were these really skeevy people backstage specifically to see Kurt – it was a couple, they were in like designer jeans and thongs on their feet and they had their little boy with them, who just idolized Kurt. Kurt responded to the boy really well, because he was a kid. But it was just so sad. The reason the parents were there was pretty obvious…"

FEBRUARY 13, 1994:

Travel day.

"IT WAS LIKE THERE WAS THE NORMAL, HAPPY BUS AND THEN THE WEIRD, TENSE SMOKING BUS."

FEBRUARY 14, 1994:

In London, the 1994 Brit Awards are taking place. Nirvana, which isn't present, loses to Crowded House for Best International Group. Over in Paris, France, the band performs at the Zenith. There was never much activity backstage at a Nirvana show, but at this gig the promoters arranged a little get-together.

"It was this weird futuristic, stadium place with metal spiral stairs and two different dressing rooms with a party going on below," says Melora. "Kurt just yelled from the balcony, 'I don't drink!' Dave and Krist were there. I think Dave was really good at saying hi to people and doing all of the industry stuff. After every show, Kurt would just lay down on a couch and just wait to leave."

Also in Paris, Melora goes shopping at flea markets, Kurt sees a homeopathic doctor for his increasingly sore throat, and the band does a very disturbing photo shoot with Paris photographer Youri Lenquette. The most shocking photo from the session is the one with the band sitting on a car and Kurt has the barrel of a rifle in his mouth.

FEBRUARY 15, 1994:

Second show at Zenith in Paris.

FEBRUARY 16, 1994:

Nirvana jams on the Knack's "My Sharona" at their show in Rennes, France at Salle Omnisports. While the shows were going very well, Kurt seemed to sink deeper into his depression, and, according to Melora, it was quite obvious how unhappy he really was on this tour.

"What I thought was weird, was that people acted like nothing's wrong," she says. "They talked around him, or through him. I didn't know what the details were, but I felt like, 'Excuse me, this guy is miserable.' Pat would tell me what's going on, but it was still very secretive. He'd tell me cryptic things and I'd hear other bits and pieces from Jennifer, and I was just trying to put it all together. [The band] didn't talk much. I felt like Krist cared a lot about Kurt, but whatever happened over the years that I wasn't privy to... he just seemed sad about Kurt's state. Kurt seemed like a really depressed guy, and I thought so much of his music and he seemed like a really nice guy too, so I just thought of him as this tortured genius."

FEBRUARY 17, 1994:

The band has a day off in Grenoble, France. Kurt begins to lose his voice from a sore throat.

FEBRUARY 18, 1994:

Nirvana plays Le Summun in Grenoble, France. It's their last show with the Buzzcocks opening. "I don't remember where it was, but one of the funniest things that happened was after a show, Kurt's skin was really messed up, he was picking at it and stuff, and after a show, he asked this girl for some foundation or base, and he took her make-up and applied it really, really well and made his skin look perfect and went to the bus. And Pat Smear is like, 'A little late, you just played for thousands of people with pizza face.' He just laughed." By all accounts, Pat has this ability to lighten things up around the otherwise tension filled entourage.

FEBRUARY 19, 1994:

Some of the band members and crew go ice-skating before their show at Patinoire de Littoral in Neuchatel, Switzerland. "All the shows were in these arenas. This one had a hockey arena connected to it, and the players – or whoever – said it was OK to go in and take skates and go skating. I think it was Krist and Shelli, Dave and Jennifer, I don't think Pat did it, and Kurt didn't go, he was, you know, kind of depressed. It was really fun, then we went straight to the show." Les Thugs, a French hardcore band on Sub Pop, opened the show on this night.

Also in Switzerland, the record label representatives there gave the band gifts. "They gave [the band] really beautiful art books and they gave me this really retarded oversized Switzerland passport – it was a book about Switzerland," says Melora.

This day's *Melody Maker* features an interview with Courtney Love titled "Hole Lotta Love" where she warns: "One thing this last terrible year has proved: if you lie about us, I will hit you, Kurt will shoot you and we will sue."

FEBRUARY 20, 1994:

Kurt Cobain turns 27. According to Melora, the band's manager John Silva, who went on to manage Dave Grohl's post-Nirvana success the Foo Fighters, got Kurt a carton of cigarettes for his birthday. "Kurt said something sarcastically, like 'Oh, he's trying to kill me.' They just seemed not to like each other and it wasn't a secret."

In fact, after leaving Gold Mountain in 1992, Danny Goldberg stayed on as a consultant for Nirvana because he was one of the few people Kurt had an easy time talking to, according to Danny. "I ended up frequently being the person that talked to Kurt specifically," explains Danny. "John certainly was in charge of all the logistics and the touring and would talk to Krist and Dave more than I did, but there came a time when Kurt mainly wanted to talk to me."

FEBRUARY 21, 1994:

Nirvana's long-time friends, the Melvins, take over the opening slot for the rest of the tour starting on this date in Modena, Italy at a venue called Palasport. The band plays "The Man Who Sold the World" totally acoustic, which they normally did electrically.

"We stayed in Bologna, a really, really amazing medieval kind of city," says Melora. "I know that Pat and Kurt went to an ancient church and the square and I think they had a decent time looking around at stuff. We all went out to dinner somewhere in Italy together, the label would sometimes take us out, other than that we didn't hang out much. Everything was always tense."

FEBRUARY 22, 1994:

Krist is outspoken and making jokes onstage about bootleggers at their show at Palagacchio in Rome. This is one of the best shows the band has done in a while, and ironically becomes one of the most popular bootleg cassettes.

"When the bus pulled into the venue, they all were really mad about the bootleggers and freaked out, which was against their normal nice-guy ways," Melora noticed. "They were saying things like, 'That's fucked up, that's our money.' They did seem concerned with money. I don't know if they were trying to impress me or if they were just kidding around, but

they were joking about how many millions each had. One was like, 'I have 1 million, you have 2 million' or 'I have 1 million you have 1.5 million.' I think it bothered Krist and Dave, but it was also totally obvious that Kurt was *the* guy, but that doesn't make anyone feel good either."

FEBRUARY 23, 1994:

Nirvana performs "Serve the Servants" and "Dumb" (featuring Melora on cello, this time) on the television show "The Tunnel" in Rome. The show is somewhat similar to "Saturday Night Live" in the States, with silly skits as well as musical performances.

"This guy is talking in Italian, blahblahblah Nirvana!," says Melora in an Italian accent. "It was kind of weird, they didn't know what they were saying and they kind of played along, they're told this is a cool show, but it didn't seem very cool. One cast member was wearing a Nirvana T-shirt and he's dressed like a grunge doofus and comes up them, speaking in Italian, it was just uncomfortable. The band just stood there and reacted."

During the day, Kurt, Pat, and Melora went to the Vatican, but it was closed. "That was the closest thing I had to a nice time with them. The sun was setting on the Vatican and we were running around, there was a sign that, I guess, means 'no short skirts' and Kurt was like 'no mini skirts allowed in the Vatican?!' He's like, 'No little girls are allowed in the Vatican?!' It was funny."

FEBRUARY 24–25, 1994:

Nirvana plays two shows in Milan, Italy at Palatrussardi. "I remember one annoying thing," says Melora. "The audience would always clap during 'Polly,' because it's acoustic and they would clap in rhythm, and Kurt thought it messed us up so he'd announce before the song, 'Please don't clap along, we're bad musicians.' And I'm like, 'I'm not a bad musician and neither are you.'" Backstage, everyone would be hanging out in the Melvins' dressing room, but Kurt just lay on the couch, according to Melora. The 24th is Kurt and Courtney's second wedding anniversary; they spend it apart.

FEBRUARY 26, 1994:

Travel day.

FEBRUARY 27, 1994:

Nirvana plays Tivoli in Ljubljana, Slovenia. Krist's relatives from Croatia, where his family is from and where he lived for a while in 1980, come to the show.

FEBRUARY 28, 1994:

Day off in Munich, Germany. According to *People* magazine, Kurt called his cousin Art Cobain and told him that "he was getting really fed up with his way of life" and Art noted that "he really seemed to be reaching out." When asked if Kurt seemed more depressed than usual at this time, Melora says, "I thought I saw somebody seriously and dangerously depressed. He was told at some point that they didn't have cancellation insurance on the tour and he was really morbid about it, and would keep going back to this and say, 'So, if someone died we'd still have to do the shows?' And everyone is like, 'If *you* died, we don't have to do the shows.' And he was just really focused on that and thought it was very strange that they didn't have insurance."

● **He *does* have a gun: February 14, 1994** ●

MARCH 1, 1994:

Nirvana plays their final show in Munich, Germany at Terminal Einz, a small airport hangar with a capacity of 3,050. The power went out momentarily during the show, so the band played an impromptu acoustic set at the front of the stage. Even though Kurt's throat was hurting him and it's just days before the Rome suicide attempt, he seemed to be having fun onstage. The band plays the Cars' "My Best Friend's Girl," which he learned to play by age 15.

"He was sick. He had a sore throat and he didn't want to play," says Melora. "They were looking for herbal cures and doctors. They didn't seem to be getting along with management either, and they had a band meeting, which was funny. They're really innocent guys, and they're like, [sarcastically] 'Well, we can change management. I'm sure we'd be a real asset to someone's alternative division. Maybe somebody else would take us.' I remember Kurt told me on the phone the first time I talked to him that Michael Meisel [part of the Gold Mountain management team] was really nice and quiet, but..."

Meanwhile, back home, the 36th annual Grammy Awards are held. Nirvana's *In Utero* loses out to U2's *Zooropa* in the Best Alternative Album category.

MARCH 2, 1994:

Nirvana cancels the rest of the tour, which is just two dates – March 2 was to be a second show at Terminal Einz in Munich and March 3 was to be in Offenbach, Germany at Stadhalle. The plan was to take a vacation after the Offenbach show, and then continue on with a second leg of the European tour.

"The reason [for the cancellation] was that Kurt was sick and we were going to have a week or two vacation anyway, starting on March 4, but now we were going to start our vacation early. Everyone went their separate ways," explains Melora. Krist went home to Seattle. Dave stayed in Germany to work on the *Backbeat* video – he's on the soundtrack. And Kurt and Pat went to Rome, where Kurt checks into Room 541 at the five-star Excelsior Hotel.

• The Excelsior, Rome •

Alex MacLeod would later tell *Rolling Stone* that Kurt saw a doctor this day who instructed him to take two to four weeks off and diagnosed him with severe laryngitis and bronchitis.

MARCH 3, 1994:

The Munich and Offenbach shows were rescheduled for April 12 and April 13, respectively. Courtney, Frances, and the nanny – coming from London where Courtney was promoting her not-yet-released *Live Through This* – join Kurt in Rome.

This evening, the Cobains order two bottles of champagne from the Excelsior's room service, and Kurt reportedly had a concierge fill his prescription for Rohypnol, a tranquilizer that can be used for insomnia. It's also known as the "Date Rape Drug" because it normally knocks a person out to the point where they're not conscious of their activities. Courtney's much-told details of the night include the two drinking some champagne. He bought her roses and a piece of the Coliseum. When he wanted to make love, she didn't. She took a Valium, and then went to sleep.

MARCH 4, 1994:

Courtney wakes up around 6:30 a.m. European Standard Time to find Kurt unconscious with blood coming out of his nose on the floor of their hotel room. Kurt is taken to the public hospital Umberto I Polyclinic after ingesting some champagne and 50–60 pills of Rohypnol, which most reports say are individually wrapped. While this was later known to be a suicide attempt, the spin on it at the time was that it was an accidental overdose. The rest of the European tour that was to start up again in Prague is officially canceled.

Rumors run rampant on the Internet that Kurt is dead, so management posts this message online: "Kurt Cobain slipped into a coma at 6 a.m. European Standard Time on 3/4/94. The coma was induced by a combination of the flu and fatigue on top of prescription painkillers and champagne. While Cobain has not awoken, he shows significant signs, said his doctors."

DGC went along with the story and issued a similar statement saying the coma was a result of Kurt "inadvertently overdosing on a mixture of prescription medication and alcohol, while suffering from severe influenza and fatigue." The spin-doctors worked overtime on this, saying that Kurt was simply celebrating with champagne with Courtney after being apart for a while.

A three-page suicide note written on hotel notepaper is found. Courtney would later tell *Rolling Stone*'s David Fricke that Kurt had written, "You don't love me anymore. I'd rather die than go through a divorce." Gold Mountain's Janet Billig added further detail when she told journalist Neil Strauss that Kurt "just took all of his and Courtney's money and was going to run away and disappear." He's said to have had $1,000 in his pocket and was wearing his brown corduroy coat.

Kurt's best friend Dylan Carlson would later say in *Kurt & Courtney* that their marriage was "obviously going through some turbulence" but that he never "flat out said anything" about divorce. If you believe Tom Grant, the private investigator Courtney hires to find her husband shortly before his death, at some point during these last months, Courtney asked their attorney Rosemary Carroll to find the best divorce lawyer around and asked if the pre-nuptial agreement could be voided.

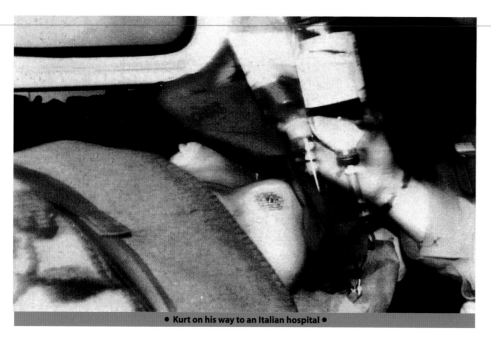

• Kurt on his way to an Italian hospital •

MARCH 5, 1994:

After being in a coma for approximately 20 hours, Kurt wakes up and is transferred to the American Hospital. He asks for a strawberry milkshake and writes a note that says, "Get these fucking tubes out of my nose."

On the way to the second hospital, Courtney kicks out of the way a photographer who was trying to get a photo of Kurt when he was moved from one hospital to the next. She later regretted doing that. "I wish Kurt could have seen [a photo of himself] because if he had, he never would get into that situation again," she told the *Los Angeles Times'* Robert Hilburn. "I don't ever want to see him on the floor like that again. He was blue. I thought I went through a lot of hard times over the years, but this has been the hardest."

MARCH 6-7, 1994:

Kurt recuperates in his hospital room from his suicide attempt. When the band's long-time sound man Craig Montgomery heard the news, he says he wasn't surprised. "None of that was surprising at all. He'd been talking for years about... I mean, he never seemed like a guy that was going to grow old and contented. You know, he just couldn't really see a way for that to happen."

MARCH 8, 1994:

Kurt leaves the hospital. Courtney later joked to the press, "He's not going to get away from me that easily. I'll follow him through hell." Back at home, *Backbeat: Music from the Motion Picture*, featuring Dave Grohl on drums, is released.

MARCH 9, 1994:

Attorneys for video director Kevin Kerslake file a lawsuit against Nirvana and Kurt Cobain in US District Court, Central District of California for copyright infringement over the "Heart-Shaped Box" video. The suit (case no. 94 1521) claims that the band allowed Kevin's video treatment for "Heart-Shaped Box" to be used by Anton Corbijn, who directed the video. Kevin hasn't worked with Geffen since this, but he has directed videos for the Rolling Stones, Smashing Pumpkins, and R.E.M.

MARCH 11, 1994:

This was the date the European tour was to start up again in Prague, and run through June with the Meat Puppets opening on about four shows. Melora Creager had already headed to Prague, planning to spend her days off there before the tour started: "Management put me in a cheaper hotel after it happened, but still told me to be ready to go. Then they sent me home, but they still wanted me ready to go. I think they still thought the tour was going to happen. It was constantly changing and even when I got back to New York, they still didn't want to cancel anything. They finally said Europe's not gonna happen, but be ready for Lollapalooza because we were still planning to do that."

MARCH 12, 1994:

The Cobains fly home from Rome to Seattle. As published in Poppy Z. Brite's biography *Courtney Love: The Real Story* (the book claims that Courtney was a friend of Poppy's while writing this book), this is a conversation that took place on that flight:

   Kurt: "Give me a Rohypnol."
   Courtney: "They're gone."
   (Five-minute pause)
   Kurt: "C'mon, give me a Rohypnol."
   Courtney: "They're gone, Kurt. They are gone. I dumped them all down the fuckin' toilet. It's over."
   Kurt: "Fuck you, you lying bitch, give me a Rohypnol… Please."

MARCH 18, 1994:

Just three weeks prior to Kurt's suicide, Courtney once again feared what would inevitably come true. She called the Seattle Police on this Friday evening because Kurt had "locked himself in a room" with a gun and "was going to kill himself," according to the Seattle Police Department report, which filed the incident as a Domestic Violence Protection Act Disturbance (incident no. 94-123078).

The police report reads, in part, "Mrs. Cobain stated that Cobain, Kurt had locked himself in a room and that he was going to kill himself. She also stated that he had a gun in the room. Officers were able to contact Cobain, Kurt and detained him pending further investigation. Cobain, Kurt stated that he had locked himself in the room to keep away from Cobain, Courtney. He continued to state that he is not suicidal and doesn't want to hurt himself."

Courtney then showed the police where the guns were and the officers confiscated four guns – a Beretta .380, a Taurus .38, a Taurus .380, and a Colt semi-automatic rifle – as well as 25 boxes of assorted .223, .380, and .38 rounds and "one bottle of assorted, unidentified pills recovered from the person of Cobain," according to the report. The report goes on to say that after further investigation, Courtney "stated that she did not see him with a gun, and he did not say he was going to kill himself. However, when he locked himself in the room, would not open the door, and knowing that he had access to guns, she contacted 911 for his safety and well-being. All parties were interviewed and released and Cobain, Kurt left the residence. The disturbance was verbal only."

Kurt, who described his relationship with Courtney in a 1993 *Details* article as "a whirling dervish of emotion, all these extremes of fighting and loving each other at once," told police there was a lot of stress in the relationship.

MARCH 25, 1994:

Those closest to Kurt stage a drug intervention on this day. According to Danny Goldberg, gathered at the couple's house on this day for five hours were himself, Courtney, Krist Novoselic, Pat Smear, Rosemary Carroll, John Silva, Janet Billig, Dylan Carlson, and Gary Gersh. Kurt is said to have kept silent, stared at the floor, and was in full denial.

One by one they each spoke, and threatened to leave or break up the band. Courtney would later tell Barbara Walters that she thinks the intervention was a mistake: "He was ganged up upon. I don't think intervention works on certain people at a certain age...I shouldn't have called for the intervention. I just panicked."

She finally convinces Kurt to go to LA with her to check into Exodus Recovery Center, the drug rehabilitation facility in Marina del Rey, California where Kurt has been treated before. But, once at the airport, he changes his mind and she goes on alone with Janet Billig, hoping that he'll follow. This was the last time Courtney saw her husband alive.

The initial plan was for drug intervention counselor Steven Chatoff to conduct the intervention, but it was canceled after Kurt found out. That night, Kurt and Pat Smear rehearsed in the basement.

MARCH 26, 1994:

Courtney checks into the Peninsula Hotel in Beverly Hills. The couple's nanny and Frances Bean soon join her. Meanwhile, an item appears in the music video column of *Billboard*, "The Eye" by Deborah Russell, about the lawsuit filed against Nirvana by Kevin Kerslake.

In the article, Kevin says, "This happens to a lot of directors. But most people don't do anything." Janet Billig says in the article, "The members of Nirvana are saddened and disappointed that Kevin is engaging in what appears to be a very expensive and protracted exercise in reality denial. We can't understand why he doesn't just get a life." Given this statement and the legal situation between Kevin and Nirvana, it's curious that at this time Kevin was still working on Nirvana's long-form home video, *Live! Tonight! Sold Out!!*, and has a director's credit on it. The details of the settlement of this lawsuit are not available for public disclosure.

MARCH 29, 1994:

In Utero is reissued in the US in response to Wal-Mart and Kmart's refusal to carry the album due to the back collage of fetuses and the controversial title of the song "Rape Me." The band decides to change the back cover, deleting the fetuses from the collage. They also change the title of "Rape Me" to the less offensive "Waif Me." (Originally, Kurt wanted to rename the song "Sexually Assault Me," but due to pressure changed it to the more non-gender-specific "Waif Me.")

Danny Goldberg maintains that the decision to make these changes was entirely Kurt's. "He wanted to change his artwork so Wal-Mart would put *In Utero* in. I wouldn't have done it because I hate that kind of stuff," says Danny. "He definitely did it because he grew up in a town where they didn't have record stores and kids bought records in Wal-Mart. He wanted very much for all of his fans to be able to get the records. He had the complete control of that. I told him not to do it. There was no pressure. Geffen was walking on eggshells; they were their biggest act. They were completely into 'don't offend the artist' mode. He wanted to do it; that was his thing. He wanted as many people as possible to hear his music."

Geffen's Bill Bennett, on the other hand, believes otherwise. "I think the record company really just pressured them. Left to their own devices, they never would have done it. By that time [Kurt] had really isolated himself. Anybody who didn't want to change it would've been Mark Kates, but I don't remember."

• One of Nirvana's last performances •

MARCH 30, 1994:

Kurt and Dylan Carlson go to Stan Baker Sports on 10,000 Lake City Way. N.E. in Seattle and buy a 20-gauge, six-pound Remington M-11 shotgun and a box of ammunition. Dylan purchased the gun for $308.37 because Kurt feared if it were in his name, the police would once again confiscate it.

Kurt claimed he bought the gun for protection. "We've got big windows and I have a baby and a wife to protect. People come into your house, not to steal your stereo, but to rape your wife and sodomize your baby. I just could not survive something like that," he told *Chicago Sun Times*' Jim DeRegotis the year before.

Dylan later told *Rolling Stone* of this day, "It seemed kind of weird that he was buying the shotgun before he was leaving [for LA]. So, I offered to hold it until he got back." Kurt kept the gun in his home instead. After much persistence from Courtney, Kurt finally gives in and flies to LA to check into Exodus and spends his first of two nights there.

MARCH 31, 1994:

Kurt spends his second and last night at Exodus. Butthole Surfers' Gibby Haynes is in the center as well. On this day, he is visited by a few friends, and speaks to Krist and his wife on the phone. And, somewhere in the last few weeks of his life, he was talking with Michael Stipe about a possible collaboration. After Kurt's death, the R.E.M. frontman issued this statement: "In the last few weeks, I was talking to Kurt a lot. We had a musical project in the works, but nothing was recorded."

APRIL 1, 1994:

Good Friday/April Fool's Day. The couple's nanny brings Frances to Exodus for a visit. Kurt calls Courtney and tells her, "No matter what happens, I want you to know that you made a really good record." When asked what he meant, he said, "Just remember, no matter what, I love you." This is the last time Courtney, who didn't visit Kurt at the center, speaks to her husband.

At 7:25 p.m., Kurt says he's stepping out to smoke a cigarette, but he jumps over the six-foot-high wall and heads back to Seattle. According to private investigator Tom Grant's report, Kurt called the Peninsula for Courtney at 8:47 p.m. and left a message.

APRIL 2, 1994:

Kurt arrives in Seattle early in the morning, around 1 a.m., and is picked up by a driver to be taken to his house. Michael DeWitt (a.k.a. Cali), the couple's former nanny who was staying at the house, has said that he had a short conversation with Kurt in his room. Courtney reportedly cancels Kurt's credit cards and begins calling around to friends and fellow musicians in LA to find him. Screaming Trees singer Mark Lanegan tells *Rolling Stone* that he'd been looking for Kurt for about a week before he was found. Kurt allegedly bought some shotgun cartridges at Seattle Guns. He's also said to have tried calling Courtney at the Peninsula again, but he never got through.

During these last few days, he was reportedly seen in a park near his house in a thick jacket and looking ill. He is also believed to have spent at least one night in their other home in Carnation with an unidentified friend. Police later found a blue sleeping bag, which Courtney says she hadn't seen before, and some cigarette butts in the house.

APRIL 3, 1994:

Easter Sunday. Courtney hires the Tom Grant Company, which she found through the Yellow Pages of the phone book, and tells him that someone is using Kurt's credit cards, which she had canceled upon the news of his skipping out on rehab. Someone tries to make charges to the cards on April 3 and 4.

APRIL 4, 1994:

Kurt's mother, Wendy O'Connor, files a missing person's report (no. 94-149669) on Kurt with the Seattle Police Department. The report states that Kurt was last seen on April 2 and describes Kurt as "not dangerous/armed with shotgun." The summary of the incident says, "Mr. Cobain ran away from California facility and flew back to Seattle. He also bought a shotgun and may be suicidal. Mr. Cobain may be at 11 Denny location for narcotics."

Back in LA, Courtney is interviewed by Robert Hilburn for a *Los Angeles Times* article to promote her forthcoming album, eerily titled and long-overdue *Live Through This*. The article appears on the cover of the *Times*' Calendar section on April 10, 1994.

APRIL 5, 1994:

Kurt Cobain, 27, barricades himself in the greenhouse above the garage at their Lake Washington home. He props a stool up against the French doors, writes a one-page note in red ink addressed to "Boddah pronounced" (Boddah was his imaginary childhood friend), sticks a pen through it and stabs it into a planter. A cigar box is by his side with drugs and drug paraphernalia and his wallet lies next to it. His TV is left on. After taking 1.52 milligrams of heroin, he places the shotgun across his body with the barrel at his head, and with his thumb pulls the trigger.

The suicide note ends with this: "I have it good. Very good. And I'm grateful. But since the age of seven, I've become hateful toward all humans in general. Only because it seems so easy for people to get along and have empathy. Empathy! Only because I love and feel for people too much. I guess. Thank you all from the pit of my burning, nauseous stomach for your letters and concern during the last years. I'm too much of an erratic, moody person and I don't have the passion anymore. So remember, it's better to burn out than to fade away. Peace, love, empathy.

"I HAVE IT GOOD. VERY GOOD. AND I'M GRATEFUL. BUT SINCE THE AGE OF SEVEN, I'VE BECOME HATEFUL TOWARD ALL HUMANS IN GENERAL ... "

To Boddah

Speaking from the tongue of an experienced simpleton who obviously would rather be an emasculated, infantile complainee. This note should be pretty easy to understand. All the warnings from the punk rock 101 courses over the years, since my first introduction to the, shall we say, ethics involved with independence and the embracement of your community has proven to be very true. I haven't felt the excitement of listening to as well as creating music along with really writing something for too many years now. I feel guilty beyond words about these things.

For example when we're backstage and the lights go out and the manic roar of the crowd begins. It doesn't affect me the way in which it did for Freddy Mercury who seemed to love, relish in the love and adoration from the crowd. Which is something I totally admire and envy. The fact is, I can't fool you, any one of you. It simply isn't fair to you or me. The worst crime I can think of would be to rip people off by faking it and pretending as if I'm having 100% fun. Sometimes I feel as if I should have a punch in time clock before I walk out on stage. I've tried everything within my power to appreciate it (and I do, God, believe me I do, but it's not enough). I appreciate the fact that I and we have affected and entertained a lot of people. I must be one of those narcissists who only appreciate things when they're gone. I'm too sensitive. I need to be slightly numb in order to regain the enthusiasm I once had as a child. On our last 3 tours I've had a much better appreciation for all the people I've known personally and as fans of our music, but I still can't get over the frustration, the guilt and empathy I have for everyone. There's good in all of us and I think I simply love people too much. So much that it makes me feel too fucking sad. The sad little, sensitive, unappreciative, pisces, Jesus man! Why don't you just enjoy it? I don't know! I have a goddess of a wife who sweats ambition and empathy and a daughter who reminds me too much of what I used to be. Full of love and joy, kissing every person she meets because everyone is good and will do her no harm. And that terrifies me to the point to where I can barely function. I can't stand the thought of Frances becoming the miserable, self destructive, death rocker that I've become. I have it good, very good, and I'm grateful, but since the age of seven I've become hateful towards all humans in general. Only because it seems so easy for people to get along and have empathy. Empathy! Only because I love and feel sorry for people too much I guess.

Thank you all from the pit of my burning, nauseous stomach for your letters and concern during the past years. I'm too much of an erratic, moody person anymore and so remember, it's better to burn out than to fade away. Peace, love, Empathy. Kurt Cobain

Frances and Courtney, I'll be at your altar.
Please keep going Courtney,
for Frances
for her life which will be so much happier
without me.   I LOVE YOU, I LOVE YOU

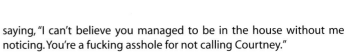

Kurt Cobain. – Frances and Courtney, I'll be at your altar. Please keep going Courtney. For Frances. For her life will be so much happier without me. I LOVE YOU. I LOVE YOU." Courtney later said that a second note was left for her as well, but that note has not surfaced. Kurt's death certificate lists April 5 as his date of death; however, there have been reports that Kurt called friends on April 6. Since no one has come forward with concrete evidence to support that, April 5 is considered accurate.

APRIL 6, 1994:

Tom Grant picks up Dylan Carlson at his apartment at 11:30 p.m. and heads to a café where they "planned our strategy for locating Kurt and finding out what was going on," according to Tom's report. Courtney has said she couldn't leave LA to help find Kurt herself because she had business to take care of in LA concerning Hole.

Meanwhile, amidst rumors that Nirvana has broken up, the official Lollapalooza line-up is announced. Lollapalooza organizer Ted Gardner issues this statement, "Although we had been negotiating with Nirvana to headline Lollapalooza '94, due to the ill health of Kurt Cobain we cannot confirm them on the bill." At this time, Janet Billig told *Billboard* that the band is "not working right now. Kurt was in a coma. Kurt's recovering. It's going to take some time. We don't know when they're going to tour again." The Smashing Pumpkins end up headlining Lollapalooza instead.

Back in Prague, where the band was supposed to start the second leg of their European *In Utero* tour, the *Prague Post* announces that their show at the Slavia-Eden Stadium has been rescheduled for April 29 and that the tour – following myriad contradictory statements – is back on.

APRIL 7, 1994:

At 2:15 a.m., Tom Grant and Dylan Carlson search the Cobains' house for Kurt. They didn't search the greenhouse. They check again at 9:45 p.m., at which time they found a note from Michael DeWitt allegedly to Kurt saying, "I can't believe you managed to be in the house without me noticing. You're a fucking asshole for not calling Courtney."

Back in LA, Courtney Love calls the front desk of the Peninsula Hotel complaining of an allergic reaction to the prescription drug Xanax, an anti-anxiety pill. The hotel calls 911 and police arrive with paramedics to find syringes and a packet of white powder in her room. Courtney is rushed to Century City Hospital around 9:30 a.m. She is then taken to the Beverly Hills police station and arrested and booked on charges of possession of a controlled substance, possession of drug paraphernalia, possession of a hypodermic syringe and possession of stolen property. She is released at 3 p.m. after posting $10,000 bail, then checks herself into Exodus and stays just one night.

The stolen property turns out to be a prescription pad left from a psychiatrist who was treating her; the controlled substance was allegedly Hindu powder called vibbhuti that was given to her for good luck by her attorney and friend Rosemary Carroll; and the syringe was said to be for her prescription to Buprenex for back pain. The news that

gets out, however, is that Courtney overdosed on heroin. However, her story pans out and she is cleared of all charges on May 5, 1994.

APRIL 8, 1994:

At approximately 8:40 a.m., Gary Smith, an electrician who came to install security lighting at the Cobains', calls 911 after seeing a body on the floor in the greenhouse of 171 Lake Washington Blvd. East. He then phones his boss at Veca Electric, who soon calls Seattle news/talk radio station KXRX saying he has "the scoop of the century." Kurt Cobain is dead. KXRX breaks the news at 9:40 a.m.

The Seattle Police Department issue the statement, "On April 8, 1994 at about 0840 hours, Smith arrived at 171 Lake Washington Blvd. East to perform some electrical work. Smith walked on to the West facing deck of the garage and observed the victim through the windowpanes in the French door. The victim was laying on the floor, with a shotgun across his body, and a visible head wound."

King County Medical Examiner, Donald T. Reay, MD, soon positively identifies the body of Kurt Cobain by fingerprints. He releases the statement: "The autopsy has shown that Kurt Cobain died of a shotgun wound to the head and at this time the wound appears to be self-inflicted."

According to Poppy Z. Brite's *Courtney Love: The Real Story*, Rosemary Carroll breaks the news to Courtney in her room at Exodus.

Courtney, Rosemary, the nanny, and Frances board a chartered plane at the Van Nuys Airport in Van Nuys, California and head to Seattle. She reportedly grabs a piece of her dead husband's hair and washes it. Kurt's mother, Wendy, would stay with her for the next few days. Wendy tells the Associated Press, "Now he's gone and joined the stupid club. I told him not to join that stupid club," referring to the premature deaths of Jimi Hendrix, Janis Joplin, and Jim Morrison at age 27.

APRIL 9, 1994:

The King County Medical Examiner officially declares the death a suicide. There are no doubts from the medical authorities that the death was anything but this. 1.52 milligrams of heroin, with traces of Valium, are found in Kurt's system. This is three times the normal fatal dose, and still considered an extremely large amount even for an addict with a very high tolerance for the drug.

Distraught fans flock to record stores to buy Nirvana CDs. The increase in sales moves all of Nirvana's albums up the charts, with *In Utero* jumping 45 positions on The Billboard 200 the week ending April 23. At home, Courtney gives an interview to MTV News while sobbing on her bed.

Sub Pop continued with their plans for their sixth anniversary party at the Crocodile Café in town, with Velocity Girl, Pond, and Sunny Day Real Estate playing. Members of Love Battery, the Posies, Young Fresh Fellows, Silkworm, and the Walkabouts were in attendance. As an editor at *Billboard* magazine at the time, I was one of the journalists flown in by Sup Pop for the party, which was surrounded by news crews trying

"NOW HE'S GONE AND JOINED THE STUPID CLUB. I TOLD HIM NOT TO JOIN THAT STUPID CLUB."

to get comments from just about anyone. The mood inside was somber and no one seemed to want to talk about it. Bruce Pavitt said a few brief words, "We should remember and celebrate the positive things about Kurt Cobain."

APRIL 10, 1994:

A public memorial service is held for Kurt at Seattle Center's Flag Pavilion, outside of the Space Needle, with an estimated 5,000 (some say as low as 4,000, others estimate higher at 7,000) fans showing up. Meanwhile, a private service is held at Unity Church of Truth in Seattle for family and friends. About 200 people are there, including the remaining band members, and many Geffen/DGC, Gold Mountain, and Sub Pop employees. Stephen Towles is the minister for the service, and Courtney and Krist are among those to speak or read poems. Two wakes are also held: one at Courtney's house and one at Krist's house.

At the public gathering, taped messages from Courtney and Krist are aired. Krist thanks fans for their concern and urged the crowd to follow their dreams: "Catch a groove and let it flow out of your heart. That's where the music will always be." Courtney's message is much longer and more emotional – calling Kurt an "asshole" for leaving and asking aloud, "Why didn't you just fucking stay?" in between reading bits and pieces of his suicide note. Here is an excerpt:

"I really don't know what to say," Courtney starts. "I feel the same way you guys do. But if you guys don't think that when I used to sit in this room and he played guitar and sang and feel so honored to be near him, you're crazy. Anyway, he left a note. It's like a letter to the fucking editor. I don't know what happened. I mean, it was going to happen. But it could have happened when he was 40. He always said he was going to outlive everybody and live to be 120. I'm not going to read you all the note because it's none of your fucking business. But some of it is to you. I don't think it takes away from his dignity to read this considering that it's addressed to most of you. He's such an asshole. I want you all to say 'asshole' really loud."

The crowd yells out "asshole!" and Courtney proceeds to read parts of the suicide note: "Over the years, it's my first introduction to shall we say ethics involved with independence and the embracement of your community has proven to be true. I haven't felt the excitement of listening to, as well as creating music along with really writing something for two years now. I feel guilty beyond words about these things. For example, when we're backstage and the lights go out and the manic roar of the crowd begins, it doesn't affect me the way in which it did for Freddie Mercury, who seemed to love and relish the love and admiration from the crowd." Courtney's taped message continues: "I'm real sorry, you guys. I don't know what I could have done. I wish I had been there."

Others speak at the public vigil, as well, such as Rev. Stephen Towles, Kurt's Uncle Larry Smith, and various local DJs such as KNDD's Marco Collins, KISW's Damen Stewart, and KXRX's Scott Vanderpool. I remember arriving at the Flag Pavilion just around 4 p.m. thinking the scene looked like a mini-Lollapalooza – kids were playing hacky sack or spread out on blankets with food. Some even passed out flyers for their own bands, a seemingly inappropriate time to be a self-promoter. Lots of young kids and flannel-clad teenagers were accompanied by their parents and well behaved. Women handed out vigil candles. Kids handed out suicide information pamphlets. Many jumped in the fountain as if to celebrate Kurt's life instead of mourn his death. Someone wore a "Kurt Died For Your Sin" T-shirt, while another brought his pet iguana, and yet another child, a 10-year-old boy, came dressed formally for a funeral while clutching his mother's hand. Later Courtney would show up with Kat Bjelland of Babes in Toyland and hand out some of Kurt's clothing to those last to leave.

APRIL 11, 1994:

In Utero is certified by the RIAA for 2 million copies. When Kurt died, his assets were estimated at a reported $1.2 million.

APRIL 12, 1994:

Although they signed with DGC two years ago, Hole's first DGC album, Live Through This, isn't released until this day. Geffen also holds an executive meeting on this day in LA. "Employees at first avoided the topic until Geffen president Eddie Rosenblatt ordered them to unload their feelings," reported Entertainment Weekly. "Rosenblatt, a close friend of Cobain and his widow, Courtney Love, opened the discussion but quickly broke down in tears."

APRIL 14, 1994:

Kurt Cobain is cremated in a uniservice crematory in Seattle at Bleitz Funeral Home. The Assistant Medical Examiner, Nikolas J. Hartshorne, MD, was the person who booked Nirvana's third show in Seattle in 1988. The death certificate is filed. It lists Kurt's occupation as Poet/Musician and his type of business as Punk Rock. Courtney soon spreads his ashes in various places, including a Buddhist monastery in Ithaca, NY, and under a willow tree in the Lake Washington Blvd. yard. Poppy Z. Brite's biography of Courtney says she makes plaster casts of Kurt's hands because she always loved them.

"People think of life as being so sacred and they feel like this is their only chance and they have to do something with their life and make an impact on everyone because it seems so realistic and the threat of dying is just so vital," Kurt told Hits magazine in October 1991. "As far as I'm concerned, it's just a little pit-stop for the afterlife. It's just a little test to see how you can handle reality." In the same interview, he was asked if he relates to a Jim Morrison type, who also died young by living fast, or if he wants to live to a ripe old age. Kurt's response was, "That's really

" ...HE ALWAYS SAID HE WAS GOING TO OUTLIVE EVERYBODY AND LIVE TO BE 120. I'M NOT GOING TO READ YOU ALL THE NOTE BECAUSE IT'S NONE OF YOUR FUCKING BUSINESS. BUT SOME OF IT IS TO YOU ..."

selfish to live to 90 years old unless you have something to offer like maybe William Burroughs. I definitely don't want to be that old. I feel more bonded with the Jim Morrison type of living on the edge – rock and roll poet in a conservative way."

APRIL 22, 1994:

The Washington State Patrol's crime laboratory report confirms that the suicide note found by Kurt's body on April 8 and the three-page suicide note from the Hotel Excelsior on March 4 were both indeed written by Kurt Cobain, therefore disproving Tom Grant's claim that someone else wrote the last four lines of the April 8 suicide note – "Frances and Courtney, I'll be at your altar. Please keep going Courtney. For Frances. For her life will be so much happier without me. I LOVE YOU. I LOVE YOU."

APRIL 23, 1994:

The news of Kurt's death on April 8 lured many consumers to the record stores, pushing all of Nirvana's albums significantly up the chart. *In Utero* leaps from No. 72 to No. 27 with a 122% gain in sales; *Nevermind* moves an astonishing 111 positions from No. 167 to No. 56 with a 197% sales gain; *Incesticide*, which has been off the chart, re-enters at No. 135 with a 300% gain in sales; and *Bleach* debuts on the Top Pop Catalog chart at No. 6.

APRIL 30, 1994:

Hole's *Live Through This* debuts at No. 55 on The Billboard 200 with weak sales of 20,000 units. Meanwhile, Danny Goldberg issues a two-page letter to LA-based *Bam* magazine in response to an April 22, 1994 article written by Jerry McCulley, who points the finger at management and Kurt's record label for his death, stating, "Kurt Cobain is dead because too many people looked the other way, or flat-out lied, for too long."

"I was one of those who begged Kurt to get treatment shortly before he died, a continuation of a conversation we seemingly had been having forever," wrote Danny in his response. "Like many of Kurt's friends, I expect to feel guilty about his death every day for the rest of my life."

Six years later, being interviewed for this book, Danny still wishes there was something more he could have done:

"I'M JUST GRATEFUL THAT I GOT TO KNOW HIM AND I JUST WISH I HAD BEEN CLOSE ENOUGH TO HIM SO THAT HE DIDN'T KILL HIMSELF."

Selected Discography In Chronological Order
(US releases except where noted)

1988

August: Scream (Dave Grohl's pre-Nirvana band) *No More Censorship*, RAS Records
November: Nirvana, "Love Buzz"/"Big Cheese" single, Sub Pop
December: Nirvana's "Spank Thru" appears on *Sub Pop 200* compilation, Sub Pop

1989

June 15: Nirvana, *Bleach*, vinyl LP, Sub Pop
July: Kurt Cobain appears on the Go Team (featuring Calvin Johnson and Tobi Vail) single "Bikini Twilight," K Records
August 12: Nirvana, *Bleach*, vinyl LP, UK, Tupelo
August: Nirvana, *Bleach*, CD/cassette, Sub Pop
November: Nirvana's "Mexican Seafood" appears on the *Teriyaki Asthma, Vol. 1* EP, C/Z Records
December: Nirvana, *Blew* EP, UK, Tupelo
1989: Scream, *Live at Van Hall in Amsterdam*, Konkurrel Records

1990

May 1: Kurt Cobain and Krist Novoselic appear on Mark Lanegan's *The Winding Sheet*, Sub Pop. "Where Did You Sleep Last Night?" features Kurt on guitar and Krist on bass; and Kurt sings backing vocals on "Down in the Dark"
August: Nirvana's "Do You Love Me?" appears on the Kiss tribute album, *Hard to Believe*, C/Z Records
September: Nirvana, "Sliver"/"Dive" single, Sub Pop

1991

January: Nirvana, "Sliver"/"Dive" single, UK, Tupelo
April: Nirvana, "Molly's Lips" split single with the Fluid's "Candy," Sub Pop
April: Nirvana, "Sliver"/"Dive"/"About a Girl" (live) single, UK, Tupelo
June: Nirvana's cover of the Velvet Underground's "Here She Comes Now" appears on the Velvet Underground tribute album *Heaven and Hell, Vol. 1*, the Communion Label. The label also released a split single with the song and the Melvins'"Venus in Furs"
June: Nirvana's "Dive" appears on *The Grunge Years* compilation, Sub Pop
August: Nirvana, "Smells Like Teen Spirit" b/w "Drain You" single, UK, DGC
August 21: Nirvana's "Beeswax" appears on the *Kill Rock Stars* compilation, Kill Rock Stars
September 9: Nirvana, "Smells Like Teen Spirit" b/w "Even in His Youth" and "Aneurysm" single, UK, DGC
September 10: Nirvana, "Smells Like Teen Spirit" b/w "Even In His Youth" and "Aneurysm" single, DGC
September 24: Nirvana, *Nevermind*, DGC
October 18: Kurt Cobain appears on backing vocals and guitar on the title track from Earth's *Bureaucratic Desire for Revenge* EP, Sub Pop
November: Nirvana's "Mexican Seafood" appears on the *Teriyaki Asthma, Vol. 1–5*, C/Z
November: Nirvana, "Smells Like Teen Spirit" b/w "Drain You," "Even In His Youth," and "Aneurysm" single, UK, DGC
1991: An early Nirvana video of "In Bloom" appears on the *Sub Pop Video Network Program* video compilation

1992

January: Nirvana, *Hormoaning* EP, Australia/Japan, DGC
February 20: Nirvana, "Come As You Are" single, UK, DGC
March 1: Nirvana, "Come As You Are"/"Endless Nameless" 7-inch, UK, DGC
March 3: Nirvana, "Come As You Are" b/w "Drain You" (live) and "School" single, DCG

March 31: Nirvana, *Nevermind: It's an Interview*, featuring band interviews, live tracks, and album cuts, DGC
March: Nirvana, "Come As You Are" b/w "School" (live) and "Drain You" (live) single, UK DGC and another UK version of the single was backed with "Endless Nameless" and "School" (live)
March: Dave Grohl demos under the name Late!, *Pocketwatch*, Simple Machines (the label estimates the release to be March 1992)
April: Nirvana, *Bleach* remastered and reissued, DGC
June 20: Nirvana's "Return of the Rat" appears on *Eight Songs for Greg Sage and the Wipers* 7-inch box set, Tim/Kerr Records
July 9: Nirvana, "Lithium" b/w "Curmudgeon" single, UK, DGC
July 20: Nirvana, "Lithium" b/w "Curmudgeon" and "Been a Son" (live) single, UK, DGC
July 21: Nirvana, "Lithium" b/w "Been a Son" (live) and "Curmudgeon" single, DGC
November 30: Nirvana, "In Bloom" single b/w "Sliver" and "Polly" (live) single, UK Geffen
December 15: Nirvana, *Incesticide*, compilation of B-sides and rarities, DGC
1992: Dave Grohl (credited as Dale Nixon) appears on Buzz Osborne's solo EP, *King Buzzo*, on vocals, guitar, bass, and drum, Boner Records.

1993

February 22: Nirvana, "Oh, the Guilt" split single with the Jesus Lizard's "Puss," Touch and Go
February: Kurt Cobain's artwork appears on Sonic Youth's Australian EP *Whores Moaning*, DGC
March 15: Nirvana's "Return of the Rat" appears on *Fourteen Songs for Greg Sage and the Wipers*, CD, Tim/Kerr Records
April 13: Dave Markey's concert documentary, *1991: The Year Punk Broke*, Geffen Home Video, featuring Sonic Youth, Nirvana, Dinosaur Jr., Babes in Toyland, Gumball, and the Ramones
July 1: Kurt Cobain and William S. Burroughs, "The 'Priest' They Called Him" 10-inch, Tim/Kerr, featuring Kurt on guitar and Burroughs' spoken word
July 21: Scream, *Fumble/Banging the Drum*, Dischord Records
August: Nirvana, "Heart-Shaped Box" b/w "Marigold" (written and sung by Dave Grohl) single, UK, DGC
September 13: Nirvana, *In Utero*, vinyl/CD/cassette, UK and other territories outside the US, Geffen. The European and Australia versions included "Gallons of Rubbing Alcohol Flow Through the Strip"
September 14: Nirvana, *In Utero*, vinyl, DGC
September 21: Nirvana, *In Utero*, CD and cassette, DGC
September 21: Kurt Cobain appears on "Sky Pup" and produced seven songs on the Melvins' *Houdini*, Atlantic Records
September 27: Nirvana, "Heart-Shaped Box" b/w "Milk It" and "Marigold" single, UK, DGC
November 9: Nirvana's "Verse Chorus Verse" appears on the *No Alternative* benefit album, Arista
November 23: Nirvana's "I Hate Myself and I Want To Die" appears on *The Beavis and Butt-Head Experience* soundtrack, Geffen
December 9: Nirvana, "All Apologies"/"Rape Me" single, UK, DGC

1994

March 8: Dave Grohl appears on drums on *Backbeat: Music from the Motion Picture*, Virgin Records
March 29: Nirvana, *In Utero*, DGC, reissued with different back artwork and "Rape Me" changed to "Waif Me" on back cover
July 5: Nirvana's "Pay to Play" appears on the *DGC Rarities, Vol. 1* compilation, DGC
October 25: Nirvana, *MTV Unplugged in New York*, vinyl, DGC
November 1: Nirvana, *MTV Unplugged in New York*, CD/cassette, DGC
November 15: Nirvana, *Live! Tonight! Sold Out!!*, long-form home video, Geffen Home Video

1995

February 28: Dave Grohl appears on drums and lap steel guitar and Krist Novoselic appears on farfisa organ on Mike Watt's *Ball-Hog or Tugboat?*, Columbia Records

June 22: Dave Grohl and Krist Novoselic appear on The Stinky Puffs' *A Little Tiny Smelly Bit Of…*, Tec Tones Records

July 4: Foo Fighters (Dave Grohl's post-Nirvana band), *Foo Fighters*, Roswell/Capitol

October: Nirvana's "Negative Creep" appears on the CD accompanying Charles Peterson's photo book *Screaming Life: A Chronicle of the Seattle Music Scene* (forward by Michael Azerrad)

November: Nirvana, *Singles*, six-CD box set, UK, DGC

1996

January 30: Krist Novoselic appears on bass on *Twisted Willie*, a tribute to Willie Nelson, Justice Records

February 20: Nirvana's live version of "Radio Friendly Unit Shifter" appears on *Home Alive: The Art of Self Defense*, Epic

March 5: Nirvana, *Nevermind*, 24-karat gold-plated CD and high-quality virgin vinyl, DGC

July 20: Dave Grohl's side-project Harlingtox AD's "Recycled Children Never To Be Grown" appears on the Laundry Room Records sampler

October 1: Nirvana's "Negative Creep" appears on the *Hype!* soundtrack, Sub Pop

October 1: Nirvana's "Come As You Are" appears on *Fender 50th Anniversary Guitar Legends*, Virgin

October 8: Nirvana, *From the Muddy Banks of the Wishkah*, live album, DGC

December 3: Dave Grohl side-project, Harlingtox AD, *Harlingtox Angel Divine* EP, Laundry Room Records

1997

February 13: Nirvana, *In Utero*, 24-karat gold-plated CD, DGC

February 25: Krist Novoselic appears on acoustic bass on Sky Cries Mary's *Moonbathing on Sleeping Leaves*, Warner Bros.

March 11: Dave Grohl/Louise Post, *Touch* soundtrack, Roswell/Capitol Records

May 20: Foo Fighters, *The Colour and the Shape*, Roswell/Capitol

August 26: Sweet 75 (Krist Novoselic's post-Nirvana band), *Sweet 75*, DGC/Geffen

October 17: Krist Novoselic, liner notes for *Help!: A Charity Project for the Children of Bosnia*, PolyGram

November 4: Foo Fighters' "This is a Call" appears on *Tibetan Freedom Concert*, Grand Royal/Capitol

November 18: Foo Fighters' "Dear Lover" appears on *Scream 2* soundtrack, Capitol

November 25: Dave Grohl appears on drums and guitar on Puff Daddy's "It's All About the Benjamins" single (rock remix), Bad Boy Entertainment

1998

January 27: Dave Grohl co-wrote "This Loving Thing" on The John Doe Thing's *For the Rest of Us*, Kill Rock Stars

February 10: Scream, *Live at the Black Cat*, Torque Records

March 26: Foo Fighters' cover of Gerry Rafferty's "Baker Street" appears on *Come Again*, a compilation album to celebrate EMI's 100-year anniversary, Capitol

April 21: Foo Fighters, *In Conversation*, interview CD

May 19: Foo Fighters' "A320" appears on *Godzilla: The Album* soundtrack Epic/

1999

January 12: Foo Fighters' "My Hero" appears on *Varsity Blues* soundtrack, Hollywood

March 23: Krist Novoselic, director, L7 home video documentary, *The Beauty Process: A Film by Krist Novoselic*, K Records

June 8: Dave Grohl, producer on Verbena's *Into the Pink*, Capitol

September 21: Nirvana's "Rape Me" appears on *SNL 25: Saturday Night Live: The Musical Performances, Volume 2*, DreamWorks Records

November 2: Foo Fighters, *There Is Nothing Left to Lose*, RCA

November 2: Foo Fighters' "I'll Stick Around" appears on *MTV The First 1000 Years: Rock*, Rhino/WEA

2000

January 25: Krist Novoselic, engineer on one track, "Sir Hanuman Chaleesa" on Krishna Das' *Live on Earth…For a Limited Time Only*, Triloka

2001

July 3: Nirvana's "Smells Like Teen Spirit" appears on *Music of the Millennium* compilation album, Universal/Polygram/Virgin/EMI

2002

October 8: Nirvana, "You Know You're Right", single release

October 29: Nirvana, *Nirvana*, DGC, best-of compilation album

2004

November 23: Nirvana, *With The Lights Out*, Universal/DGC, CD/DVD box set

2005

March 22: Nirvana, *Classic Albums: Nirvana – Nevermind*, Eagle Vision, documentary DVD

November 1: Nirvana, *Sliver: The Best of the Box*, DGC, compilation including rarities

November 4: Nirvana's "Something In The Way" appears on soundtrack to *Jarhead* movie, Universal Pictures

2006

November 7: Nirvana, *Live! Tonight! Sold Out!!*, Geffen, DVD

2007

November 20: Nirvana, *MTV Unplugged in New York*, DGC, DVD of the band's iconic 1993 acoustic set

2009

November 3: Nirvana, *Live at Reading*, Geffen, CD/DVD release of band's 1992 performance at Reading Festival

2010

August 31: Nirvana, *Icon*, Universal/DGC, compilation album

2011

September 27: Nirvana, *Live at the Paramount*, DGC, recording of the October 31 1991, performance in Seattle

Pg 145 Hugo Dixon

Corbis
Pg 10/11 Lynn Goldsmith, pg 28 Ian Tilton, pg 59 Ian Tilton, pg 83 Louise Rhodes, pg 84 Allen Ginsberg, pg 87r Karen Mason Blair, pg 93, 103 Neal Preston, pg 104, 157 Steve Jennings, pg 136 Bettmann/Corbis, pg 153 Henry Diltz Charles Hoselton 97, Youri Lenquette 175, 176

Kevin Estrada pg 101, 168

Glen E. Friedman © Photography 1981, Reprinted with permission from the book *Fuck You Heroes* (Burning Flags Press) pg 15

Jeff Kravitz pg 119t, 149, 152, 160

London Features
Andrew Catlin pg 48, 14 Tim Paton pg 49, Hashimoto pg 54, Mat Ankor pg 64, Kristin Callahan pg 81, Gie Knaeps pg 76, 90, Geoff Swaine pg 108, 120 Kevin Mazur pg 118 Frank Micelotta pg 3, 161

Lindsay Brice pg 151

Courtesy Nirvanaclub.com pg 181

Outline Press
Greg Watermann pg 85, 89, 94 Dora Handel pg 99, 125, 192 Chris Cuffaro pg 130, 170 Jesse Frohman pg 148

Charles Peterson pg 13, 146

Redferns
George Chin pg 64 Paul Bergen pg 75 Michel Linssen pg 80, 91, 95, 132 Erica Echenberg pg 128

Retna
David Atlas pg 102 A J Barratt pg 7, 156 Jay Blakesburg pg 66, 87, 156 Steve Double pg 43, 60tl Steve Eichner, pg 51, 96. Darren Filkins pg 60br Charles Hoselton pg 97, Youri Lenquette pg 175, 176 Sam Levi pg 134 Tom Mottram pg 63, Charles Peterson pg 20, 22/23, 23, 26/27, 35, 38, 39, 50, 55, 67. 68, 73, 108, 116, 121, 122, 127, 130tr, 138, 141, Steve Pike pg 76, 84 Retna pg 169, Ed Sirrs

Tilton pg 34, 35, 36, 58, Alice Wheeler pg 25, 29, 30, 31, 33, 185

Rex
Rex/Sipa pg 2, 70, 71, 158, 171, 182, 183, 184, 186, Rex/Today Pg 8, 9, 114 Charles Sykes pg 74 Stephen Sweet pg 144, 155

S.I.N
Mark Benney pg 18, Ian Tilton pg 24, 28, 37, 40, 61, 65 Martyn Goodacre pg 38, 63 Steve Double pg 41, 47, 56, 57, 66, 111, 112 Ian Lawton pg 44, Tim Owen pg 65, 82, Peter Morris pg 69 Phil Nichols 72, 159 Doralba Picerno pg 76 Roy Tee pg 92 Jana pg 147

Stephen Sweet pg160, 187

Ian Wallace pg 107

Alice Wheeler pg 32, 52/53, 62, 164, 166/7

Wireimage
Pg 78, 131, 137, 142